Foreign Aid
Toward the Millennium

Foreign Aid Toward the Millennium

edited by
Steven W. Hook

LYNNE
RIENNER
PUBLISHERS

BOULDER
LONDON

Published in the United States of America in 1996 by
Lynne Rienner Publishers, Inc.
1800 30th Street, Boulder, Colorado 80301

and in the United Kingdom by
Lynne Rienner Publishers, Inc.
3 Henrietta Street, Covent Garden, London WC2E 8LU

Library of Congress Cataloging-in-Publication Data
Foreign aid toward the millennium / edited by Steven W. Hook.
     p.   cm.
   Includes bibliographical references and index.
   ISBN 1-55587-504-1 (alk. paper)
   1. Economic assistance.   I. Hook, Steven W., 1959– .
HC60.F59158 1996
338.91—dc20   96-14827
                                          CIP

British Cataloguing in Publication Data
A Cataloguing in Publication record for this book
is available from the British Library.

Printed and bound in the United States of America

The paper used in this publication meets the requirements
of the American National Standard for Permanence of
Paper for Printed Library Materials Z39.48-1984.

5 4 3 2 1

Contents

Figures and Tables

Preface

Few aspects of world politics in the late twentieth century have been as controversial as foreign aid.

The practice of sharing wealth with impoverished peoples has emerged as a norm among industrialized countries, and nearly every state in the world has participated as a donor or recipient of foreign aid since World War II. Donors created permanent aid bureaucracies, international development agencies established explicit qualitative standards for aid flows, and all parties to the emerging aid regime thoroughly documented the volume, direction, and terms of nearly $1 trillion in concessional loans and grants disbursed during the half century since World War II.

Yet, amid the growth and institutionalization of aid flows, the practice has been constantly subject to intense criticism and debate. Critics from all points on the ideological spectrum—in both rich and poor countries—have found fault with various aspects of foreign aid, and their debates have assumed a central role in North-South relations and international political economy.

The scholarly literature on foreign aid has reflected its controversial history. Realists charged that foreign aid reflected naive assumptions about world politics and insisted that aid programs should be either related to narrowly defined donor self-interests or eliminated outright. Pluralists generally defended aid programs in principle but criticized the inefficiencies of top-heavy aid bureaucracies and the provision of aid to repressive regimes. Neo-Marxists, meanwhile, typically dismissed foreign aid as an extension of capitalist control to the periphery of the world system and as an agent for continuing exploitation. Thus, foreign aid has endured relentless criticism while remaining a central feature of global economic relations in the late twentieth century.

Although scholars have produced numerous volumes addressing various aspects of global development, the literature has heretofore lacked a comprehensive, cross-national treatment of foreign assistance. Responding to this lacuna, the contributors to this book examine profound changes in the aid regime since the Cold War: the initial expectations for expanded aid flows in the pursuit of sustainable development, the subsequent cutbacks in many aid programs, the redirection of aid to Eastern Europe and the former

Soviet Union, the broadened scope of UN peacekeeping efforts, the prominence of economic versus military aid, the role of aid in the ongoing debt crisis, and the boom in private capital transfers to developing regions. They explore the role of major donors in shaping the post–Cold War aid regime and the experience of recipients whose development strategies and outcomes have varied widely. Military aid is examined in several chapters and receives detailed attention in Chapter 3, but the focus of the volume is on the much larger and widespread transfers of economic, or development, assistance.

We have endeavored to be as precise as possible in our terminology, although the language of international development is often ambiguous and notoriously value-laden. The contributors have avoided references to the "Third World," for example, a term born of the Cold War struggle and relevant only in that limited context. The terms "less developed" or "developing" countries are often employed, given their parsimony and widespread acceptance in the development literature. We recognize their shortcomings, however, and we do not wish to imply a singular or linear path of development. Furthermore, the terms "North" and "South" are used guardedly to represent the basic socioeconomic divisions between the industrialized states of Western Europe and North America (along with Japan) and the less affluent areas of Africa, Latin America, South Asia, and Oceania.

The authors were encouraged to advance their own perspectives and to allude to related essays in this volume. Although they do not share a single ideological coloration, they commonly believe in the potential benefits of economic aid in improving living conditions in poor areas of the world, and they express a collective concern that aid flows have yet to achieve their full potential for sound international development.

As editor I would like to express my gratitude to all the contributors and my admiration for their far-flung but parallel efforts to enhance our understanding of foreign assistance. The authors are, in turn, thankful for the cooperation of the diverse government and private sources who provided interviews and essential data. As the editing process proceeded, I received invaluable assistance from many officials at the OECD, particularly Jean-Louis Grolleau. The World Bank and the United Nations provided excellent summary data regarding both aid flows and the socioeconomic conditions in developing countries. At the U.S. Agency for International Development, Dan Israel was most helpful in responding to requests for documentation on U.S. economic and military aid, which was employed in several chapters.

The American Political Science Association facilitated this project in August 1994 by bringing these scholars together for a roundtable discussion as part of its annual meeting. This session and the subsequent contacts among contributors, policymakers, and other students of foreign aid generated new ideas and greatly improved this anthology.

I received generous support from the Department of Political Science at the University of Missouri, where I taught a variety of courses in international relations while compiling this volume. Herbert Tillema, Birol Yesilada, and Annette Wenda were particularly helpful at Missouri. My colleagues at Kent State University, where I am now teaching, were enthusiastic as the project neared fruition. I am grateful to Lynne Rienner, as always, for her support for such scholarly endeavors, and to editors Bridget Julian, Larry Borowsky, and Gia Hamilton for their skillful treatment of this manuscript. I attribute the strengths of this volume to them while accepting personal responsibility for its deficiencies. Finally, I owe a substantial debt to my wife, Debra-Lynn, and my children, Emily and Christopher, for enduring the final preparation of this manuscript.

—*S. W. H.*

1

Introduction: Foreign Aid in a Transformed World

Steven W. Hook

Great expectations followed the collapse of the Cold War in December 1991. Leaders and mass publics welcomed the departure of troops from Central Europe, the reduction of nuclear stockpiles, and the ambitious plans for political and economic reform. Members of the European Union sought new members and a common foreign policy, and in the United States a "peace dividend" was widely anticipated.

The end of the East-West conflict was also expected to bring overdue relief to North-South relations, subordinated for nearly half a century to the Cold War rivalry. The United Nations declared sustainable development the centerpiece of its post–Cold War mission. At the 1992 UN Conference on Environment and Development, the largest assembly of world leaders in history confronted transnational problems such as rapid population growth, global warming, habitat destruction, AIDS, and terrorism. To pay for the expensive remedies to these problems, along with a growing list of UN peacekeeping missions, wealthy governments pledged higher levels of foreign aid. The impoverished regions of Africa, Latin America, and South Asia were to receive more support, as were the transition states of Eastern Europe and the former Soviet Union. For a fleeting moment it appeared that foreign aid, for so long contaminated by the Cold War, would finally achieve its vast potential.

As subsequent events have demonstrated, however, these expectations of a new world order were unfounded. Global collaboration in the mid-1990s instead succumbed to the domestic priorities of wealthy governments, to intensifying economic competition, and to the resurgence of ethnic and religious violence. Rather than growing, as widely expected, economic aid flows *decreased* in absolute terms between 1992 and 1994, and the percentage of donor states' income devoted to aid fell to its lowest levels in two decades (OECD, 1996a: 89).

In the United States, the primary source of economic and military aid throughout the Cold War, massive budget and trade deficits, and a runaway national debt dominated the federal government's agenda. Newly elected president Bill Clinton, who as a candidate in 1992 emphasized domestic rather than foreign policy, devoted his energy to cutting the federal deficit, stimulating trade, improving education and health care, and combatting social problems such as racism, teenage pregnancy, and drug abuse. Although he did not emphasize foreign policy, Clinton adopted the cause of sustainable development and redirected the U.S. Agency for International Development (USAID) to address global problems. His attempt languished, however, in the midst of sharp cutbacks in U.S. foreign aid and a direct attack on USAID by the Republican-led U.S. Congress. Its leaders sought unilateral solutions to U.S. foreign-policy problems, proposing higher defense spending and reduced allocations for the UN and most aid recipients.[1]

Western European governments confronted similar domestic pressures. Germany fell into a protracted economic slump after covering the enormous costs of unification, and its restrictive monetary policies dampened economic growth across the European Union (EU). Economic strains provoked nationalist uprisings in major German cities and across France and Great Britain, where sluggish growth and high unemployment were increasingly blamed on unfair trade practices and foreign laborers. Scandinavian leaders, long the leading foreign-aid donors on qualitative terms, scaled back aid commitments after conservative parties rose to power and demanded deep cuts in government spending. Even the government of Japan, the world's largest donor since 1989, temporarily curbed many aid programs as it struggled to overcome a recession and political crisis.

The circumstances in many recipient states were equally precarious in the wake of the Cold War. In Russia, Boris Yeltsin's hold on power faltered as political rivals from the left and right opposed his reforms and the Russian public turned against him. Western fears of a collapse of Russian reform led to a $10 billion loan from the International Monetary Fund (IMF), $4 billion of which was made immediately available as Yeltsin campaigned for reelection in the spring of 1996. Elsewhere in the Soviet bloc, Communist leaders regained power and appealed to the disenchantment of mass populations.

As during the Cold War, the scale of human suffering remained greatest by far in less developed countries (LDCs), where living conditions in many areas deteriorated. Real per capita income in fifty-one low- and middle-income countries was lower in 1993 than in 1980, and overall gross domestic product fell in fourteen countries (World Bank, 1995a: 162; World Bank 1982a: 110).[2] Life expectancy among low-income countries averaged 62 years in 1993, compared to 77 years for high-income economies; infant mortality in the poorest countries averaged 64 per 1,000 live births, nine times the level recorded in affluent states (World Bank, 1995a: 214). Gaps in living standards widened as the consequences of underdevelopment—overcrowding, air and water pollution, social unrest, and armed conflict—plagued the world's most distressed areas. As many newly industrialized countries (NICs) enjoyed rapid economic growth and attracted large amounts of both public and private capital, the growing income gaps shattered what little remained of a cohesive "Third World."

This is the setting in which the contributors to this volume explore the current status and future prospects of foreign aid. In this introductory chapter I will review the basic trends in post–Cold War aid flows below before comparing the new paradigm in development theory to its predecessors. I then will describe some general socioeconomic trends within the developing world to provide further context for the chapters to follow.

TRENDS IN GLOBAL AID FLOWS

After rising steadily through the 1980s and peaking at $60.9 billion in 1992, development-aid flows declined to $59.2 billion by 1994 (OECD, 1996a: 89). Members of the Organization for Economic Cooperation and Development (OECD) committed .30 percent of their combined GNP to development aid in 1994, the lowest rate in twenty-one years and less than half the international standard of .70 percent. Eleven members of the OECD's Development Assistance Committee (DAC) disbursed less bilateral aid in real terms in 1994 than in 1992, and overall multilateral aid flows fell from 35 percent of total aid in the early 1980s to less than 30 percent.[3] The absolute levels of aid rebounded in 1994 from their levels a year earlier, suggesting that the steep long-term decline anticipated by many was not likely.

As the net reductions in aid were recorded between 1992 and 1994, *private* capital flows from rich to poor states rapidly expanded (see Figure 1.1). These market-based transfers—direct investments, commercial bank lending, and bond lending—amounted to $110 billion in 1994 and represented more than 60 percent of all capital flows from industrialized to developing countries. When these transfers of economic resources are added to the equation, LDCs absorbed a record $184 billion in foreign capital, and the transition states of Eastern Europe and the former Soviet Union received an additional $20 billion.[4]

Despite the widespread cutbacks in development aid, the number of donor states continued to grow. Ireland, Portugal, and Spain established ongoing aid relationships, and South Korea was scheduled to join the OECD in 1996. Japan emerged as the leading source of development aid, with

Figure 1.1
Economic Flows to Developing Countries[a]

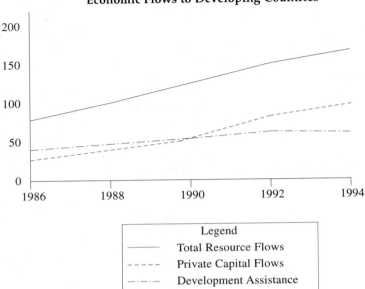

Source: OECD (1996a)
Note:
a. Figures in billions of current U.S. dollars.

$35.6 billion in transfers during the first three years of the post–Cold War period, followed by the United States, France, and Germany (see Table 1.1). Major cutbacks were reported by the United States, Germany, Italy, the Netherlands, Belgium, and Finland, whose governments were forced to retreat from their pledges to subsidize many aspects of sustainable development.[5]

The cutbacks in aid commitments during the immediate post–Cold War period were unevenly distributed, and many LDCs continued to accept massive volumes of development assistance each year. Eleven states received more than $3 billion in official development assistance (ODA) during the 1992–1994 period (see Table 1.2). Four recipients—Egypt ($9.7 billion), the People's Republic of China ($9.6 billion), India ($9.1 billion), and Indonesia ($7.9 billion)—received the lion's share of this aid.[6] Several LDCs received large increases in development assistance during the three-year period, including Bolivia, Ethiopia, Uganda, and Vietnam. Overall, thirty-one LDCs received at least $1 billion in concessional loans and grants during the three-year period.

Critics of foreign aid welcomed the decline of aid flows, arguing that

Table 1.1   Major Donors of Development Assistance, 1988–1994

	1988	1990	1992	1994	1992–1994 Totals (Average ODA/GNP)
Canada	$2,347[a]	$2,470	$2,515	$2,250	$7,138
	(.50)[b]	(.44)	(.46)	(.43)	(.45)
Denmark	922	1,171	1,392	1,446	4,178
	(.89)	(.94)	(1.02)	(1.03)	(1.03)
France	5,463	7,163	8,270	8,466	24,651
	(.58)	(.60)	(.63)	(.64)	(.63)
Germany	4,731	6,320	7,583	6,818	21,355
	(.39)	(.42)	(.38)	(.34)	(.36)
Italy	3,193	3,395	4,122	2,705	9,870
	(.39)	(.31)	(.34)	(.27)	(.30)
Japan	9,134	9,069	11,151	13,239	35,649
	(.32)	(.31)	(.30)	(.29)	(.29)
Netherlands	2,231	2,538	2,753	2,517	7,795
	(.98)	(.92)	(.86)	(.76)	(.81)
Sweden	1,534	2,007	2,460	1,819	6,048
	(.86)	(.91)	(1.03)	(.96)	(.99)
United Kingdom	2,645	2,638	3,243	3,197	9,360
	(.32)	(.27)	(.31)	(.31)	(.31)
United States	10,141	11,394	11,709	9,927	31,759
	(.21)	(.21)	(.20)	(.15)	(.17)
Total	47,063	52,961	60,850	59,152	176,474
	(.34)	(.33)	(.33)	(.30)	(.32)

Source: OECD (1996a: A7–A8)
Notes:
a. Figures reflect aid disbursements by OECD donors in millions of current U.S. dollars.
b. Figures in parentheses indicate ODA as percentage of donor gross national product.

Table 1.2   Major Recipients of Development Assistance, 1988–1994

	1988	1990	1992	1994	1992–1994 Totals
Bangladesh	$1,610[a]	$2,024	$1,552	$1,869	$4,692
China	3,313	1,920	3,224	3,013	9,639
Egypt	2,147	13,495	3,569	2,587	9,708
India	3,186	2,486	3,963	3,357	9,087
Indonesia	2,673	2,899	2,569	2,630	7,851
Israel	1,547	1,402	2,026	1,396	4,871
Mozambique	1,070	786	1,545	1,152	3,749
Pakistan	1,770	1,511	1,191	1,604	4,555
Philippines	1,841	2,138	1,526	1,810	4,911
Thailand	1,071	1,265	712	1,104	3,934

Source: OECD (1995c)
Note:
a. Figures reflect aid commitments in millions of current U.S. dollars.

aid was less effective than private investments and commercial loans in stimulating long-term economic growth. Other critics pointed to the dubious Cold War record of foreign aid in subsidizing autocratic regimes, fostering neocolonialism, and inflaming regional conflicts. They further criticized the bloated and top-heavy bureaucracies of many aid agencies, which often spent much of the aid on themselves rather than providing it to LDCs and misappropriated funds for luxurious capital-intensive projects that did little to improve overall living standards. To all of these critics, the rise of private capital as the principal mechanism for transferring wealth from rich to poor states was an encouraging trend.

Among defenders of foreign aid, many were alarmed by U.S. cutbacks, which lowered its global share of development aid from nearly 40 percent in 1980 to less than 20 percent by 1994. Officials at the OECD and within recipient governments worried that the widely publicized reductions in U.S. aid would lead to a domino effect among donor governments. "This seeming withdrawal from traditional leadership is so grave that it poses a risk of undermining [overall] support for development cooperation," the OECD warned in April 1995. Private cash flows, aid supporters further argued, were driven by motivations far different from those that guided the volume, direction, and terms of foreign aid. Given that multinational corporations (MNCs) and commercial banks explicitly sought to profit from their overseas investments, they targeted developing areas that had already exhibited a track record of sustained economic growth. By contrast, foreign-aid funding decisions presumably included considerations of human needs within recipient states, transnational problems, and other factors that did not make likely a tangible, short-term return for the donors.

Indeed, the vast majority of private capital transferred from wealthy states to LDCs in the early 1990s went to a handful of NICs. East Asian states such as China and Indonesia got the most private capital, but the transition states of Eastern Europe and the former Soviet Union also benefited. Only 6 percent of private investments and commercial loans was directed toward Africa in 1994, only 2 percent toward least developed countries (LLDCs) throughout the world. Thus, the growing integration of public and private capital flows exacerbated the widening chasm not just between rich and poor states but within the developing world as well.

NEW PARADIGMS AND OLD PROBLEMS

Global flows of foreign aid have historically been intertwined with broader trends in world politics and economics, and this remained the case in the Cold War's aftermath. Within the global development-aid regime, which originated in the early 1960s at the peak of African decolonization, aid policies conformed to a "new development paradigm based on markets, competition, and private initiative and enterprise" (OECD, 1995a: 12). As in the case of private capital, aid transfers were predicated upon the ability of recipients to convert the concessional resources into prolonged economic growth, a process that presumably would not only benefit recipients but create markets and expanding investment opportunities for donors.

This new paradigm may be contrasted with previous phases in the evolution of foreign aid, which focused on the role of aid in facilitating the takeoff of nascent economies, in meeting basic human needs or promoting human rights, and in redressing structural inequities between North and South. Although a comprehensive review of development doctrine is beyond the scope of this chapter, a brief overview of the most influential schools of thought may help illustrate the ongoing tensions between the economic and political determinants of foreign aid and between the self-interests of donors and the developmental needs of recipients (see Gilpin, 1987; or Chilcote, 1985 and 1981, for elaboration).

In the 1950s and 1960s, amid the decolonization process and the creation of more than sixty new nation-states, prominent economists and political scientists devised linear models of economic and political development they perceived to be more or less common to all economies (see Rostow, 1971; Nisbet, 1969; and Organski, 1965). Their models, based upon projected stages of growth, were compatible with the liberal international economic order (LIEO) led by the United States following World War II and codified in the Bretton Woods system. By 1970 they had been widely adopted by major development organizations and multilateral financial institutions that served as conduits for foreign aid.

Finding fault with these "deterministic" models, other scholars (e.g., Cardoso, 1972; Myrdal, 1971; and Gunder Frank, 1967) called attention to the subordination of LDCs to the preferences of wealthy states. They encouraged leaders of poor states to pursue independent, self-sufficient paths to economic development directed toward meeting basic human needs, reducing material inequalities, and minimizing their economic (and often political and military) dependence on industrialized countries. This approach favored assertive state intervention in economic development, import-substitution strategies designed to promote self-sufficiency, and the protection of developing countries from foreign competitors. Within the UN General Assembly and the UN Conference on Trade and Development (UNCTAD), leaders from developing regions pressed their case for a new international economic order (NIEO) that would encourage economic self-determination and greatly expand aid transfers from North to South.

The Third World, never a coherent or cohesive collectivity, fragmented along several lines in the 1970s and 1980s, and the uneven progress of LDCs led to a reappraisal of both orthodox and revisionist development theories. Among the first such fissures occurred in the early 1970s after members of the Organization of Petroleum Exporting Countries (OPEC) suspended oil exports to several industrialized states and precipitated the first of two energy crises. OPEC's ability to exploit the vulnerability of industrialized economies encouraged other commodity cartels in the developing world to attempt (unsuccessfully) to emulate the OPEC model. The OPEC states pledged to share their oil profits with other LDCs and to exploit their newfound political leverage to recast the terms of the North-South dialogue. Their promises to share their wealth were largely unfulfilled, however, as OPEC fell victim in the 1980s to internal discord and growing competition from other oil-producing regions.

Also during this decade, Japan and NICs along the Pacific Rim demonstrated how a combination of low labor costs, government protection, and export-led industrialization could produce rapid economic growth (see Johnson, 1982). Japan's model of guided capitalism, replicated by other states in East Asia, stood in stark contrast to the development models advanced by advocates of the NIEO, whose efforts to foster self-sufficiency and to compel the redistribution of wealth from rich to poor foundered in the 1980s.

Most other LDCs, however, struggled with economic stagnation, social and political unrest, and ongoing dependence on affluent states. Their needs for development aid grew as their populations swelled and as the availability of productive farmland diminished because of inefficient planting and harvesting techniques. With their leaders barely able to retain power, and then only through repression, these countries were hardly in a position to recreate the East Asian "miracle" (World Bank, 1993c). Flows of development aid to these states nonetheless continued, provided largely by the United States and other OECD donors, which by now had discovered foreign aid to be an effective tool in achieving their foreign-policy goals. For the United States, aid relationships with more than 100 LDCs continued into the 1980s, solidifying an American presence at a time when neo-Marxist development models competed for influence in many poor areas. In this respect U.S. foreign aid was primarily designed to strengthen political ties to elites in the developing world; its impact on long-term economic development was at most a secondary consideration (see Hook, 1995; Zimmerman, 1993; Baldwin, 1985).

The Cold War's collapse prompted yet another reevaluation of foreign aid and a shift toward sustainable development as the guiding principle of the aid regime. Specific environmental issues identified at the 1992 Earth Summit included global warming, soil degradation, and the loss of biodiversity in tropical forests. All of these problems were aggravated by rapid population growth in the developing world, further limiting the abilities of governments to control development and its impacts. Although market factors received growing emphasis in development aid, leaders recognized that "environmental protection is one area in which government must maintain a central role. Private markets provide little or no incentive for curbing pollution" (World Bank, 1992: 1). Political leaders, at least rhetorically, accepted responsibility for ensuring that long-term development was sensitive to these environmental and demographic concerns. The UN encouraged this effort by establishing a Commission on Sustainable Development, and forty countries established their own such agencies in 1992 and 1993. Together, they devised dozens of standards for environmental protection and applied them to private industrial development and aid programs.

This effort, however, was fraught with problems. Signatories to environmental protocols did not specify their costs and did not address their domestic policy ramifications, the interpretation of which was ultimately left to member states. As a result, conditionalities attached to aid packages were often ambiguous, inconsistent, and unenforceable. The emphasis among aid donors on "good governance" proved equally problematic. Unresolved debates over the meaning and connotations of democratic development were revived, and the presumed causal linkage between such political considerations and long-term economic growth in LDCs was unclear.

Skeptics of this view observed that during the 1970s and 1980s the most rapidly expanding economies—including Japan, China, South Korea, Taiwan, and several Latin American NICs—often violated widely accepted standards of good governance with little criticism from wealthy states. The United States, for example, renewed China's preferential trading status despite its repression of human rights. The United States also established closer economic relations with Mexico through the North American Free Trade Agreement (NAFTA) despite the ongoing dominance and autocratic practices of its one-party government. In the texts of many World Bank reports exalting the East Asian "miracle," these countries were held up as blueprints for modernization and economic integration to be emulated by other LDCs.

Given this controversial history, it may not be surprising that support for foreign aid in many industrialized states has eroded in the 1990s. In response to the changing priorities among foreign-aid donors, heightened emphasis has been placed upon integrating aid with other capital flows between rich and poor countries. Aid donors in 1995 acknowledged the "basic recognition" that aid is "less important than healthy access to markets, capital, and technology, but it can serve as a key, strategic catalyst to help foster such an enabling environment" (OECD, 1995a: 9). Donors stressed long-term "capability building" as a central tenet of the new paradigm, and aid programs called for specialists in poor countries, rather than personnel from donor states, to plan and manage development projects. To the OECD (1995a: 41), the capability-building process presumed that long-term economic growth must "be solidly underpinned by [recipients'] own human, scientific, technological, organizational, institutional, and resource capabilities."

What troubled development experts was that the rapid expansion of private financial flows was limited to NICs that had already experienced rising economic growth. A few less developed but populous states such as China and India also attracted large volumes of private capital, along with large sums of development aid. Left out, however, were the majority of LDCs and LLDCs in sub-Saharan Africa and South Asia, whose standards of living worsened in the 1980s, widely considered the "lost decade" of international development. In many African states, including Liberia, Rwanda, and Somalia, socioeconomic problems brought on the collapse of political order, widespread bloodshed, and foreign intervention.

The smaller aid flows available to the world's poorest states were often consumed by debt repayments from previous concessional loans, leaving little or nothing to generate sustainable development.[7] As their overall debts reached a record $1.7 trillion in 1994—up by $140 billion over the 1993 total—such "reverse flow" of capital merely compounded the problem. Aid to the poorest states, which amounted to 27 percent of total aid flows in 1983–1984, fell to 24 percent of the total by 1994; thirteen of the eighteen DAC members in 1983–1984 devoted a smaller share of their development assistance to LLDCs a decade later (OECD, 1996a: A58).

In both respects, a growing gap appeared in the post–Cold War period between the poorest states (the former Fourth World) and more prosperous developing countries. Private banks and multinational corporations generally limited their investments to growing economies with established records of export-led industrialization. The poorest countries, primarily those in sub-Saharan Africa, continued to rely on foreign assistance as their primary source of foreign capital, but their prospects for continued aid were diminished by the shrinking aid budgets of many wealthy states and by the new development paradigm, which rewarded states with proven records.[8] Thus, leaders of the world's most impoverished states, already marginalized by the sudden withdrawal of support from the Cold War superpowers, faced the additional prospect of being left out of the market-oriented aid regime of the mid-1990s.

TRENDS IN GLOBAL DEVELOPMENT

As the availability of aid funds tightened in the mid-1990s, industrialized states increasingly sought assurances that their aid transfers were achieving appreciable benefits in the developing world. Timothy Wirth, the U.S.

undersecretary of state for global affairs, observed that the days of "leaving money on the table in the middle of the night" had long since passed. In this context, it is worth briefly reviewing the record of economic development and living standards in the poorest regions of the world during the period since 1960.

Among important economic indicators, growth rates among LDCs in the 1960s averaged 6.2 percent in the 1960s, well above the UN's target of 5 percent annual growth for the first "development decade." Average life expectancy increased rapidly during the period from 1950 through 1980, from 43 to 59 years; average literacy rates increased from 33 to 59 percent; and the rate of child mortality fell by more than two-thirds (OECD, 1985a: 270). The problem of overpopulation received widespread attention during this period, and educational programs and effective family planning led to rapid reductions in birthrates in many countries.

Progress in living conditions across the developing world varied widely, of course, and many LDCs did not share in the economic growth that occurred elsewhere. Although inhabitants of East Asia and, to a lesser extent, Latin America experienced considerable improvements in living standards, those in sub-Saharan Africa and parts of South Asia suffered from deteriorating conditions. Of the twenty-three low-income countries that experienced negative per capita income between 1980 and 1993, seventeen were in sub-Saharan Africa (World Bank, 1995a: 162).[9] Furthermore, the economic growth rates experienced by many LDCs in the 1960s and 1970s slowed considerably in the 1980s and in some cases reversed direction. Low-income economies (excluding China and India) grew at an annual rate of .1 percent between 1980 and 1993, whereas high-income economies enjoyed a growth rate of 2.2 percent.

These statistics reflect both the positive and negative aspects of international development in the late twentieth century. They fail, however, to capture several important quality-of-life indicators, most notably the often considerable variations in living conditions *within* developing countries. Despite their shortcomings, however, the figures suggest an impressive record within large segments of the developing world. Given the lack of private capital available to these areas, both internally and from overseas sources, foreign assistance must receive considerable credit in contributing to the improved living standards.

Yet the continuing plight of the world's poorest states, and the growing disparities in global wealth, remain unavoidable realities in the post–Cold War era. The world has witnessed massive waves of refugees from such areas as Rwanda, Haiti, and the former Yugoslavia, and these problems have had a serious impact on neighboring states. As the consequences of environmental decay and overpopulation are more acutely felt, it becomes less possible to dismiss problems in "isolated" parts of the world.

As the following chapters in this volume will remind us, patterns of economic growth have varied widely in the latter half of the twentieth century,
and "universal" models have largely failed to explain or predict developmental outcomes in a variety of diverse settings. The role of foreign aid in
this process has further discouraged generalizations, despite the best efforts
by the OECD and World Bank to establish singular criteria and qualitative
standards for aid flows. A comprehensive understanding of aid and economic development must include focused study of the different forms of foreign
assistance, of the diverse aid policies and objectives of donor states, and of
the utilization of foreign aid by developing countries. These are the subjects
of the twelve chapters to follow. The final chapter offers reasoned speculation about the future of foreign aid as the Cold War recedes further into history and as new problems and opportunities come into focus.

OUTLINE OF THE ANTHOLOGY

This book is divided into four parts, three of which focus on a distinctive
piece of the foreign-assistance puzzle. In Part 1 we consider the machina-
tions of foreign assistance in contemporary world politics. Part 2 and Part 3
focus on donors and recipients of foreign aid, respectively, and on their
adaptation to the post–Cold War aid regime; and Chapter 14, in Part 4, offers
some conclusions.

In Chapter 2, Robert Wood considers the evolution, status, and future of
the development-assistance regime. Drawing on his earlier application of
regime theory to ODA, Wood considers the proliferation of donors and
recipients, their evolving roles within the aid regime, and the complex
norms and practices that have been established to guide concessional financing to the developing world. Wood believes the ODA regime has assumed
complex institutional features that accommodate both the policy interests of
donors and the developmental needs of recipients. Thus, it will likely remain
a pervasive aspect of North-South relations even as aggregate aid flows are
curtailed by many donors, particularly the United States.

In Chapter 3, Michael Klare and Dan Volman confront the flip side of
the foreign-assistance coin, security assistance. They identify military aid as
a central component of the Cold War competition and place it in the broader context of North-South relations during this volatile period. Klare and
Volman then delineate the consequences for LDCs of military transfers,
which are comparable whether they are delivered on concessional or market
terms. The authors review the dramatic shift in arms transfers from aid to
cash sales in the Cold War's wake. In the final section of their chapter, they
call for an arms-transfer-control regime modeled after regimes that have

prevented the proliferation of nuclear weapons and other means of mass destruction.

In Chapter 4 Robert Zimmerman and I review the central role of the United States as a source of both economic and security assistance to most LDCs in the international system throughout the Cold War. We consider the bureaucratic problems that plagued USAID during its first three decades and consider the ongoing assault on the agency by Congress and large segments of the public. Not only were levels of U.S. economic aid cut sharply in the mid-1990s, we argue, but the surviving programs were not effectively directed toward long-term political reform or economic development that empowered large portions of LDC populations.

Beginning in 1989, U.S. preponderance within the development-aid regime was eclipsed, as Japan disbursed greater sums of concessional aid to LDCs. In Chapter 5, Alan Rix explores the distinctive Japanese approach to foreign assistance, which in many ways reflects the country's broad foreign economic policies. As Rix observes, Japanese aid has served as a powerful vehicle for the country's own economic development. Its expanded scope portends greater Japanese involvement in the economic destinies of many LDCs, particularly those neighboring Japan along the Pacific Rim. The Japanese government's ability to exploit its elevated status, however, may be jeopardized by internal strains that have emerged during the 1990s. The future of Japanese aid, Rix concludes, may well hinge on the government's ability to resolve these domestic difficulties.

Similarly, the central U.S. presence among aid donors has been over-shadowed by many West European countries and the combined economic contribution of the European Union. In Chapter 6 M. Leann Brown and Joanne M. O'Connor examine the performance of several West European donors, particularly France, Germany, and the United Kingdom. As former recipients of Marshall Plan assistance, these countries experienced the benefits of concessional aid and have applied some of these lessons to their aid programs. Brown and O'Connor find that the aid policies of West European donors have clearly changed since the end of the Cold War, but their emerging policies have been less clear as new tensions emerged between the self-interests of the individual donors, the collective goals of the European Union, and the needs of recipient states.

In Chapter 7, Katie Verlin Laatikainen compares the aid policies of Nordic donors and contrasts their evolving aid strategies in the 1990s. She recalls how during the Cold War these donors adopted a distinctive normative approach to foreign assistance, reflecting cultural traditions of the Nordic region emphasizing egalitarian social-welfare policies, neutralism, and pacifism. Foreign assistance served as a vital expression of all three traditions as Denmark, Finland, Norway, and Sweden became assertive aid donors, leading the OECD in most categories of aid quality. Like the countries of Western Europe, however, these donors have recently confronted domestic economic strains and political challenges that have threatened not only the aggregate volumes of Nordic aid but its quality as well.

Nations of the Gulf region also have played an important role in dispensing concessional assistance. Timothy Luke in Chapter 8 reviews the sudden emergence of OPEC states as aid donors following the oil shocks of the 1970s and their similarly abrupt decline as aid donors during the 1980s. Luke finds that OPEC members, like other donors, tailored aid packages to accommodate their own domestic interests, a fact made readily apparent in his review of intra-OPEC disputes and aid policies in the 1990s.

Turning to recipients of foreign aid, Janine R. Wedel in Chapter 9 examines the Central and Eastern European countries and the new independent states of the former Soviet Union (CEEC/NIS). As Wedel demonstrates, the urgent needs in this region have profoundly altered the calculi of bilateral aid donors and multilateral development agencies. Wedel explores the pattern of "frustration and resentment" that emerged within the Visegrad states of Poland, Hungary, and the former Czechoslovakia, then describes how leaders in these states and their Western counterparts have attempted to learn from past mistakes and to make subsequent aid programs more effective.

We explore the status of foreign aid in the recipient states of the former Third World in our next four chapters. In Chapter 10 David I. Steinberg analyzes the LDCs of South Asia and reviews their widely varying developmental experiences. As Steinberg observes, security assistance played a central role in facilitating the geopolitical objectives of both superpowers during the Cold War. In some countries, particularly India, economic aid produced tangible results and contributed to the "green revolution," which improved living standards for millions of people. Japan propelled its own economic expansion by providing aid to East Asian LDCs, which were encouraged to replicate Japan's model of "guided capitalism."

In Chapter 11, Peter J. Schraeder analyzes the recipient states of francophone Africa. Schraeder illustrates how the French government utilized foreign assistance as a central means of controlling these LDCs. He then considers the prospects for a continuation of this approach given France's loss of its self-proclaimed role as an ideological alternative to the Cold War superpowers and given the growing role of other donors, particularly Japan, in African development during the 1990s. In Chapter 12, Goran Hyden looks to the anglophone and lusophone states of southern Africa, many of which continue to rely on foreign aid as their principal sources of income. Hyden finds that aid donors to southern Africa have imposed their foreign-policy agendas onto their aid relationships, often with pernicious effects on the recipients' prospects for economic growth. Hyden contrasts the overlapping aid flows from several industrialized states to southern Africa. He then turns to the phenomenon of "developmentalism," which in many cases merely compounded LDCs' dependency on outside assistance, and suggests a variety of reforms to make future aid flows to Africa more responsive to recipient needs.

Latin America is another traditional destination of foreign aid; its political and economic relationship to industrialized states, particularly the United States, was largely determined by Cold War considerations. In Chapter 13, David Louis Cingranelli and SimonPeter Gomez examine the efforts by various recipients to overcome their dependence on the United States—their resort to commercial lenders, the subsequent debt crisis, and current attempts to accelerate economic development and consolidate democratic reforms. To Cingranelli and Gomez, the outlook for Latin American aid is encouraging despite its clouded past. They outline a "progressive trend" in aid to this region by which aid flows, though not increasing in absolute terms, have increased in important qualitative categories.

All of these contributors highlight the pervasive and malleable role of foreign aid in furthering the foreign policies of donors and the development efforts of recipients. Along the way they emphasize the proclaimed and implicit objectives of aid transfers, often referred to as policy interests. Though the authors do not embrace a monolithic conception of national interest—diverse substate and transnational pressures are emphasized throughout—it is clear that decisionmaking outcomes in the area of foreign aid, resulting in documented allocations of public resources on terms dictated by donors, reflect prevalent governmental priorities. David Baldwin's (1966: 3) statement of three decades ago remains true today:

> Foreign aid is first and foremost a technique of statecraft. It is, in other words, a means by which one nation tries to get other nations to act in desired ways. . . . Thus, foreign aid policy is foreign policy, and as such it is a subject of controversy in both the international and the domestic political arenas.[10]

This convergence of donor interests and recipient needs and the tension between national self-interest and global concerns make the study of foreign aid fascinating but often troublesome. These chapters are designed to serve the essential function of moving beyond generalities in post–Cold War foreign aid toward a focused understanding of its role and prospects throughout the world. As aid budgets stabilize in the mid-1990s and begin to recover from their earlier cutbacks, it is inevitable that foreign aid will continue to play a key role in foreign policy and international development well into the new millennium.

NOTES

1. Senator Jesse Helms, the committee's chairman, also sought to downsize or eliminate the U.S. Information Agency and the U.S. Arms Control and Disarmament

Agency. As chairman he was able to hold up much of U.S. foreign policy—including key diplomatic nominations and arms-control treaties—until his demands for restructuring these agencies were met.

2. These were dominated by the former territories of the Soviet bloc, including Albania, Armenia, Azerbaijan, Georgia, Kazakhstan, Latvia, Lithuania, Moldova, Romania, Russia, and Tajikistan. Other states included Nicaragua, Niger, and Peru (World Bank, 1995a: 162).

3. The Development Assistance Committee, which provides more than 90 percent of aid flows in the mid-1990s, includes Australia, Austria, Belgium, Canada, Denmark, Finland, France, Germany, Ireland, Italy, Japan, Luxembourg, the Netherlands, New Zealand, Norway, Portugal, Spain, Sweden, Switzerland, the United Kingdom, and the United States.

4. Of this transfer of private capital, $47 billion was reported in the form of direct investments, $33 billion in bond lending, and $21 billion in international bank lending (OECD, 1996a: A1–A2).

5. In some respects these figures were misleading. The United States, with more than $12 billion in net military transfers during the three-year period, provided the most overall aid during the period (USAID, 1996a). Also, additional German economic aid to the former Soviet bloc, not technically considered ODA by the OECD, would render Germany the third-largest aid source.

6. Egypt's total receipts amounted to $13.6 billion and Israel's to $10.3 billion when U.S. military assistance was included (see USAID, 1996a).

7. Developing countries with the highest percentages of debt relative to GNP in 1994 included São Tomé and Principe (623 percent), Nicaragua (577 percent), Guyana (575 percent), Myanmar (381 percent), and Guinea Bissau (248 percent).

8. See Khadiagala (1993) for an illustrative study of Uganda's ongoing struggle to stimulate economic growth in the context of domestic, regional, and global uncertainty.

9. These included Benin, Central African Republic, Côte d'Ivoire, Gambia, Lesotho, Madagascar, Malawi, Mali, Mauritania, Mozambique, Niger, Nigeria, Rwanda, Sierra Leone, Togo, Zambia, and Zimbabwe.

10. In *National Interest and Foreign Aid* (1995), I demonstrated empirical linkages between U.S. ODA flows and the level of military spending and conscription within recipient states during the 1980s. Japan's aid flows, meanwhile, were positively and significantly related to its bilateral trade networks, and Swedish aid flowed disproportionately to LDCs with the greatest social-welfare needs. Although these findings do not provide conclusive evidence of discrete foreign-policy interests, they add empirical weight to such assertions and in many cases contradict the rhetoric of political leaders and aid administrators.

Part 1

Machinations of Foreign Assistance

2

Rethinking Economic Aid

Robert E. Wood

Global economic aid has survived the transition to the post–Cold War era despite its origins and intimate role in the superpower conflict. The aid regime, which incorporates dozens of bilateral and multilateral aid programs, continues to subsidize development efforts in nearly every poor country. Many donors have reduced aid allotments in the mid-1990s, but the plight of the world's poor, the growing severity and recognition of ecological threats, and the confluence of donor and recipient interests underlying most current aid programs ensure their extension well into the next century.

Because development aid's relationship to the Cold War was always complex, the demise of the Cold War has left an ambiguous legacy. Old rationales for many aid programs have disappeared, and new threats to wealthy states and new development problems and opportunities have emerged. Most important, the social, economic, and political problems of LDCs—many of which became independent during the peak of the Cold War—remain largely unresolved in the late 1990s.

It is inconceivable that the massive aid programs established during the post–World War II period would have originated or been sustained without the Cold War rivalry between the United States and the Soviet Union and China. Beginning with the Marshall Plan in 1947 and continuing through the construction of an international regime of aid provided in the name of development, the rhetoric of anticommunism and superpower rivalry was critical in harnessing the necessary political support in the United States, for many years the main source of bilateral aid.[1]

Cold War politics were important but of varying significance to most other donors. Within these states diverse interest groups, policymakers, and public administrators continually sought to build popular support for economic aid on other grounds, appealing to everything from self-interested export promotion to religious and secular humanitarianism. These efforts ensured special political protection for certain forms of aid, most notably food aid, but it is hard to imagine that even they would have existed in the absence of the Cold War.

Yet in many ways the institutional mechanisms for delivering econom-ic assistance are more elaborate than ever in the late 1990s. The World Bank, the OECD, and regional development banks announce hundreds of new commitments each year. The number of aid donors and recipients has con-tinued to increase steadily, with South Korea most recently "graduating" from aid recipient to donor, and the former Soviet bloc changing roles in the reverse direction. Official development assistance (ODA), the most com-mon and the most concessional form of economic assistance, is transferred annually to more than 120 impoverished states and expected as a de facto obligation from the world's affluent societies.

The proposal to reclassify the successor states to the Soviet Union and its former Eastern European clients as middle-income developing countries (MIDCs) in need of the same kind of assistance formerly extended to the Third World—an idea that would have been absurd in the late 1980s—was quickly accepted by both leaders and publics in the advanced industrialized countries.[2] Indeed, per capita flows of ODA to these formerly state-socialist states matched the average for all LDCs in 1992 (World Bank 1993d: 13), and official aid to Russia far surpassed aid to any other single recipient. The IMF established a temporary facility in 1993 to aid former state-socialist countries in their transition to market economies, thus becoming, along with the World Bank, a universal institution for the first time, including as mem-bers virtually all internationally recognized states.

Reflecting the growing complexity of world politics since the Cold War, "the tasks of foreign aid have multiplied dramatically" (Nelson 1992: 4). In addition to facilitating the transition of the former state-socialist societies to market economies, other proposed uses of aid in the post–Cold War era have included mitigating a wide range of environmental problems, ranging from deforestation and fossil-fuel emissions to the disappearance of African ele-phants; combatting AIDS; cutting the international flow of narcotics; pro-moting democratization, political pluralism, and human rights; helping immigrants and refugees; and controlling world population growth. These objectives now exist alongside long-standing uses of ODA: capturing new markets, consolidating bilateral security ties, and rewarding domestic ethnic constituencies.

In this context, proponents of development aid cannot hope to reap much of a financial dividend from the end of the Cold War. The claims on the pool of available resources have multiplied, not contracted. At the same time, the gradual evolution of the Cold War–inspired patchwork of aid pro-grams into an international regime means that ODA is significantly institu-tionalized within the global political economy. The fact that the regime has been only mildly affected by the United States' diminished role indicates the degree to which aid provision has become adopted as an international stan-dard.

Development aid's survival into the post–Cold War era reflects a wide range of factors, from bureaucratic inertia to the development of new rationales and constituencies in the face of new realities. Although the Cold War provided a discursive framework into which virtually every international issue was placed, the actual workings of foreign aid always served additional goals. Studies of the Marshall Plan, for example, have shown clearly how its goal was much less to oppose communism than to promote the kind of national capitalism espoused by many Western leaders and intellectuals (see Wood, 1986; Block, 1977; and Kolko and Kolko, 1972).

Subsequent U.S. aid policy in the developing world, despite the anticommunist rhetoric, showed an abiding concern with protecting the interests of U.S. multinational corporations and subverting radical development strategies based on local redistribution and economic nationalism (see Hayter, 1985, 1971; Lappé, Collins, and Kinley, 1980; Weissman, 1974; and Payer, 1982). Since the signing of the Camp David accords in 1978, U.S. aid has been heavily weighted toward Israel and Egypt, less for reasons of the Cold War (although anti-Soviet rhetoric was often used) than for reasons of domestic ethnic politics, regional stability, and economic interests. In most European countries, aid politics were equally complicated, often focusing on the preservation of postcolonial relationships (see Chapters 10–13). Everywhere, special business interests sought to use aid programs as vehicles for export promotion, often with considerable success.

In this respect Cold War discourse imposed on aid a uniformity of purpose more apparent than real. It gradually assimilated a commitment to development as an antidote to the appeals of communism. At the same time, Cold War competition introduced perennial instability into aid programs—yesterday's enemy could become today's ally. Combined with the perviousness of aid programs to special interests, the overall system of development assistance often lacked coherence or integrity.

Such a perception of incoherence, however, underestimates the degree to which an international system of aid provision evolved during the late twentieth century into an international *regime*—a set of "principles, norms, rules, and decision-making procedures" relating to a specific issue area in international relations (Krasner 1982: 186). The ODA regime was based on very particular assumptions both about what development meant and about what means were appropriate to assist it, assumptions much more widely shared among aid providers than among recipients.[3] The relationship of this regime to the Cold War was intimate but nebulous.

As already noted, Cold War anticommunism provided the major impetus to a regime of economic assistance centered on Third World development. At the same time, temporary and often opportunistic Cold War concerns constantly impinged on the regime, often violating its basic principles and norms and distorting the volume and direction of aid flows. In this respect, the post–Cold War aid regime has been liberated from the geopolitical factors that previously distorted its functions. Indeed, aid officials and supporters hoped that the Cold War's demise would make possible a new and more durable consensus in support of development aid.

Freed from Cold War distortions, the aid regime in the post–Cold War period probably has more power than ever to shape development choices and processes among aid recipients. It is much harder now for aid recipients to avoid regime discipline by playing donors off against each other. Even if aid levels decline for several years, the liberation of regime norms from Cold War distractions could mean the aid regime will have a stronger chance of achieving its considerable potential in the years to come.

In this chapter I seek to provide an overview of the development-aid regime—how it evolved during the Cold War and how it is changing in its wake. I first briefly review its evolution in the aftermath of World War II, then examine the more specific relationship between the aid regime and international development, identifying some central elements of the logic that continues to lie behind patterns of aid allocation and practice. I then explore how this logic led the regime into trouble in the 1980s, culminating in a debilitating debt crisis. The shift in focus from development to structural adjustment in the 1990s will also be examined before I assess the status and future of the ODA regime.

SOURCES OF DEVELOPMENT ASSISTANCE

Official development assistance, the most pervasive form of economic aid, consists of public grants and low-interest loans.[4] Surely any borrower would prefer ODA-level terms, but other forms of aid are still preferable to private capital available on international financial markets. Indeed, ODA is considered *supplemental* to market flows: Donor states will only provide assistance if private foreign investors or commercial lenders are unavailable.

In the analysis that follows, ODA will be given an expansive definition, incorporating everything from grants to loans to equity investments and guarantees, as long as they are extended by official institutions ostensibly for developmental purposes. The common thread linking these diverse activities and terms is that it is the disinterest of market forces that triggers a government or multilateral response. Viewed in institutional terms, the ODA regime involves several primary actors, which will be reviewed below.[5]

Bilateral Aid Institutions

About thirty industrialized states provide development aid on a regular basis. Most of them participate in the ODA regime through the OECD's

Development Assistance Committee, whose membership of twenty-one countries has grown steadily and is expected to include several newly industrialized countries by 2010. Each of these donors commits a certain proportion of its aid directly to recipient governments for the purpose of fostering economic development.

The United States was the primary source of bilateral development aid during the Cold War. U.S. aid programs started under the 1947 Marshall Plan, which was primarily designed to revive decimated U.S. allies in Western Europe but also involved more than $2 billion in economic aid to LDCs in the Middle East and South Asia. Though the Cold War served as a catalyst for many U.S. bilateral programs, it created frequent shifts in the geographical focus of U.S. aid: to Western Europe in the late 1940s, Latin America in the early 1960s, Indochina in the late 1960s and early 1970s, the Middle East in the 1980s, and Eastern Europe and the Soviet Union in the 1990s (see Chapter 4).

The Japanese government graduated from recipient to donor status in the 1960s and became in the 1990s the leading donor of bilateral ODA. Foreign aid served as a catalyst of Japan's own economic growth, strengthening relations with surrounding states, which became active trading partners. Given the fact that military rearmament was proscribed under Japan's postwar constitution, the government identified economic growth as a primary objective and utilized foreign aid to facilitate this goal (see Hook, 1995). Faced with a prolonged economic recession and political crisis in the 1990s, the Japanese government scaled back many of its bilateral aid programs but remained the primary donor because the United States and other nations cut back their aid programs (see Chapter 5).

By the early 1960s, most Western European and Scandinavian countries, along with Canada, Australia, and New Zealand, had initiated bilateral aid programs. Coordinating their aid programs through the OECD, these donors provided smaller net volumes of bilateral flows but often disbursed aid of higher quality than that offered by the United States and Japan. This pattern was affirmed in OECD documents along several qualitative dimensions: ODA as a percentage of GNP, per capita ODA, the proportion of grants versus loans, and the proportion of aid to least developed countries (LLDCs), among others (see Chapters 6 and 7).

The Soviet Union and the People's Republic of China initiated small aid programs in the late 1950s, and the specter of communist aid led the United States to press its allies to initiate and expand their bilateral aid programs. Cold War concerns were so central in the development of U.S. aid programs, in fact, that Soviet leader Nikita Khrushchev once suggested that aid from capitalist countries should be seen "as a particular kind of Soviet aid," as it would not have been extended without the challenge posed by the Soviet Union (Tansky 1967: 5).

In addition, several members of OPEC emerged as significant bilateral donors after the 1973 oil-price increases. OPEC aid peaked in the late 1970s and fell from \$9.5 billion in 1980 to \$2.7 billion in 1991. Only Saudi Arabia remains a significant Arab donor. Contrary to the expectations of many developing countries, OPEC aid was never widely disbursed beyond the Middle East; most OPEC funds were transferred to non-oil-producing Arab states. The modest level of OPEC aid to other regions was largely eliminated as the cartel succumbed to internal disarray and a prolonged slump in petroleum prices (see Chapter 8).

The collapse of Soviet aid after 1991 had major consequences for Cuba, Afghanistan, Mongolia, Vietnam, and Angola but relatively little impact elsewhere (Webber, 1993). Among the indirect consequences, however, it reduced the ability of recipients to play off the great-power donors against each other. In addition, the transformation of the former Soviet Union and its territories from aid donors to recipients has increased competition for ODA resources (see Chapter 9).

Aid donors vary in many critical ways, including in the manner in which they manage their aid bureaucracies. In the United States, for example, responsibility for setting aid policy is scattered among roughly thirty agencies, but the main one since 1961 has been USAID. Japan, by contrast, has no central aid agency, and many Western European states manage economic aid through their foreign ministries. The widely varying institutional arrangements for ODA reflect the multiple purposes it serves in promoting the political, economic, and security objectives of aid donors.

In each case, however, development aid has become a central part of affluent states' international relations. Their bilateral aid programs, most often renewed from year to year, have served as crucial and tangible links to the developing world.

Multilateral Institutions

Though the wholesale shift to multilateral aid advocated by the United Nations and leaders of LDCs in the 1970s never occurred, multilateral institutions have become steadily more central to the ODA regime. It is widely agreed that multilateral aid often meets recipient needs more directly than resources transferred directly from donors, which commonly are more "political" and have more strings attached. Multilateral aid channels presumably wash out these donor self-interests and serve recipient-oriented development goals.

The World Bank Group constitutes the core of the multilateral institutional sector of the aid regime.[6] Technically, it consists of three separate organizations: the International Bank for Reconstruction and Development (IBRD), the International Development Association (IDA), and the

International Finance Corporation (IFC). The IBRD is the World Bank's "hard-loan window," from which it transfers funds borrowed on international financial markets. Because the bank has an excellent credit rating and low fees, the terms of IBRD lending are generally slightly better than average market rates. As noted above, however, the bank will generally only lend if no private-sector lender or investor is interested.

The IDA raises funds through periodic replenishments from its richer members, then provides concessional loans with a modest service fee. Its loans meet the criteria of ODA; only countries with a per capita income below a certain standard ($765 for the tenth replenishment period, running to 1996) are eligible for IDA loans.[7] The IFC, meanwhile, makes loans to and equity investments in *private* companies operating in LDCs. Although the IFC's financing has historically been dwarfed by that of its two World Bank affiliates, it has rapidly increased in recent years, from $700 million in 1984 to more than $4 billion in the mid-1990s.

Two other UN agencies have taken an active role in the area of development aid—the UN Development Programme (UNDP), which provides extensive technical assistance and small project grants, often in conjunction with other UN agencies; and the World Food Program, the major arena for the articulation of norms for food aid allocation (Hopkins, 1992). The UN's development goals and aid efforts have been aggressively promoted since the early 1960s within the General Assembly, in which LDCs became a majority and formed a cohesive voting bloc.

The IBRD/IDA model was adopted by a series of regional development banks (RDBs), of which by far the most prominent are the Inter-American Development Bank (IDB) and the Asian Development Bank (ADB). The African Development Bank and Fund, though comparatively small, expanded its lending rapidly in the late 1980s and early 1990s. Several smaller RDBs also exist, most of which were established in the 1960s. In the 1970s, Middle East oil-producing countries established a number of multilateral institutions, including the OPEC Fund for International Development, but disbursements from most of them tapered off rapidly in the late 1980s. European Union members collectively supported several multilateral aid funds and institutions, most notably the European Investment Bank and the European Development Fund (EDF), through the periodically negotiated Lomé Conventions.

The existence of an international ODA regime implies the existence of some mechanism for the creation of norms and principles and for ongoing negotiation and implementation. The development-aid regime, however, lacks a central treaty or organizational structure. As noted above, the organization that was created with such a role most closely in mind and which has sought, with only limited success, to play such a role, is the OECD's Development Assistance Committee (DAC).[8] The DAC has been more successful in establishing target norms than in eliciting compliance with them (witness, for example, its largely unfulfilled 0.7 percent of GNP target for ODA); it continues to conduct annual reviews of individual donor policies and to hold high-level ministerial meetings.

The end of the Cold War has removed a number of the constraints upon the ODA regime. As the millennium approaches, a sufficient body of shared norms and principles for aid has been established to warrant the extension of the regime framework for many years. Let us now examine the shape of this ODA regime by looking at the long-debated relationship between aid and development.

THE AID REGIME AND DEVELOPMENT

A half century of aid programs in LDCs has not yielded any firm conclusions about the relationship between aid and development. Statistical studies have produced inconsistent and inconclusive findings. Even the DAC conceded in 1980 that "there can be no rigorous scientific proof that in the past the aggregate of everything officially designated as ODA has had an identifiable, assignable, positive and cost-effective impact on Third World development." The widely respected Cassen Report was more positive, but it too admitted that "inter-country statistic analyses do not show anything conclusive about the impact of aid on growth" (Cassen and Associates, 1986: 33), a general conclusion supported by several other analyses (Lele and Nabi, 1991; Mosley, 1987; Riddell, 1987).

This doubt has been accentuated by the inability of many studies of bilateral aid to find patterns—beyond fairly crude ones, such as historical ties and small-country bias—in donor allocations. Certainly, neither recipient need nor development performance seems to be a strong predictor of aid allocation. Some observers have simply thrown up their hands, concluding, in the words of one, that "it is impossible to discern the slightest rhyme or reason to the way in which funds have been distributed among countries" (Uri, 1976: 36).

The conclusion that there is no empirically verifiable relationship between aid and development should hardly come as a surprise. Development outcomes are extremely variable and are conditioned by the complex interactions of a vast number of factors (Booth, 1993). Yet despite these widely acknowledged ambiguities, the ODA regime has been more deeply implicated in some of the failures of development than suggested by much of the current literature, which stresses government policy failures. Development-aid lending has indeed been subject to fads of questionable value, to the narrow self-interests of both donors and recipients, and to the shifting systemic environment. But it is not primarily responsible for under-development.

Despite these problems a distinctive aid regime has emerged since the 1960s whose members generally accept recognizable "rules of the game." This regime typically lies at the crossroads of donor and recipient interests and at the intersection of individual state interests and transnational concerns such as overpopulation and global warming. In the rest of this section, I examine several of the rules that have had significance for the options and choices of recipient countries.

Institutionalized Noncompetition

Assuming a natural desire to avoid debt, we would expect aid-seeking governments first to approach those agencies offering grants and then reluctantly to move across the financial spectrum to agencies offering progressively harder terms. However, regime norms clearly specify that the opposite is supposed to happen. No aid at all is supposed to be offered if private-sector financing is available, and no softer form of aid is supposed to be made available if capital can be obtained on more commercial terms. Hence, in theory at least, the potential recipient is supposed to go first to the *least* competitive source of aid (and only after private financing has been found unavailable) and to approach sources with easier terms only as others express their lack of interest. The aid-seeking government is thus offered the form of aid that comes as close to market terms as the profitability of the proposed use of aid and the creditworthiness of the recipient allow.

The degree to which development assistance departs from market terms varies greatly. One may envision a spectrum extending from rigid market terms to outright cash grants; all aid programs can then be viewed at varying points along this spectrum.

At what might be called the "market edge" of the development aid regime are institutions such as the IFC—the arm of the World Bank that makes equity investments in, and loans to, private enterprises. Even the IFC, with its goal of promoting private-sector development, is prohibited by its charter from "undertaking any financing for which in its opinion sufficient private capital could be obtained on reasonable terms" (IFC, 1992: 3). To the companies in which it invests, the IFC's appeal lies less in the concessionality of its terms, which are barely distinguishable from the market's, than in the political protection it tends to bring as a member of the powerful World Bank Group.

Located slightly further away from market terms are bans from bilateral export-credit agencies. Such loans are not generally considered development assistance, as export promotion (rather than development per se) is the avowed purpose of these agencies. However, export credits are often blended with development loans in ways that obscure the distinction; they are at least ostensibly for development, and their terms are at least mildly concessional. A fair proportion of these mixed, or "tied-aid," credits can therefore be considered part of the flow of aid resources.

A short step further away from private capital markets are the hard-loan windows of multilateral development banks. Average loan terms from these banks tend to be slightly more favorable than official export credits, an advantage increased by the fact that multilateral loans are not tied to a specific source.[9] Next come concessional loans, which generally meet ODA standards and originate from bilateral aid agencies, and some soft-loan windows of regional development banks, followed by the no-interest loans of the World Bank's soft-loan window. Furthest from market terms are outright grants, made primarily by donor governments, the EU, OPEC, and various UN agencies. The practices of blending and cofinancing further complicate this spectrum in terms of aggregate aid.[10]

The regime norm of institutionalized noncompetition is formally embodied in the legislative mandates of many agencies; they are prohibited from making loans if an agency offering harder terms is prepared to do so. It is also embodied in the practice of graduation from softer loans to harder loans, a step a recipient takes when it reaches a set level of per capita income or attains a certain level of access to commercial bank lending. These norms limit the systemwide cost of financing concessional transfers to LDCs and reinforce the role of market principles.

The Negotiating Framework:
Asymmetrical Bilateralism

Virtually all aid transfers are directly negotiated by providers (either singly or jointly) and individual recipients, despite a half century of efforts by LDCs to establish a more automatic and collective format. Whether bilateral or multilateral, aid has remained ultimately a matter of discretionary choice by donors, subject to requests by and negotiations with prospective recipients. Thus, the national interests of donors, extending far beyond the aid relationships, inevitably take center stage, and the prospects for support to LDCs are limited to cases of perceived *mutual* interest.

The asymmetrical bilateralism of the aid process serves not only to solidify the advantages of the world's wealthiest states but also to isolate recipients from each other and to separate aid negotiations from other issues and from arenas in which recipients could express a collective voice.

Despite efforts by LDCs to link them, donors have successfully insisted that international monetary issues, trade, and debt relief be dealt with in contexts separated from development financing.

Appropriate Uses of Aid: Strategic Nonlending

For years, Baldwin (1985, 1969, 1966, 1965) reminded us that one of the most effective ways to use aid as an instrument of economic statecraft is to withhold it. Donors may either keep the total amount of aid small relative to its potential uses or withhold it altogether from uses deemed inappropriate. As noted, a central determinant of appropriateness is whether private investors or lenders exist as a viable alternative. Written into the statutes of almost every major aid agency, whether bilateral or multilateral, is the requirement that aid not be extended if private-sector financing is available (or would be available given specified changes in government policy). Nonlending, then, is a strategic way of encouraging recipients to be more open to private capital, both local or foreign.

Because most aid in the first instance goes to governments, some observers (most notably Bauer, 1981, 1972) have drawn the conclusion that aid promotes statism. In reality, a great deal of aid simply passes through the recipient government on its way to the private sector, and most of the rest is limited to physical and social infrastructure. A U.S. Treasury Department study during the Reagan administration tested the statism proposition by classifying all the 1980 loans of regional development banks in terms of whether the activity financed would have been undertaken in the private sector in the United States. On this basis, only 8.2 percent of IBRD/IDA lending, 5.6 percent of IDB lending, and 5.8 percent of Asian Development Bank were competitive with the private sector (U.S. Department of the Treasury, 1982).

Strategic nonlending has generally denied aid for the expansion of state-owned means of production, thereby encouraging LDCs to be both politically and financially dependent on processes of private capital accumulation—to occupy the structural position of a capitalist state (Wood, 1980). Indeed, it was primarily the availability of commercial bank lending in the 1970s that enabled some LDCs temporarily to escape this regime constraint.

Two other sets of regime norms will be examined in the next section. The first involves the servicing of debt, an issue that directly affects the financial and political viability of recipient states as well as of aid institutions themselves. The second involves the linkage of aid and development policy through conditionality—a linkage accentuated by the debt crisis that emerged in the 1980s and continues in the late 1990s.

CRISES IN THE AID REGIME:
DEBT AND STRUCTURAL ADJUSTMENT

The Marshall Plan, universally viewed as the most successful aid program of the Cold War era, distributed aid almost entirely in the form of grants. When Marshall Plan funds were disbursed to LDCs, however, most took the form of concessional loans. These loans created debts, which had to be repaid with interest. Unless new loans increased faster than debt service, it was inevitable that aid transfers would become effectively *negative* (more money flowing back to aid donors than received by LDCs). This would not constitute a problem if an adequate level of economic development had been reached. Short of that, however, any situation approaching negative transfers was likely to raise the question of both the ability and willingness of debtors to pay. Economists might consider such reverse capital flows perverse; people in countries still poor were more likely to call them unjust or unacceptable.

This problem emerged early in the aid regime. It has been argued (Libby, 1975) that the creation in 1960 of the IDA soft-loan window in the World Bank was primarily an effort to help LDCs service their IBRD debts and to ensure a continued role for the bank by broadening its constituency. Constant DAC and World Bank efforts to increase aid flows have to be seen at least in part as a strategy to ensure the repayment of past aid. As Payer (1989: 9) suggests, the resulting system increasingly resembled a Ponzi scheme in which new aid became the way of financing old aid. As we shall see, Ponzi techniques have reached new levels of sophistication—and contradiction—in the era of debt crisis.

It is not widely recognized how a crisis of aid-based debt emerged prior to and contributed to the crisis of commercial bank debt that exploded onto the global economy in 1982. For DAC bilateral aid, debt service as a percentage of gross disbursements steadily increased from 23 percent in 1968 to 39 percent in 1980. Only a flurry of seventeen Paris Club debt reschedulings between 1980 and 1982 brought the proportion down to 31 percent in 1982. After an additional 150 Paris Club agreements and a 91 percent increase in DAC aid commitments, debt service on past aid offset 37 percent of new DAC bilateral disbursements in 1991. More lenient debt rescheduling and reduction options adopted by the industrialized countries in Toronto in 1988 and enhanced in 1991 proved insufficient to stem the combined problems of rising official debt and declining net transfers, particularly for the group of countries classified as the "severely indebted low-income countries."[11] Even after the enhanced terms were approved, twenty-one of these poor states had debt ratios in excess of 200 percent, prompting the World Bank to endorse a one-time debt reduction for these countries (World Bank 1993d: 44–47).

The ODA regime's strategy for dealing with debt since 1982—to increase new lending, reschedule debt repayments, and sponsor negotiated and limited debt reduction—did not prevent the doubling of Third World debt between 1982 and the early 1990s. The use of long-term development loans alongside short- and medium-term IMF lending greatly increased the share of debt service going to official creditors, from 21.5 percent in 1982 to 42.7 percent in 1993; for multilateral institutions (not including the IMF), the share rose from 6.7 percent to 22.8 percent.[12] This latter increase was particularly significant because multilateral institutions often refuse to reschedule interest and repayments on their loans, so the room to maneuver was considerably reduced.

There is a certain irony to the solicitousness of the multilateral aid institutions toward the interests of the commercial banks. During the 1970s, the cheap terms and easy access offered by commercial banks led some LDCs to shun both foreign private investors and the IMF. The IFC (1981: 12) complained that the availability of these loans had "led developing countries to adopt a less welcoming policy towards direct (foreign) investors," and the DAC (OECD, 1979a: 96) lamented, "Ample alternative private financing has thus tended to weaken the role of the IMF, and a major part of its resources remains idle." Commercial bank lending was enabling borrowers to escape from regime discipline—but at the cost of an enormous accumulation of debt.

It is tempting to conclude that the debt crisis, now in its second decade, has become a permanent feature of the international economy in general and of the aid regime in particular. Indeed, Griffin (1991: 678) concluded that "the debt burden, not economic development, has become the legacy of forty years of foreign aid." After a short period of viewing the debt problem as a liquidity issue, both bilateral and multilateral institutions have concluded that the resumption of long-term economic growth is critical to the continued success of their debt strategies. Their prescribed route to growth has been structural adjustment, and it is to this central category of regime discourse and policy that we now turn.

In the midst of the debt crisis that began in the early 1980s, a discourse of structural adjustment increasingly displaced the discourse of development. Theoretically, at least, adjustment was merely a means to get the development process back on track, but so dominant did it become for a decade that it might be said that the development-aid regime became an adjustment-aid regime during the 1980s and early 1990s. But adjustment to what? And who was to do the adjusting?

Obviously, LDCs bore the burden of adjustment, especially at first. The ODA regime, though softening the pain of adjustment, nonetheless functioned effectively to shield others, most notably commercial banks, from this burden. Policy choices of LDC governments in previous decades exacerbated the problem of adjustment when it came, but these choices were associated with significant growth in many countries as long as the external environment remained supportive. The advantages of hindsight are evident: Aid institutions criticized poor countries for not anticipating changes the donors had failed to anticipate themselves.

To summarize briefly, LDCs had to adjust to six interrelated changes in their external environment, including:

- The collapse of the commodity boom of the mid-1970s and the resumption of a long-term downward trend in the prices of primary products;
- Deflationary policies in industrialized countries, which pushed up interest rates to record highs for most of the 1980s and plunged the global economy into a prolonged recession;
- The emergence of a creditor cartel, including aid institutions, which successfully asserted the absolute priority of interest payments on international debt over other obligations and succeeded in making outright default unthinkable;
- Reduced private capital flows from commercial banks, resulting in overall negative long-term financial transfers from all sources for LDCs between 1984 and 1988;
- The failure of the ODA regime to increase aid flows sufficiently to offset the loss of export income and sharply reduced private capital inflows; and
- The counterrevolution in development theory that by 1982 had come to dominate the thinking and policies of multilateral and bilateral aid institutions.[13] Indeed, a substantial part of the adjustment process involved adjustment to a much more constraining ODA regime.

Toye (1987) and others have called the resurgence of classical, anti-Keynesian economics "a counter-revolution in development theory and practice." Although this emergent neoliberalism, like any school of thought, has its own diversity, its refraction through the aid regime involved a number of common themes. The first was an overwhelming focus on domestic policy failure as the root cause of the debt and development problems that plagued LDCs in the 1980s. Adverse changes in the international economy were admitted but minimized. The second theme, closely related, connected state minimalism with the superiority of the market. The outcomes of state intervention were seen as virtually always inferior to the outcomes of unfettered markets.

The third, more specific major theme involved a rejection of import substitution in favor of export-oriented policies. The evidence in support of the latter rested very heavily on the experiences of Japan, South Korea, and

Taiwan, and the World Bank energetically promoted the view that the success of export-led growth was based on "market-friendly economic policies," not, as much of the academic literature suggested, on state guidance and intervention (e.g., Wade, 1993, 1990; Woo, 1991; Haggard, 1990; and Amsden, 1989). The World Bank continues to promote these views to a broad audience in the late 1990s.

Neoliberalism's most immediate impact on the provision of ODA has been the rise of structural-adjustment programs in more than seventy countries. Although the IMF and the World Bank take great pains to emphasize that these programs are tailored to the circumstances and wishes of individual countries, virtually all involve the "four Ds": devalue, decontrol, deflate, and denationalize (Lipton and Toye, 1990: 101).

There is evidence, however, that both the focus of aid donors on structural adjustment and the dominance of neoliberal ideas are in gradual decline. This trend can be seen in a series of contradictions in the regime-guided adjustment process. First, although it was largely debt-servicing problems that brought LDCs to adjustment borrowing, aid institutions were torn between the rapid disbursement necessary if current debt obligations were to be met and the hard bargaining and tough discipline required to impose the high-level conditionality envisioned in structural-adjustment lending. Second, a learning process has taken place, particularly within the World Bank, about the political dimensions of successful reform processes.[14] What has been called the "orthodox paradox"—the attempt to use the state to dismantle its own power and shift decisionmaking to markets—has drawn increased attention to issues of state efficacy and institution building (e.g., Streeten, 1993; and Callaghy, 1989).

Third, a combination of domestic and international pressures has forced adjustment programs to acquire more of a "human face." UNICEF's two-volume study of the largely adverse consequences of early adjustment programs on women and children (Cornia et al., 1987) was an important step in the process.[15] The result, as Hyden and Karlstrom (1993: 1395) suggested, is that "the [structural adjustment] concept itself has become increasingly ambiguous." Fourth, despite agreement among adjusting countries, the World Bank, the IMF, and the DAC that successful structural adjustment requires substantial increases in ODA, the aid regime has by and large been unable to deliver them.

Finally, just as one source of structural-adjustment lending was "project fatigue," there is evidence in the late 1990s of "adjustment fatigue." This phenomenon stems first and foremost from the inconclusive results of structural-adjustment programs to date. Attempts to determine the relationship between aid and development have always produced nebulous results, so it should not be surprising that the effects of structural-adjustment programs have proven equally unclear.

Together, these considerations suggest that structural adjustment by the turn of the century will have been consigned to the already rather long list of failed panaceas for development. The basic truth—that in the absence of international reform LDCs have little choice but to respond to global changes beyond their control—will remain. It is likely, however, that the reforms suggested by the adjustment concept will be increasingly broadened to go beyond neoliberal prescriptions and that the need for changes in the global economy to enable, support, and extend these reforms will be increasingly recognized.

CONCLUSION

In the wake of the Cold War, USAID official Richard Bissell (1992: 32) lauded U.S. economic assistance as "an instrument, sometimes as effective as arms, in confronting and containing communism in the main streets and remote corners of the world." As development experts (e.g., Ruttan, 1989: 414) have noted, the effectiveness of aid, including military transfers, in promoting Cold War security and political objectives has been subject to far less scrutiny than the effectiveness of aid in promoting development. Whatever the truth or falsity of Bissell's claim, it appears clear that the use of economic assistance to "confront and contain communism" frequently conflicted with its use in promoting sound economic and social development. The long-term legacies of the Cold War aid policies are only beginning to be fully grasped.

The ODA regime's position in the international political economy appears secure, although its roles will likely remain ambiguous, controversial, and in some cases contradictory. On the one hand, the end of the Cold War has in some respects freed the regime from pernicious external constraints and pressures; an important set of nondevelopmental factors that often impinged on the regime has been largely removed. In this respect the regime has in some ways been liberated. On the other hand, with the elimination of the Cold War justification for development aid, other types of foreign aid are likely to become increasingly important. The most important of these so far is aid for the transition economies of the former state-socialist countries. As noted earlier, ODA to these countries as a group was equal in per capita terms to ODA to LDCs in 1992, and aid to Russia currently dwarfs aid to any other single recipient.[16] But there are other contending uses for foreign aid in the post–Cold War era as well, most notably the promotion of sustainable development, which the UN, OECD, and most major donor states embraced in the early 1990s.[17]

Some recent events provide clues to the ODA regime's future. As the Cold War wound down, the U.S. government quickly withdrew its aid from strategic allies such as Zaire and eased its opposition to World Bank lending to socialist countries, including Vietnam. In this new context, we are likely to see the extension and consolidation of a number of currently tentative regime norms linking aid allocation and concessionality more closely to economic performance and to programs focused on food security, poverty alleviation, and sustainable development. In a context of increased competition for aid resources, graduation practices within the aid regime will likely be tightened, shifting countries sooner from more to less concessional aid and then to market mechanisms.

As this process occurs, the increasingly aid-dependent majority of sub-Saharan African countries will become the main focus and challenge of the ODA regime. Neoliberal prescriptions and conventional structural-adjustment programs seem increasingly irrelevant with respect to the desperate plight of these LLDCs. Further, the end of the Cold War should give the epistemic community of development experts and activists (both North and South) a better chance to be heard as the influence of the rather narrowly based neoliberal community declines.[18]

Prior to 1991, aid not related to the Cold War could be assumed, at least in general intention, to be development aid. This assumption, however, did not preclude an array of goals subsumed under the rubric of development.[19] Still, the demise of Cold War goals makes it likely that other goals will become more salient. In addition, the casino-like quality of the global financial system is likely to generate a regular sequence of crises, such as the Mexican peso crisis of 1995 and the $10 billion Russian loan of 1996, calling for various kinds of aid and loan guarantees to protect the interests of powerful international investors and lenders.

In sum, trends in economic assistance are likely to reflect two opposing tendencies: a more coherent focus on development, at least as aid donors define it, and an increasing use of other forms and purposes of aid whose relationship to development may be problematic. Ideally, the outcome will be a creative tension, spurring innovation and synthesis, but the potential exists for the kind of displacement of development goals that too often occurred during the Cold War.

NOTES

1. Coincidentally, the United States was displaced by Japan as the largest provider of official development assistance in 1989—the year the Berlin Wall came down.

2. The way had been paved by the belated official designation of China as a developing country in 1980, but who could have predicted how that category would expand after 1989?

3. Some observers have expressed doubt about whether a development-aid regime actually exists. Ruggie (1983: 435), for example, labeled it a "quasi regime." An important outlet of regime theorists, *International Organization,* carried articles on the closely related "balance-of-payments financing regime" (Cohen, 1982), the "debt regime" (Lipson, 1981), the "trade finance regime" (Moravcsik, 1989), and the "food-aid regime" (Hopkins, 1992, 1987; Uvin, 1992) but has never taken up the development-aid regime as such. Kardam (1993) assumed the existence of a "development-assistance regime" in his analysis of policy advocacy in multilateral organizations but treated it narrowly in terms of external pressure. Another attempt to apply the regime concept to economic assistance is Wood (1986).

4. About three-quarters of bilateral aid (not including export credits) meets ODA standards established by the OECD.

5. An accessible survey of the OECD, the IMF, multilateral development banks, UN specialized agencies and programs, and related NGOs is contained in Morrison and Purcell (1988).

6. The World Bank group is technically part of the United Nations system but most often operates independently.

7. Combined IBRD/IDA commitments reached $23.7 billion in 1993, up from $14.5 billion a decade earlier.

8. Members of the Organization for European Economic Cooperation (OEEC) created the Development Assistance Group (DAG) in 1960, the precursor to the DAC. Subsequently, Japan, Australia, and New Zealand became members of the DAC; Spain and Portugal, which originally were recipients of aid, joined the DAC in 1991.

9. Tied aid is aid that must be used to purchase the goods and services of a source country. Studies indicate that the tying of aid lowers the real value of aid by an average of 15–30 percent, effectively increasing the interest rate. In individual projects however, tying has been shown to increase costs by as much as 225 percent (Jepma, 1991: 15, 59).

10. "Blending" refers to the deliberate mix of aid carrying different terms to achieve a specified aggregate set of loan terms for a given country. For example, the World Bank classifies countries as IDA-only countries, IBRD-only countries, and blend countries. By varying the proportions of IDA and IBRD lending for blend countries, it can achieve a range of aggregate terms. "Cofinancing" involves blending at the project level, where loans from different aid agencies and sometimes private lenders and investors are linked together in a package of financing. Cofinancing allows official lenders to leverage their money into larger financial packages, and it offers private lenders and investors political risk protection.

11. According to the World Bank's 1993–1994 annual report on debt, the debt-service ratio (scheduled debt service as a proportion of exports) for these countries at the end of 1992 ranged from a low of 183 percent for Egypt to more than 2,000 percent for Sudan, Nicaragua, and Somalia.

12. In addition to providing money to service commercial debt, the World Bank in 1990 established a debt-reduction facility for IDA-only countries. This facility provided grants to retire commercial debt at market-determined discounted rates. The Inter-American Development Bank established a similar facility.

13. As Woo (1990: 415) suggests, the triumph of this counterrevolution in development thought was symbolized in 1982 by the replacement of Hollis Chenery by Anne Krueger as vice president of development policy at the World Bank. See Stallings (1992) for a useful attempt to link changes in development thought to the debt crisis and subsequent adjustment strategies.

14. World Bank research has paid increasing attention to political processes and to the political correlates of success and failure, and its research has been supplemented by a number of excellent independent studies (e.g., Haggard and Kaufman, 1992; Mosley, et al., 1991a, 1991b; and Nelson, et al., 1989). Though the findings of these studies are too complex and varied to be summarized here, they consistently suggest that significant departures from neoliberal rectitude are necessary for the sustainability of adjustment. For example, some losers from reform must be bought off, and the interests of both vulnerable and aggrieved popular classes need to be accommodated (Nelson, 1993, 1989).

15. Researchers and activists alike documented the variety of adjustment strategies, which carried widely variable social implications (e.g., Nelson, 1993; Clark, 1990; and Taylor, 1988).

16. In addition, Russia received more official debt relief in 1993 than all LDCs combined.

17. A thoughtful review of possible new roles for ODA may be found in Moore and Robinson (1994).

18. International regime theory pays considerable attention to the role of communities of experts, known as epistemic communities, in facilitating both regime initiation and change (see Haas, 1992).

19. A U.S. congressional task force in 1989 found no fewer than thirty-three independent statutory goals and objectives and seventy-five priority areas that USAID was obliged to pursue in formulating its aid program—along with 288 reporting requirements in implementing it (Wharton, 1993: 528; Rondinelli, 1989: 76).

3

From Military Aid to Military Markets

Michael T. Klare & Daniel Volman

As the first two chapters of this book describe, foreign aid since World War II has been disbursed in two primary forms—economic and military. Most of this book will focus on economic assistance, given its larger volume and geographic scope, particularly in the post–Cold War era. But readers should also understand the flip side of the foreign-aid coin—military assistance—which played a crucial role in projecting great-power influence during the Cold War and which continues to shape North-South relations in the late 1990s.

In this chapter we will first review the role of military aid in the Cold War international system. We will then consider the transition from military *assistance* to market-driven military *sales* in the 1990s, with particular attention devoted to the growing and pivotal role played by the United States in this process. Finally, we consider the consequences of these trends for international stability and outline our proposal for an arms-transfer-control regime.

The crucial point is this: Regardless of whether weapons are shipped to LDCs on concessional or market terms, their effects on the internal governance of recipients—on their prospects for sustained and equitable economic development, domestic order, and regional stability—are identical. Heavily militarized LDCs are among the most volatile, repressive, and crisis-prone in the world; large stockpiles of weaponry often take on a life of their own. Moreover, the relationship between the source and recipient of military hardware extends far beyond the transfer of weaponry, providing wealthy states great and enduring leverage over LDCs. Finally, arms transfers on concessional and cash terms alike contribute to global militarization at a time of great uncertainty in the international system.

THE HISTORICAL CONTEXT OF MILITARY AID

Economic aid, ostensibly intended to improve socioeconomic conditions in the world's poorest countries, is usually considered the most appropriate form of foreign assistance. However, concessional transfers of military hardware—munitions, spare parts, and expertise—have for centuries played a key part in the security policies of major powers. During the Cold War the United States, the Soviet Union, the People's Republic of China, and other states attracted clients by promising military assistance. Unlike development aid, however, the volume and economic value of these transfers were often confidential, and no international regime emerged that attempted to document military aid. But given the massive volume of military transfers and the integral role they played in the manufacturing sectors of many industrialized states, these military-aid relationships had significant impact on the domestic economies of donor nations. In many cases, official development assistance and military aid flowed simultaneously from donor to recipient, creating complex and overlapping relationships that endured for decades, even after the Cold War ended. Fungibility has always been a central aspect of foreign aid, and the line between economic and military aid has been routinely crossed.

A substantial proportion of arms transfers from the major powers was provided free or subsidized through loans at submarket interest rates. The United States alone recorded more than $145 billion in military assistance between 1946 and 1991, 71 percent in the form of grants (USACDA, 1992: 4). Of this total, more than $73 billion was transferred to the Near East and South Asia, $40 billion to East Asia, $5 billion to Latin America, and $4 billion to Africa. The remaining military aid, just 13 percent of the total, was designated for industrialized states (USACDA, 1992).

These and other concessional transfers of military resources to "friendly" states projected the security interests of the donors, strengthened clients' hold on power in the face of internal challenges, and tipped regional balances of power. The provision of military training established intimate links between donors and recipients and gave the sources of weaponry leverage in other aspects of their bilateral relations. Finally, military transfers increased the revenues of arms manufacturers and, perversely, provided them with foreign battlefields to serve as testing grounds for their products.

Since the end of the Cold War the volume of foreign military assistance has dramatically decreased. According to the best estimates, the annual value of arms transfers to the developing world declined from levels in excess of $50 billion in the 1980s to $20.4 billion in 1993, with about 60 percent of the latter total originating in the United States (Grimmett, 1994: 49). Substantial reductions have been documented in the level of arms transfers by Russia and China, which continue to export large volumes of weapons but emphasize basic products such as machine guns, ammunition, and rocket launchers rather than more sophisticated (and expensive) missile systems, aircraft, and computer-support networks. Transfers by France, the United Kingdom, Germany, and other middle-range producers have fluctuated widely but have generally decreased in real terms in the 1990s.

These changes in the level of arms transfers to the developing world have been due, in large part, to the general decline in military-aid programs. The best known—and most precipitous—reduction, of course, occurred in the Soviet Union, which provided a large proportion of global military assistance until the late 1980s. This military aid was being reduced even before the collapse of the Soviet Union in 1991, and it disappeared almost entirely thereafter (although Russia was reported to have provided some military hardware to Tajikistan and other unstable Central Asian republics during the mid-1990s as part of its effort to combat Islamic fundamentalism in the region).

Whereas the Soviet Union in its heyday supplied billions of dollars of arms each year to favored clients such as Cuba and Vietnam for no cost (or for overvalued supplies of raw materials), its successors are in no position to provide arms for free or even at concessional rates. Instead, they have asked for payment in hard currencies. But many of their major clients, including Cuba and Vietnam, are themselves effectively bankrupt or would rather spend their hard currencies on Western, especially U.S. weapons, which were deemed to have performed better than Soviet weapons in the Gulf War. (The defeat of Iraq in 1991 also accounts for much of the decline in French and Chinese arms exports, as Saddam Hussein had been one of their major customers.)

The PRC has also made some cuts in its military-aid programs, which provided small but significant quantities of arms to governments and insurgent forces in a number of developing countries—particularly in Africa—during the 1960s and 1970s. Since the late 1980s the level of Chinese aid has dropped in real terms as the PRC has sought to reduce spending on the armed forces and to increase cash arms exports as part of its policy of economic modernization.[1] During the 1980s the PRC continued to transfer "very modest quantities of arms at concessional rates or as military aid to mostly African countries in its attempt to counter Soviet influence, and to add to its credentials as a Third World champion" (Eikenberry, 1995: 10). But as cash sales gained in importance, Chinese arms transfers to Africa (both sales and aid) fell from 17.1 percent of total transfers in the 1974–1978 period to 2.8 percent in the mid-1980s, and Chinese arms transfers to Africa have continued to decline in the 1990s.[2]

Among European arms exporters, France and Great Britain have consistently provided the largest amounts of military assistance. As in the case of development aid, they have provided military aid primarily to their former colonies in Africa and South Asia. In both cases, military transfers on both concessional and market terms have decreased in the 1990s, for a variety of reasons (USACDA, 1995: 111, 135). Arms transfers as a percentage of total exports have also decreased during the decade.

Only Nigeria, Zimbabwe, and Mauritius received concessional arms transfers from Great Britain in the early 1990s, and before that British leaders generally deferred to the United States in dictating the volume and direction of military-aid flows. Since the end of the Cold War, British arms transfers have occurred almost entirely on market terms and largely have been directed toward affluent states, including Saudi Arabia and South Korea.

Most French arms transfers to Africa in the mid-1990s have been in the form of cash sales to Nigeria rather than military aid to former colonies, which France continues to regard as de facto protectorates. In the 1991–1993 period, the French government sold $50 million worth of weapons to Nigeria, more than half the $85 million in arms sales the French government recorded during the period.[3] The new French government, headed by Jacque Chirac, reevaluated France's long-standing relationship with its former colonies in light of its desire to cut the budget and to devote more attention and resources to promoting European economic and political integration. This shift in priorities is likely to lead to further reductions in French military-aid programs.

Another major change in the international arms network has been the emergence of East Asia as a major market. Buoyed by an increase in national income due to highly successful trade policies, the NICs of the Pacific Rim have become avid consumers of modern weaponry. Taiwan, for instance, has ordered 150 F-16 fighters from the United States and 60 Mirage-2000 fighters from France. South Korea and Thailand have also increased their arms purchases, producing a new arms race in the area (Klare, 1993: 136–152). And because those countries tend to favor U.S. weaponry, they have further contributed to the U.S. domination of the arms trade. These arms transfers have been conducted on market rather than concessional terms, reflecting a worldwide trend in this industry.

At first blush, the overall decline in military aid would appear to be a most welcome and encouraging consequence of the Cold War's demise. After all, the historical record is filled with cases in which military aid from the superpowers inflamed regional conflicts in the developing world and militarized fragile nation-states just emerging from colonial rule. The massive transfers of military hardware often strengthened autocratic leaders and left the vast majority of LDC populations impoverished and politically powerless. These trends, visible from Central America across Africa to much of

South Asia, left a legacy of political unrest, socioeconomic despair, and military control that remains palpable long after the Cold War.

Unfortunately, the decline of foreign military aid has not ended the flow of arms from North to South. It has merely changed the *terms* of these transactions, which had been largely executed on a concessional basis but increasingly have taken the form of cash and barter sales. Military aid has largely given way to military markets in the late 1990s, reflecting broader realignments in the foreign policies of the post–Cold War great powers and in the international political economy.

THE U.S. ARMS BAZAAR

As global arms transfers have declined since the end of the Cold War, the importance of U.S. arms transfers has expanded significantly.[4] The proportion of global arms transfers originating in the United States rose from 16.7 percent of the total in 1988 to 55.8 percent in 1993, making the United States by far the preeminent source of military hardware and materiel in the immediate post–Cold War era.[5] Given the primacy of the United States in the arms trade of the mid-1990s—its sales to foreign governments exceeded $12 billion in 1994 alone—it is useful to review its major arms programs in detail.

Although the number of recipients of U.S. military aid under the Foreign Military Sales (FMS) program has been cut sharply, the United States remains the most important supplier of free and low-cost weaponry to the developing world. Grant aid and credit for all African and most South Asian LDCs has been largely eliminated, but large-scale transfers of grant aid continued in fiscal year 1995 to strategically important clients such as Israel ($1.8 billion) and Egypt ($1.3 billion). At the same time, significant funds were shifted from the FMS program to support LDCs' efforts to control international narcotics trafficking, terrorism, and crime. In FY 1995, ten Latin American countries were scheduled to receive a total of $80.2 million in grant military assistance for these purposes.[6]

After cutting its support for the International Military Education and Training (IMET) Program, the United States in the mid-1990s revived spending for this program, which provided military training both at U.S. facilities and abroad. For FY 1995, Congress authorized $26.4 million for the IMET program, an increase of more than 10 percent. European countries were to receive the largest share of this assistance, but allocations in excess of $3 million were approved for recipients in Africa, the Near East, South Asia, and Latin America (U.S. Department of State, 1995).[7]

U.S. grant and concessional military aid therefore remains a significant factor in the developing world. U.S. military sales, which have replaced concessional military assistance as the principal mechanism for arming friendly LDCs, were seen both as a tool of foreign policy and as a means of reducing the U.S. trade deficit. Arms sales were also used to recoup some of the enormous costs of developing and producing high-technology weapons and to prop up the ailing aerospace industry. Spurred by such motivations, U.S. leaders tended to favor a high level of arms exports to the developing world (see Klare, 1984: Chapters 2–3; see also Pierre, 1982: 45–72).

After the 1991 Gulf War, President George Bush called for vigorous international efforts to constrain the flow of advanced weaponry to developing countries. Arguing that unrestrained arms trafficking had contributed to Iraq's aggression, he proposed new restraints on unconventional (i.e., nuclear, chemical, and biological) munitions and announced a number of separate initiatives aimed at limiting the global trade in conventional weapons.

The president's commitment to arms control did not survive for long, however. Driven by the same sorts of arguments that had inspired his predecessors, Bush announced a series of major new military sales to Egypt, Israel, Turkey, and the United Arab Emirates (UAE), setting in motion intensive arms marketing by the other major suppliers. By late 1991, international arms trafficking had returned to pre–Gulf War levels, and the United States was riding the crest of a global arms boom. Proponents of a permissive arms-export policy in the United States argued that high levels of military sales were needed in the post–Cold War era to cushion the economic consequences of reduced spending by the U.S. Department of Defense and to protect allied regimes in unstable regions.

However, critics of the current policy (including the authors of this chapter) argue that unrestrained arms sales pose significant risks for U.S. and international security. By stimulating regional arms races in areas of potential or actual conflict, such sales exacerbate tensions and increase the likelihood that ethnic and territorial disputes will be resolved through force rather than through peaceful negotiation. They also divert scarce resources from vital socioeconomic needs and thus contribute to continuing underdevelopment and instability in the developing world (see Hartung, 1994: Chapter 10; Klare, 1984: Chapters 6–7; and Pierre, 1982: 136–231).

Clearly, U.S. policymakers face something of a dilemma regarding arms transfers. On the one hand, many within Congress, the executive branch, and the military-industrial complex favor the continuation of unfettered arms transfers to LDCs. On the other hand, many arms-control experts and some members of Congress favor a tightening of U.S. arms export controls and fresh efforts to adopt multilateral controls of the sort considered by the five major powers in 1991. The struggle between these two groups is likely to intensify in the late 1990s as regional arms races accelerate and as U.S. arms sales continue their upward climb (see Hartung, 1994).

The outcome of this debate will have a significant impact on the future of international security. With the Cold War over, many experts believe the greatest threat to world peace and security is posed by the growing frequency and intensity of regional and ethnic conflicts. In this environment, the relative tempo and scale of international arms trafficking could prove critical. If the arms flow expands, we are likely to see an increase in the duration and destructiveness of regional conflicts. If we can reduce this flow, we might stand a better chance of curbing the virulence and frequency of such conflicts.

The U.S. government's permissive stance toward arms transfers—both concessional and market-rate—first arose during the early Cold War era, when both superpowers began to use them as a device for winning and retaining the loyalty of LDCs, especially in South Asia, Latin America, and the Middle East. Many U.S. policymakers continue to cling to these beliefs in the post–Cold War era, even though Moscow is no longer in a position to challenge Washington for the loyalty of developing nations and despite the fact that many once-vulnerable clients are now engaged in regional power struggles of their own.

Immediately following the 1992 election, Bill Clinton promised to initiate the development of new multilateral controls on the arms trade. "I expect to review our arms sales policy and to take it up with the other major arms sellers of the world as part of a long-term effort to reduce the proliferation of weapons of destruction in the hands of people who might use them in very destructive ways," Clinton told reporters in Washington. In February 1995 the White House revised its policy on conventional-arms transfers, offering greater support for documentation of arms transfers and discouraging those to expansionist states. But this policy, too, defended the continuation of massive arms sales, and Clinton, like Bush, approved major sales of U.S. weapons to long-term customers.

Although a disjointed policy of this sort is undoubtedly attractive to U.S. policymakers, who perennially seek to accommodate competing pressures, it cannot be sustained indefinitely. Given the multiplicity of suppliers in the global arms market and the strong pressure to increase foreign sales (due largely to cutbacks in Cold War–related military spending), any rise in U.S. military transfers will undoubtedly be viewed by other suppliers as justifying corresponding increases in their own arms exports. And because what is viewed as defensive by one country is often seen as offensive by others, an increase in U.S. arms sales to a particular country in a region will inevitably spur its neighbors and rivals to increase *their* arms acquisitions.

The result, in all likelihood, will be an intensified regional arms race and an increased risk of miscalculation and conflict.

The impact of unrestrained U.S. sales on other suppliers is readily apparent in statements by Russian leaders concerning their own country's sales policies. "I think if other countries would have started reducing arms deliveries, this would have had some effect" on Russian policy, Andrei Kokoshin, a senior Russian military expert, observed in February 1992. However, "it turned out that most democratic countries are not stopping arms sales, but increasing them." For these reasons, he noted, it is unrealistic and unfair to expect Russian arms companies to reduce their own military transfers. In fact, after weathering the downfall of many arms programs in the wake of the Soviet Union's demise, Russian firms have stepped up their arms-marketing activities in such areas as the Middle East, South Asia, and the Far East. Russian arms exports grew from $2.4 billion in 1992 to $2.6 billion in 1993 in constant dollars (USACDA, 1995: 128). They were expected to grow further in the late 1990s, as conservative challengers to President Boris Yeltsin advocated greater arms production as a means to revive the Russian economy.

It is evident, therefore, that despite Washington's best efforts to balance competing policy concerns, there is a contradiction between selling large numbers of weapons to foreign governments and pursuing multilateral constraints on arms transfers. The United States cannot pursue both goals simultaneously and expect to accomplish its stated objective of curbing arms proliferation. If progress is to be made at the international level, the United States must demonstrate its willingness to impose restraints on its own arms exports. This, in turn, will require leaders to confront the arguments that have traditionally been used to justify U.S. military transfers.

Given this assessment, it is abundantly clear that the United States's long-term security interests—and those of its friends and allies—would best be served by exploiting the Cold War's end to reduce dramatically the flow of arms from rich to poor states. The great powers face a historic opportunity to constrain the flow of conventional arms to areas of conflict and to persuade LDCs to join in regional peace talks aimed at reducing tensions and shrinking military arsenals.

Indeed, this was precisely the position adopted by Congress in Section 401 of the Foreign Relations Authorization Act for FY 1993: "Future security and stability in the Middle East and Persian Gulf region would be enhanced by establishing a stable military balance among regional powers by *restraining and reducing* both conventional and unconventional weapons" (emphasis added). The act called upon the president to work with other major arms suppliers to establish a multilateral arms-transfer–control regime similar to those now covering exports of nuclear, chemical, and missile technology. We will consider this proposal below and advance our own recommendations for such a regime.

NEEDED: A VIABLE ARMS-TRANSFER–CONTROL REGIME

Assuming that official U.S. policy shifts toward curtailment of arms trade in the late 1990s, it will be necessary to develop the functioning components of an arms-transfer-control regime. Such a regime will begin, in all likelihood, with supplier restraints of the sort discussed by the major powers in 1991. To be fully effective, however, it will also require the adoption of regional peace and security pacts in the Middle East and other areas of tension (so as to reduce the *demand* for arms) and economic conversion efforts in the major arms-producing countries (so as to reduce the pressure to *supply* weapons).

In developing such mechanisms, advocates of conventional-arms-transfer control can draw on several earlier attempts. The earliest of these was the voluntary register of arms transfers maintained by the League of Nations during the interwar period. Although not notably successful in restraining military sales during this period, the League effort did provide a model for more recent proposals aimed at promoting openness, or transparency, in the arms trade. A second example was the 1974 Declaration of Ayacucho, under which eight South American nations pledged to restrain their purchases of offensive weapons. This initiative also failed to slow the spread of weapons, but it, too, contained features that were incorporated into subsequent proposals (Pierre, 1982: 281–285).

The arms-restraint policy of President Jimmy Carter provides a further model. Announced on May 19, 1977, the Carter plan included an annual ceiling on U.S. sales to most non-NATO nations and a ban on new-technology arms deliveries to LDCs not already possessing such weapons. The Carter policy also called upon the United States to meet with other major suppliers, particularly the Soviet Union, to negotiate multilateral controls on the arms trade. Though the resulting Conventional Arms Transfer Talks (CATT) of 1977–1978 failed to result in any concrete agreements, they produced a model for multilateral arms-export controls and established a negotiating history that can be drawn upon in future agreements (Pierre, 1982: 52–62).

To supplement these few examples, proponents of conventional arms control are looking at other treaties and agreements as possible models for action. Though not directly applicable to conventional-arms transfers, these prototypes often incorporate specific features that can be woven into a conventional arms-transfer-control regime. These models include the Nuclear Non-Proliferation Treaty (NPT); the Missile Technology Control Regime (MTCR); and the Conventional Forces in Europe (CFE) Disarmament Agreement of 1990. By building on these prior initiatives, it is possible to conceive of a comprehensive arms-transfer-control regime that would enable the world community to curb the flow of arms to areas of tension and conflict.[8] Such a regime should feature several key components.

Transparency

The first step in imposing greater international control over the arms trade is to promote greater transparency in arms imports and exports. Proponents of transparency argue that greater openness in the arms trade will counteract the tendency of nations to overarm in response to ambiguous or incomplete data regarding their rivals' arms purchases (a tendency fed by the common, and perhaps rational, inclination to assume the worst about an enemy's military capabilities). Full disclosure may also provide an early-warning system that can be used to detect major military buildups by potential belligerents (see United Nations, 1991: 36–40). In line with these views, the UN General Assembly voted 150 to 0 (with 2 abstentions) in December 1991 to establish a voluntary register of conventional-arms transfers. The register, when fully functioning, will collect and publish data on arms imports and exports by all member states (see SIPRI, 1992: 299–301, 305–307).

Critics of transparency as a route to arms control charge that it will be impossible to gain support for such measures from many key countries and that even if such support does materialize it will be impossible to prevent cheating by those with something to conceal. They believe both the sources and recipients of arms transfers will consider these exchanges as classified national-security secrets, a position the U.S. Central Intelligence Agency steadfastly defended throughout the Cold War.

In response, proponents argue that transparency is not an all-or-nothing proposition but rather an evolutionary process that can develop over time into a comprehensive, mandatory system as the world gains confidence in such procedures. Proponents also suggest that it is possible and desirable to develop new systems of verification—including a UN monitoring agency—to support more advanced forms of transparency (see Brzoska, 1983). It is in the interest of all countries to have accurate data regarding global arms movements.

Supply-side Restraints

Although the technology to produce arms has been widely diffused, a few countries, led by the United States, continue to dominate the trade in high-technology armaments. It is possible, therefore, to establish supply-side restraints, or supplier cartels, to control the spread of arms to particular regions. Such measures have been tested by the major Western powers in the past, notably through the 1950 Tripartite Declaration on the Middle East, but have generally proved to be of limited effectiveness because of the nonparticipation of the Soviet Union and the People's Republic of China. In the aftermath of the successful UN embargo of arms to Iraq, however, it is possible to conceive of agreements that include all major suppliers. This was the basis of the negotiations among major powers initiated in Paris in July 1991.

Assuming that these negotiations can continue in the late 1990s, what sort of measures should the major suppliers adopt? The goal of such restraints should not be to cut off the flow of arms entirely, as that will only boost the black-market traffic in arms. Rather, the goals should be to constrict significantly the arms flow to areas of tension and to preclude deliveries of weapons that would have a destabilizing effect. To accomplish the former, the major suppliers should set an annual ceiling on total sales by any single supplier to any individual recipient.[9] To accomplish the latter, the suppliers should set maximum-allowable-force levels for major weapons systems of regional protagonists and ban the sale of any equipment that would exceed these levels (see Nolan, 1991a).

It is possible, of course, that supplier restraints of this sort would merely spur recipient countries to seek out other suppliers of such hardware or to develop or expand their own arms-production capabilities. Therefore, supply-side restraints should be accompanied by regional arms-control agreements, and the talks among the major suppliers should be expanded to include mid-level sources such as Italy, Spain, Israel, and Brazil.

Regional Arms Control Agreements

It will be impossible to halt the flow of arms into a region unless the nations of that region agree among themselves to exercise restraint in the acquisition of arms. Supplier restraints of the sort described above can never halt the delivery of all weapons to an area, because the technology to produce conventional arms is now so widespread. Moreover, such cartels are widely resented by many leaders of LDCs because of their association with imperial systems of control. Thus, any system for arms control within a region should rely as much on recipient restraint as on supplier restraint—with the latter used as a stimulus for the former or as a substitute when recipient restraint does not appear to be forthcoming.

Previous attempts at regional self-restraint—notably the Declaration of Ayacucho—have not been particularly successful. With the signing of the CFE agreement, however, arms-control proponents can point to a new and highly successful model of regional arms control. Arms-control analysts have suggested the establishment of similar mechanisms in other areas. These proposals envisage a similar approach to that adopted in the Conference on Security and Cooperation in Europe (CSCE), which involves consultations, increased transparency, confidence-building measures, and other steps leading over time to specific arms-control agreements (see Kemp, 1992: 124–128).

Technology Control

With the establishment of the Missile Technology Control Regime (MTCR) in 1987, major Western powers created a prototype for multilateral controls on the proliferation of military systems. Although limited in its applicability and lacking effective provisions for inspection and enforcement, the MTCR has been credited with a significant slowdown in the spread of missile technology. Moreover, the regime has gained international legitimacy through the decisions by such nations as China, Israel, and Russia to join the regime or to abide by its provisions (see Nolan, 1991b: 145–155).

The imposition of MTCR-type controls on other military systems, however, is not likely to prove effective in curbing the spread of basic combat systems that are produced in many countries and whose design principles are widely known. It would also be unwise to view such controls as a substitute for more inclusive constraints on the arms trade. However, this approach can and should be used to slow the spread of particular weapons whose introduction into areas of conflict would have a destabilizing effect. Using these criteria, the best candidates for MTCR-like controls are submarines, cruise missiles, and deep-penetration bombers.

Economic Carrots and Sticks

Except in a few of the wealthier LDCs, arms imports constitute luxury items in that they contribute little or nothing to development and consume scarce hard currencies and/or overseas credit. For this reason, excessive military spending by debt-burdened LDCs has produced great concern among officials of the international lending agencies, notably the World Bank and the IMF. The linkage between military spending and international lending was first raised by World Bank president Barber B. Conable, who observed in 1989, "It is important to place military spending decisions on the same footing as other fiscal decisions and to explore ways to bring military spending into better balance with development priorities."

On the basis of such remarks, it is possible to imagine an arms-transfer-restraint regime based on the use of economic incentives, including the awarding of supplemental ODA to states that reduce their arms spending and the denial of such aid to states that devote more than a certain percentage of their national income to military purposes. Such a regime would rely both on international measures, notably those adopted by the World Bank, and on cooperation by major donor nations.

At the same time, economic incentives—in the form of grants, loans, and technical assistance—should be provided to weapons firms in the supplying countries that agree to convert their production to nonmilitary products. Because many military contractors and the communities in which they are located depend on foreign sales to make up for declines in domestic demand, there is an ever-present lobby opposed to arms-export restraints. If these pressures are to be neutralized, it is essential that proposals for arms-transfer control include assistance to firms and communities affected by such restrictions.

Each of these mechanisms, operating independently, would provide government leaders with an effective instrument for constraining the transfer of conventional weapons. None of them, however, can address all of the major concerns identified in this chapter. As in the nuclear- and chemical-weapons fields, a number of mechanisms—each addressing one or more fundamental problems—must be brought together into a comprehensive arms-transfer-control regime. Ultimately, it will not be possible to constrain the arms trade until all the nations of the world are brought into regional and international security systems designed to overcome local hostilities and eliminate the need for large military arsenals (see Johansen, 1994).

CONCLUSION

The demise of many programs of foreign military assistance has been a welcome trend in the aftermath of the Cold War. No longer are the world's major powers providing massive amounts of weaponry to developing countries, either as gifts or on favorable terms. Military assistance served as a common strategy during the Cold War, promoting superpower geostrategies at the cost of domestic development and regional stability in the former Third World. Now that the race for clients is over, and now that many LDCs have created peaceful, democratic governments, this chapter of global militarization has mercifully come to a close.

But the transition from military aid to military markets poses its own risks for international security. These risks, which have been outlined above, suggest that continued vigilance is essential if the promising trends of the early 1990s are to continue. In today's uncertain world, most arms transfers raise proliferation risks rather than assuring military and economic security. No doubt there will still be some cases in which it will be deemed necessary to supply certain weapons to friendly nations in danger of being overrun by a hostile power. However, the top priority of all industrialized states should be to pursue the development of a multilateral arms-transfer-control regime and to intensify efforts to produce comprehensive peace settlements in heavily militarized areas of conflict such as the Middle East.

Arms-transfer restraint on the part of the United States and other major suppliers will be a crucial condition of global restraint and will advance other objectives as well. To promote stability, development, and democracy in poor regions, it is essential that states increase their investments in education, health, agriculture, and basic infrastructure. But the more these countries spend on imported arms, the less they have for nonmilitary purposes (see Ball, 1988). Inasmuch as some LDCs spend a considerable portion of government revenues on armaments, any reductions in weapons spending could release significant funds for social and economic development, which is needed much more urgently than arms in these impoverished regions.

Ultimately, it matters little whether LDCs receive their guns, tanks, and military training in the form of gifts or in exchange for cash. History has shown that the flow of weaponry imposes its own independent effects on regional tensions and global stability. If the promise of the post–Cold War period is to be realized, restraining military assistance and market-rate arms transfers should be a top priority of the world's wealthiest states.

NOTES

1. The overall, inflation-adjusted level of Chinese military transfers—both aid and cash sales—dropped from more than $3 billion annually in the late 1980s to $950 million in 1993 (USACDA, 1995: 106). Arms transfers as a percentage of total Chinese exports fell during this period from about 6 percent to 1 percent.

2. Although the Chinese government does not reveal the value of its military-aid programs, a clear indication of its small size is provided by USACDA data. According to USACDA (1995: 139–140), the total value of Chinese arms transfers to countries other than Zimbabwe and oil-rich Nigeria, both of which paid for arms imports, was $60 million between 1991 and 1993. Recipients of Chinese military aid in these years included Burundi, Chad, Djibouti, Gambia, Mozambique, Zaire, and Zambia.

3. According to USACDA (1995: 139–140), other major recipients were Malawi ($20 million), Burkina Faso ($10 million), and Burundi ($5 million).

4. Though the proportion of U.S. arms sales has increased, U.S. sales declined in constant 1993 dollars from a peak of $15.4 billion in 1987 to $10.3 billion six years later (USACDA, 1995: 135). It was in 1987 that U.S. arms exports reached a record 5.5 percent of total U.S. exports, a figure that fell to 2.2 percent in 1993.

5. The French proportion of global arms transfers rose from 2.3 percent to 15.8 percent over the same period. The share of the trade accounted for by Russia, however, fell from 26.6 percent to 5.9 percent, and Chinese arms transfers fell from 4.8 percent to 1.2 percent of the total (Grimmett, 1994: 51).

6. The largest portions of this funding were designated for Columbia ($29 million), Bolivia ($26 million), and Peru ($16 million).

7. African countries were scheduled to receive $4.9 million worth of IMET support, including $600,000 for Botswana, $450,000 for Senegal, $280,000 for Kenya, and $250,000 for both Ethiopia and South Africa. Another $4.9 million was directed to countries in the Near East and South Asia, including $1 million to both Egypt and Jordan. Latin American countries were to receive $4.8 million in IMET funds in fiscal year 1995, with the primary recipients including Colombia ($600,000), El Salvador ($400,000), Bolivia ($350,000), Honduras and Peru ($325,000), and Ecuador ($300,000). U.S. military-training assistance for East Asian countries was scheduled to rise to $3.4 million, most of it destined for the Philippines ($1.2 million), Thailand ($1 million), and Malaysia ($500,000).

8. For an elaboration of this proposal see Klare (1992, 1991).

9. Analysts have proposed various ceilings for bilateral arms transfers, with levels of about $250 million representing the middle ground.

Part 2

Donors of Foreign Assistance

4

The Assault on U.S. Foreign Aid

Robert F. Zimmerman & Steven W. Hook

World War II and its aftermath forced U.S. leaders to recognize their country's preeminent world role and to identify the foreign policy necessary to preserve that role. Underlying their deliberations was a consensus that long-term U.S. security ultimately depended on events overseas. As the Cold War set in and extended across Asia, this assumption would have profound implications for developing countries.

U.S. foreign policy makers rarely address the country's world role without reference to its perceived moral responsibilities (see Spanier and Hook, 1995). After World War II they had such confidence in these values that they attempted to transfer them wholesale to other countries through many instruments of foreign policy (see Bellah, et al., 1991). This practice would include the worldwide distribution of foreign assistance, both economic and military, to nearly every LDC that sided with the United States in the Cold War. For as long as the competition lasted, the United States held the distinction of being the world's foremost aid donor.[1]

For a brief period in the early 1990s, it appeared the United States would retain this status while redirecting its aid programs toward transnational problems and sustainable development in the world's poorest and most densely populated regions. USAID (1994: 1) reflected and encouraged this optimism, noting, "With the end of the Cold War, the international community can now view the challenge of development directly, free from the demands of superpower competition."

Contrary to expectations that the peace dividend would be directed toward an expanded foreign-aid program, however, the 1990s have witnessed a fundamental reappraisal of U.S. foreign aid and major cutbacks in bilateral aid flows. Efforts to shift attention to transnational issues reflecting the priorities of the United Nations, World Bank, OECD, and many nongovernmental organizations (NGOs) have given way to a struggle for the very existence of the U.S. aid program. Foreign leaders in both rich and poor states have closely watched this political showdown, a result of the 1994 congressional elections, which brought the Republican Party to power. In the absence of an assertive U.S. role, the global development-aid regime, which the United States has led since World War II, is in peril.

Congressional Republicans followed the lead of Sen. Jesse Helms of North Carolina, who became chairman of the Senate Foreign Relations Committee after the 1994 midterm elections. Helms held hostage much of U.S. foreign policy—including nearly 400 foreign-service nominations and several important treaties—and pressed his own demands for major changes in U.S. foreign policy. "At the heart of the matter is his long-standing disdain for foreign aid," Phillips (1995: 7A) observed. "His reorganization proposal strikes at the core of foreign aid." Specifically, Helms sought to bring three autonomous agencies—USAID, the U.S. Arms Control and Disarmament Agency (USACDA), and the U.S. Information Agency (USIA)—under the direct control of the State Department. He encountered strong resistance from the Clinton administration, the agencies themselves, other parts of the federal bureaucracy, and many of his congressional colleagues. All of these parties felt the agencies should remain independent and hence less political. The dispute reflected profound differences over the role of the United States in the post–Cold War world, disrupting its bilateral and multilateral relations and creating a dangerous void in global leadership.

In this chapter, we explore the role played by U.S. foreign aid, particularly economic aid, throughout the post–World War II period and consider its presumed and actual connection to broader U.S. foreign-policy objectives. Along the way we critically examine the frontal assault on foreign aid in the mid-1990s, which already was among the least popular spending programs of the federal government. Public and congressional opposition to U.S. foreign aid is largely attributable to misuse of such aid during the Cold War, when it was principally applied to serve U.S. security interests rather than to achieve recipients' developmental goals.

The forces of change the United States helped set in motion not only have obscured a recognition of what has been achieved but also have dissolved the national consensus regarding the country's world role. From this paralyzing dissensus must come an appreciation of the country's immense potential as a partner in global development. Thus far, unfortunately, a new vision for global collaboration has failed to supplant the security concerns that previously governed U.S. aid allocations. A historic opportunity may be lost if the United States fails to live up to its commitment to improve the living conditions of the world's poor.

THE ROOTS OF U.S. FOREIGN AID

Among their other preoccupations, the architects of U.S. postwar foreign policy were determined to avoid a recurrence of the Great Depression and the subsequent degeneration into world war. Their pursuit of a liberal international economic order was designed to foster economic growth and the diffusion of stable, democratic governments (see Isaak, 1995). As Eberstadt (1988: 20–21) observed, they sought "to capture the most beneficial economic workings of the trade and finance arrangements associated with the Age of Imperialism and at the same time to protect the weaker peoples of the world against imperial subjugation and anti-democratic oppression."

The $13 billion Marshall Plan was the first massive government-sponsored aid program, funding the postwar reconstruction of Western Europe and other decimated societies.[2] Though there were obvious differences between postwar Western Europe and the former colonies of Africa, Asia, and Latin America, the Marshall Plan became a blueprint for U.S. foreign aid. More than 90 percent of these funds were disbursed in the form of grants rather than low-interest loans; about two-thirds were designated for economic rather than military purposes.

Compromises in these objectives emerged, however, soon after the Marshall Plan programs were terminated in 1952 and the Mutual Security Act was passed. During the Eisenhower administration—tense Cold War years preceding the decolonization of Africa—military and development aid were separated, and the former became by far the more prominent. Whereas military aid to friendly countries accounted for only one-sixth of total U.S. foreign aid between 1949 and 1953, between 1953 and 1961 it constituted more than half (Eberstadt, 1988: 31). Real and imagined communist threats not only in Europe but across Asia and into the Southern Hemisphere compelled these changes. The United States designed its security aid, primarily in the form of support for police and paramilitary forces engaged in counterinsurgency, to help struggling governments maintain political stability and resist potential Marxist challengers.[3]

The tone and substance of U.S. foreign aid changed dramatically in the early 1960s after the Kennedy administration implemented its Alliance for Progress. Ambassador George C. McGhee, a key advocate of the idealistic new effort, defined the moral dimensions of the challenge and argued that the cohesion of democratic states depended on impoverished peoples' making progress toward economic development through peaceful and orderly methods:

Our response to the challenge of development has become, in our time, a great crusade in the light of which most historical movements fail. . . . *The interests of neither the United States nor the host country will be promoted by aid programs which do not face up to this challenge. . . .* [It is] a question of making sure that our aid, in responding to the economic and political needs of the moment, *does so in ways which contribute to the long-term development goals that we and the host country share* (emphasis added).[4]

President Kennedy's message to Congress in March 1961 directly linked political and developmental objectives. Kennedy (1961: 325–326) believed the United States's freedom and the prospects for democratic development around the world depended "on the ability to build growing and independent nations where men can live in dignity, liberated from the bonds of hunger, ignorance, and poverty." Congress approved Kennedy's ambitious aid program—including the Peace Corps—in the Foreign Assistance Act of 1961, creating USAID to administer the growing volumes of economic assistance.

Kennedy refined the security-development linkage by equating development and security aid—both contributed to a more peaceful and secure global environment. He believed this linkage would encourage the public and Congress to support economic aid, and he argued that to preserve its security and advance other national interests the United States must promote long-term socioeconomic development at the peak of global decolonization (see Nathan and Oliver, 1987: Chapter 2). U.S. military and economic aid became critical vehicles for this goal and provoked other wealthy states and multilateral organizations to undertake their own aid efforts.

AID AND U.S. FOREIGN POLICY

Three decades have passed since Kennedy raised these moral challenges and articulated the United States's stakes in global development. Since World War II, the U.S. government has dispensed $452 billion in foreign aid, 66 percent in economic aid (versus military assistance) and 77 percent in the form of grants rather than low-interest loans through 1994 (USAID, 1996: 4). The Near East region received the largest aid volumes—$117 billion between 1946 and 1994—followed by Asia and Europe, with Latin America and sub-Saharan Africa receiving a combined total of less than $50 billion (see Table 4.1).[5]

Before being overtaken by Japan in 1989, the United States long held the distinction of being the world's primary donor of official development assistance.[6] Annual U.S. ODA flows peaked at $11.7 billion in 1990 before dropping in current dollars to $9.9 billion by 1994, signaling what is anticipated to be an extended period of ODA cutbacks (OECD, 1996a: A7, A8). Most states have received less bilateral assistance from the United States in the post–Cold War period, and the Clinton administration went forward with plans to close twenty-one overseas aid missions by the end of 1996. Entire ODA programs to many countries, including Afghanistan, Costa Rica, and Zaire, were eliminated for various reasons.[7]

Among the few nations to which the United States increased its aid

Table 4.1   Regional and Functional Distribution of U.S. Foreign Aid, 1946–1994

	Total U.S. Aid Disbursements	Economic Assistance	Military Assistance
Near East	$117[a]	$54	$63
Asia	101	58	43
Europe	80	39	41
Latin America	35	30	5
Sub-Saharan Africa	23	21	2
Interregional	91	86	5

Source: USAID (1996a)
Note:
a. Figures in billions of current U.S. dollars.

flows were the new independent states of the former Soviet Union, particularly Russia. The U.S. government approved transfers of $1.7 billion in 1993 and $2.4 billion in 1994 to this region, dispensing aid primarily through multilateral channels but also bilaterally. These aid programs, which were often linked to private investments to the region, were expanded, whereas programs to traditional recipients were curtailed or eliminated, reflecting a widely held belief that the most pressing U.S. foreign-policy interests of the time were tied to the stability of the former Second World.

At the same time, private capital flows from the United States to LDCs increased in the mid-1990s, reflecting a broader trend in North-South capital flows (see Chapter 1). U.S.-based private investment grew from $17.7 billion to $46.3 billion between 1992 and 1994 (OECD, 1996a: A9, A10), an increase of more than 150 percent in current dollars. These private transfers—including direct investment, private export credits, and bilateral portfolio investment—raised the total volume of U.S. capital flows to developing countries to $59.7 billion, more than double the Japanese total of $28.5 billion in 1994. Thus, critics of U.S. foreign aid argued that LDCs were receiving continued and in some cases expanded economic support through more efficient channels—private investors and multinational corporations which sought a profit from their infusions of capital, technology, and expertise.

Even in the heyday of U.S. ODA, its quality was among the lowest of all industrialized countries. In the early 1990s, however, these levels descended to unprecedented depths. In 1994 U.S. ODA flows represented .15 percent of GNP, far below the .7 percent standard established by the OECD and the lowest level among the twenty-one members of the DAC.[8]

Per capita U.S. ODA amounted to $38 in 1993–1994, less than half the DAC average of $77. A scant .04 percent of U.S. aid was allocated to LLDCs; only Spain distributed a smaller share of its GNP to LLDCs. Thus, the chronic gap between the quantity and quality of U.S. aid remained wide.

Military aid, which more explicitly reflected the security preoccupations of the U.S. aid program, increased from 25 percent of total aid in 1978 to 37 percent in 1988 in real terms before decreasing significantly in the wake of the Cold War. Over the same period, development aid decreased from 33 percent in 1978 to 26 percent. Economic support funds (ESF), which focused on countries where the United States had high political and strategic security interests, remained at or near 50 percent of all economic aid throughout the period. Food aid, meanwhile, steadily fell from record highs in the 1950s and 1960s to $1.6 billion in 1990.[9]

The shifting regional focus of U.S. foreign aid during the Cold War reflected the high priority of political over development objectives. Geopolitical priorities for U.S. aid began with the European recovery effort after World War II. South Asia and Southeast Asia became priority areas during the 1950s and remained such throughout the Vietnam War. Israel and Egypt have received nearly half of U.S. economic aid since the signing of the Camp David accords in 1978. During the 1980s, U.S. assistance to Central America (particularly El Salvador, Guatemala, and Honduras) rose sharply to $1.3 billion in 1989, surpassing aid to Asia. Flows to sub-Saharan Africa, relatively modest given the region's large number of nation-states and high degree of human need, stabilized at about $1.5 billion in the early 1990s. In the Cold War's immediate aftermath the geographic focus shifted once again, to Eastern Europe and the CIS. The United States transferred $1.4 billion to Russia despite worsening internal conditions in the country and an impending political and economic crisis.[10]

As this process continues in the late 1990s and U.S. aid flows continue to shift in response to changing conditions and policy goals, some reflection on the country's track record in utilizing development aid can provide useful lessons for the future.

THE MULTIPLE GOALS OF U.S. AID

The primary global objective of U.S. foreign aid was—and remains—preserving the territorial and political security of the United States. During the Cold War this objective involved containing perceived threats to vital U.S. interests, primarily from the Soviet Union and its Eastern European satellites but also from the People's Republic of China and other communist regimes in developing areas of the world. The closely related second objective of U.S. aid was to ensure the political security and cooperation of strategically important allies. Such efforts included promoting friendly governments, strengthening military forces, providing food, and creating a supportive international environment—all in countries where the establishment of communist regimes was seen as directly threatening U.S. security.

Promoting economic growth constituted a third distinct foreign-policy priority of U.S. aid. This objective entailed active opposition to acts that harmed the U.S. economy or, more generally, the liberal international economic order (LIEO) established and led by the United States. The LIEO rested upon open markets, foreign investment opportunities, access to technology and raw materials, and limited government intrusion in economic activity. The fourth major objective, promoting humanitarian concerns, was the one most frequently proclaimed by U.S. leaders. It derived from long-held assumptions of U.S. exceptionalism and a related belief that the U.S. socioeconomic and political system could be shared with foreign countries to their advantage. This goal required that the United States be willing and able to respond to human catastrophes, whether man-made or natural, anywhere in the world.

Development aid was used to pursue each of these objectives in various ways. Underlying all the stated objectives was the appeal to the moral principles and cultural values of a country flushed with a new sense of destiny following World War II.

The Marshall Plan established the essential link between economic health and political stability. Its underlying tenet was a variant of the "trickle-down theory" of development. According to this view, consistent economic advances would increasingly benefit the poorer elements in society by creating more jobs, improving public and private economic and social infrastructure, and increasing per capita and overall incomes. The theory seemed to hold true in the case of Western Europe, so it was replicated as the U.S. aid program reached a global scale.

In most cases, U.S. bilateral and multilateral aid programs depend heavily on the operational strategy that a rising tide will lift all boats, a central assumption of liberal economic theory that has driven U.S. policy for half a century. One of the few consistent aspects of U.S. economic aid, it has persisted amid constantly shifting geographical priorities and relations between the United States and other great powers.

Greatly complicating matters is the fact that the overarching objectives mentioned above have been coupled with specific secondary goals. For example, diplomatic and political objectives almost invariably have included obtaining rights for U.S. military bases, gaining support for issues of importance to the U.S. in the United Nations, and maintaining diplomatic access to recipient governments. U.S. aid diplomacy during the Cold War ultimately sought to maintain stable relationships with recipients that supported short- and medium-term U.S. security interests.

In time, this emphasis fostered a credibility crisis. Accusations were commonly made that U.S. aid was wasted on corrupt and repressive governments. Not only did the United States have little to show developmentally for its funding, but its generosity was often not repaid with UN votes, concessions to U.S. exporters, or political reforms (see Kegley and Hook, 1991). Many Third World governments persisted in subsidizing a dizzying array of inefficient state-owned enterprises, for example, and expected donors to relieve the burden on their national budgets.

Had it not been for the Cold War, the U.S. would likely have depended more on multilateral development institutions, which became particularly influential after the weakening of the U.S.-led Bretton Woods regime in 1971. This multilateral effort included a growing World Bank program in basic infrastructure, coupled with the United Nations Development Programme and a host of specialized technical assistance agencies (see Chapter 2). Though the World Bank and UN agencies served developmental objectives and enhanced the credibility of economic aid, the Cold War compelled the United States to sustain a large bilateral program so it could fly the flag over its friends and allies. Multilateral aid was presumably invisible with respect to specific donor countries, and in the Cold War context it was essential that the U.S. get full credit for its largesse. Consequently, U.S. funds often flowed into a country from a variety of sources for a variety of purposes—and not always in a coordinated or coherent manner.

It fell largely to USAID to make the case to an increasingly skeptical Congress and public that extending aid flows through multiple channels served U.S. security and economic interests and was consistent with the development priorities of LDCs. Given the well-publicized cases of mismanagement of U.S. aid under these circumstances, it is little wonder the credibility of USAID was stretched to the limit. The Department of State was satisfied with the security rationale for aid flows and did not see the need, as USAID did, to define success in developmental rather than political-security terms. In time, the pressure to broaden the definition of the U.S. national interest to include foreign aid generated a multiplicity of objectives and amended legislation. It also produced an identity crisis at USAID, the primary locus of bilateral U.S. assistance.

In the wake of the Vietnam War, USAID became, in a sense, a symptom of U.S. ambivalence about foreign policy in general and relations with LDCs in particular. Americans questioned whether the country was truly committed or able to lead a war on global poverty. Across Africa and Latin America, it could hardly be said that U.S. economic aid had consistently helped promote constructive social, economic, and political change. Frequent support for repressive dictators only fueled cynicism regarding aid efforts. USAID continued its struggle to justify its multiple, even competing objectives, a condition masked for years by uncritical Cold War rationales but revealed in endless amendments to foreign-aid legislation.

As a result, U.S. leaders engaged in a virtually nonstop reexamination of aid objectives and program rationales. Each initiative, from the Marshall Plan through Eisenhower's New Directions and Kennedy's Alliance for Progress, reflected a distinct period in U.S. strategic interests and development thought. The Carter administration emphasized basic human needs and poverty alleviation and made a strong effort to establish human rights as a criterion in judging the development performance of aid recipients. The Reagan administration revived the trickle-down theory, emphasized military aid, and promoted private enterprise as "the engine of growth."

Presidents Bush and Clinton placed greater emphasis on sustainable development, defined by greater attention to environmental and population concerns and promotion of democracy. Though the emphasis on sustainable development suggested a possible new paradigm for U.S. foreign policy in the 1990s, in practice many established aid programs remained unchanged, with only their rhetorical goals changing. The Bush administration was in practice reticent about sustainable development—and the implicit expectation for larger U.S. aid commitments—and the Clinton administration only began making tangible adjustments within USAID when the midterm elections of 1994 resulted in the frontal assault on the aid program.

Because of such constant changes, the U.S. foreign aid program has tried to serve multiple and often incompatible masters. Foreign-aid proponents have offered everything from feeding the hungry to opening new commercial markets for U.S. industry. Under successive administrators, USAID studied itself and changed directions under the watchful eye of a Congress that imposed ever tighter controls and made amendments for special interests. The result was an endemic lack of credibility for U.S. foreign aid and the further erosion of its support both within Congress and across the country.

SOME ACCOMPLISHMENTS OF U.S. AID

Despite the many shortcomings outlined above, U.S. foreign aid has achieved several significant successes. During the Cold War, in a struggle against authoritarian regimes in both the Soviet Union and the PRC (whose atrocities are still being revealed almost daily), aid flows and related security guarantees protected allies and solidified bilateral relations. The success of the Marshall Plan is beyond dispute, and subsequent programs to stimulate economic growth in Japan and other newly industrialized countries achieved comparable results. Meanwhile, infusions of U.S. capital to UN agencies, the World Bank, and the IMF have contributed to documented improvements in living conditions in many LDCs since World War II (see Chapter 1).

More specifically, the massive volumes of aid to Israel and Egypt have sustained a dialogue between these former enemies and have facilitated an expanded peace process in the Middle East. A related objective was to enable Egypt to endure the 1973 break in its relations with other Arab states, especially the cutoff of oil. Most of these countries resumed relations with Egypt in the early 1990s. U.S. aid was instrumental in achieving peace accords between Israel and the Palestine Liberation Organization (PLO) in 1993, with Jordan signing on in 1994. It was among the primary carrots Secretary of State Warren Christopher dangled before Syrian leaders in his trips to Damascus in 1995 and 1996. The United States has also provided major funding for democratic and electoral reforms in South Africa, Namibia, Cambodia, Panama, and Haiti.

A less prominent success was obtaining Pakistan's cooperation in providing support to Afghan rebels resisting the Soviet occupation of Afghanistan. Ironically, the United States earlier had cut its aid allocations in response to Pakistan's refusal to suspend its nuclear program. Resisting the Soviet invasion of Afghanistan became a higher political objective, forcing the U.S. government to resume a massive aid program. Pakistan's cooperation was essential in producing the military stalemate that led to Soviet withdrawal from Afghanistan. An unexpected additional result was the impetus this outcome gave toward political reform in the Soviet Union itself and toward Soviet withdrawal from Eastern Europe. After this success, the original nuclear nonproliferation concern once again took priority, and Congress ended the Pakistani aid program.

Today there are more opportunities to promote sustainable development than ever before, and standards of living continue to deteriorate in many of the world's poorest and most congested states, but substantial U.S. resources and interests are diverted toward the drug war in the Andes Mountains, economic partners in East Asia, or newly liberated republics in Eastern Europe and the Commonwealth of Independent States (CIS). The rationale for many current programs remains rooted in old definitions of U.S. security interests rather than a search for partnerships leading to continuing economic, social, and political development. Although these regions clearly merit U.S. assistance, their leaders have frequently been unable to absorb for development purposes the resources allocated to them (see Chapter 8). Making matters more difficult, the United States still encounters the legacy of LDC distrust and resentment that stems from misdeeds during the Cold War.

CONFRONTING THE DEVELOPMENT DILEMMA

Economic aid clearly has advanced U.S. political objectives since World War II. Unfortunately, the United States too often has supported political leaders who resisted necessary reforms and postponed hard decisions about economic restructuring and reallocation of resources. As a result, many aid recipients became more rather than less dependent on foreign aid. The considerable tension between U.S. political objectives and development objectives has severely limited the economic-aid program's achievements as well as its prospects for the future. Given the policy vacuum that has existed since November 1994, little is being done to resolve this central tension in U.S. aid.

The failure to establish a coherent policy framework integrating global development objectives with more immediate security objectives has left a gap between promise and performance. In Haiti, for example, talk in 1995 of jump-starting the economy suggested that the old reliance on unrealistic quick fixes still drove policy. Previous failures to establish policies that effectively reconciled political and developmental goals spelled disaster in Indonesia, Iran, Nicaragua, Liberia, and Somalia, among other developing countries, but little was learned from these mistakes.

In most other donor states, development policy is more concerned with empowering mass publics and creating civil societies than with establishing intimate security ties between elites of the donor and recipient states. Much of U.S. aid administrators' rhetoric has suggested an effort to support the development of self-sufficient governmental and private institutions capable of determining and effectively responding to their peoples' economic, social, and political needs. Such institutions and organizations presumably would be able to design and implement programs to increase agricultural and industrial productivity, expand educational opportunities, improve basic health services, and empower people to define and pursue their own personal destinies rather than continually expect material relief from the wealthiest states.

Unfortunately, the fragmented U.S. economic aid program has hardly begun to elicit measurable progress toward such enlightened objectives (see Zimmerman, 1993). Gaps between word and deed may have been inevitable throughout the Cold War; their continuation since the collapse of the Soviet Union is more difficult to rationalize. But as U.S. aid appropriations were being reduced dramatically in the mid-1990s, with only the most established recipients (especially Israel and Egypt) continuing to receive substantial funding, prospects for a move toward development-oriented aid became dimmer, not brighter. Leaders in many LDCs clearly recognize political linkages as the real preconditions for obtaining U.S. foreign aid. Understandably, these LDCs often ignore U.S. pressure to reform. This reaction may not be clearly visible, but the alienation of these LDCs from the United States is palpable to those in USAID who maintain regular contacts with their leaders.

Ultimately, U.S. foreign-policy self-interests, such as regional stability, human rights, environmental protection, and free trade—all of which indirectly contribute to the security of the United States—depend on the progress other countries make toward building responsive political systems and self-sustaining economies. Success in these areas will help solidify earlier gains and facilitate the diplomatic dialogue that will be necessary to advance future U.S. objectives. Alternatively, maintaining support for short-term political objectives becomes more difficult when the longer-term development objectives are not being attained. This represents the core of the development dilemma and a primary reason that support for the poorest states in the world has declined in the 1990s.

No discussion of the tensions between political and development objectives can ignore the role of special interests, which continue to influence the direction and volume of U.S. economic aid and its impact on diplomatic and development goals. Domestic interests often distort or undermine development objectives, especially when congressional earmarks limit resources available to countries with the greatest needs. Special interests, such as farmers or producers of heavy machinery, can divert resources from sustainable development in order to subsidize their own commercial interests or preserve U.S. business advantages overseas. The Egyptian and the Israeli aid programs illustrate how U.S. domestic politics can interfere with sound foreign-aid policy. In January 1990 Senator Robert Dole proposed that the Bush administration obtain additional resources for Eastern Europe by cutting aid to several recipients, including Israel and Egypt. Dole's proposal drew immediate fire from the Israeli government, the America-Israel Public Affairs Committee (AIPAC), and many of Dole's colleagues in Congress (Diehl, 1990). His effort was rejected, and aid to both countries continued; in the case of Egypt, the U.S. government approved a massive debt-relief package that boosted its 1990 ODA disbursement by several billion dollars.

If policies and standards of conduct cannot be established to reduce the impact of special interests, U.S. foreign political and development-related aid programs will remain bogged down. When domestic political interests prevail, the availability of aid funds for the most deserving recipients diminishes.[11] Valued partners have learned they cannot rely on the United States as a source of support in their development process. Cutbacks or elimination of anticipated funds for much-needed projects has damaged U.S. credibility and undermined its influence throughout the developing world. More important, such actions have frustrated development efforts in the South at a time when its needs, particularly in the areas of population and environmental protection, have become ever more acute.

PROSPECTS TOWARD THE MILLENNIUM

Just half a decade after the Cold War's conclusion, it is already obvious that many opportunities to promote real international development—defined as empowering social, economic, and political processes—have been lost. Leaders of LDCs are less able than they were during the period of bipolar confrontation to use political leverage to obtain high levels of aid from both East and West. The end of communism, the dismal record of past foreign-aid programs, and the Republican revolution in the U.S. Congress have all worked against U.S. foreign aid. Japan has become the world's leading donor of economic aid, and NICs elsewhere in East Asia have created aid programs that reflect their growing roles in the international economy. All of these factors reduce the willingness of the U.S. public to increase support for aid, suggesting that the already marginal role played by the United States within the global aid regime will continue to erode.

The end of the Cold War has forced fundamental changes in all donor nations' aid and trade priorities. The United States has given higher priority to Eastern Europe and the states of the new Russian federation, with Latin America not far behind and the LLDCs of sub-Saharan Africa and South Asia lost in the shuffle. The Japanese government has given more priority to the PRC, whereas Western European donors are focused primarily on Eastern Europe, the CIS, and their former colonies. Scandinavian nations, traditionally the most generous donors of foreign aid on qualitative grounds, have curbed their ODA programs in response to domestic economic pressures. The cumulative effect of these aid patterns is that fewer funds are available for the countries with the highest rates of poverty and population growth.

Nevertheless, there are new opportunities in the late 1990s for the United States to promote peace and human freedom and to use foreign aid for constructive sociopolitical change rather than against foreign ideologies. There are new threats to U.S. security that are far more real than was the threat of Soviet aggression during the Cold War. These threats include increased environmental degradation; the chronic debt crisis that reflects the failure of past aid programs; mass emigration from the poorest parts of the world, driven by the lack of economic, political, and social opportunity; and growing disenchantment of LDCs and donors with outmoded development projects.

Given these political realities and the fallacy of equating economic growth with development, a clearer understanding of the differences between modernization and development is required. History provides clear evidence that authoritarian political systems and highly centralized bureaucracies can initiate basic modernization of institutions and infrastructure to stimulate significant social and economic change. They can modernize basic education, health care, and agricultural systems. All of this modernizing infrastructure can greatly facilitate social and economic development, but going beyond modernization and creating self-sufficient political and economic institutions requires the active involvement of leaders and mass publics in the developing world.

Outside the United States, there appears to be increased appreciation among individual donors and multilateral aid institutions of the need to redefine development as a process that empowers people, organizations, and institutions to articulate and control their own destinies. Measuring such a process will require realistic indicators that relate economic-growth statistics to broader processes that expand political and economic power and create wealth based on the products of skilled, educated, and free peoples. By gaining a clearer understanding of these relationships, U.S. leaders and policymakers will be better able to use foreign aid to attain the development objectives they rhetorically support.

In the first two years of the Clinton administration, it appeared the United States would be receptive to this new approach to foreign aid. Under the leadership of its new administrator, J. Brian Atwood, USAID in March 1994 set forth its new post–Cold War *Strategy for Sustainable Development,* outlining five objectives: 1) protecting the environment; 2) building democracy; 3) stabilizing world population growth and protecting human health; 4) encouraging broad-based economic growth; and 5) providing humanitarian assistance and aiding postcrisis transitions. All of USAID's programs addressing these objectives "will aim at building indigenous capacity, enhancing participation, and encouraging accountability, transparency, decentralization, and the empowerment of communities and individuals" (USAID, 1994: 3).[12]

The most notable element of the strategy statement was its emphasis on empowering mass populations in LDCs and achieving the widest possible participation by people and political organizations. Development was explicitly recognized as a process that sparks reform and changes the distribution of power throughout a society. Such statements were impossible during the Cold War, when economic aid merely complemented military support and was used primarily to establish, promote, and consolidate intimate ties between the United States and strategically important LDCs.

Unfortunately, although the strategy introduced important new objectives, it rationalized many existing practices that had not contributed to the progress of LDCs. U.S. leaders seem to understand the importance of concepts such as self-determination, ownership, and empowerment, but their aid strategies and project proposals continue to reflect established bureaucratic and political routines. The inability of USAID to convert its new principles into practice, largely a result of the withdrawal of congressional support, has compounded the already fractured relations between the U.S. government and the developing world.

As the millennium approaches, a national debate is urgently needed to set a course for U.S. foreign aid in the next century. The era demands a redefinition of U.S. interests through a major reform effort that educates the public about the potentially vital role of foreign aid in U.S. policy and international development. The public is largely unaware of the many ways foreign aid serves U.S. national interests, leaving the door open for gross distortions in the battle for scarce taxpayer dollars.[13]

CONCLUSION

As we have observed, U.S. foreign aid survived the Cold War's demise but has since suffered from elite and public criticism. Efforts by Helms and others in Congress to reduce U.S. aid—and to truncate USAID and eliminate its political autonomy—have been witnessed by foreign audiences, who have long followed the lead of the United States. Thus, the uncertainties over U.S. foreign aid radiate outward and ultimately threaten the viability of the development regime outlined in Chapter 2.

The U.S. government must now confront the following questions: Is it prepared to use foreign aid as a change agent, regardless of short-term U.S. self-interests? Is it now possible that, given its global preeminence, the United States may yet emerge as a creative force in development? Can the U.S. define development goals in ways that complement those of international organizations? Finally, can the United States and LDCs jointly identify with these new objectives and translate them into practice?

In the end, only the governments of developing countries and their citizens can create the socioeconomic and political processes required for truly sustainable development. They will never be able to utilize foreign aid effectively until they have begun to take charge of their own destinies. But the path to economic and political power lies in giving more of such power to the people themselves rather than to autocratic rulers or corrupt bureaucrats. Ultimately this transformation is a function of the political process, particularly its capacity to provide the broadest possible opportunity for people to make the most of their limited resources. Foreign assistance, wisely applied, can effectively foster such changes.

It is worth remembering that truly effective foreign aid—that which enables recipients and their people to establish and control their own destinies—will enhance the credibility of the U.S. people and their government. Americans are not diminished as a consequence of progress in other lands. Indeed, they are enhanced whenever they contribute successfully to such progress. That was the lesson of the Marshall Plan period, the high-water mark of U.S. foreign aid, and it has been the lesson in several countries, many of them in Latin America, that have instituted democratic governments in the 1980s and early 1990s. These countries moved not only toward democratic rule but also toward economic growth, which has conferred its own benefits on the United States.

In this regard draconian cutbacks of the U.S. aid program not only will disrupt social and economic progress in many LDCs but also may damage U.S. self-interests. In an issue area so fraught with ironies, many of them tragic, this would be the greatest irony of all.

NOTES

1. Although flows of military assistance were substantial throughout the Cold War (see Chapter 3), the focus of this chapter is on economic assistance, specifically development aid.

2. The Soviet Union did not permit those parts of Europe under its occupation forces to participate in the West's reconstruction program. Instead, Joseph Stalin and his successors sponsored their own aid program, known as COMECON.

3. USAID provided aid (both equipment and technical advisers) to such security forces, particularly in Latin America and Southeast Asia, throughout the 1960s and early 1970s, until Congress prohibited such programs. During the 1980s some aid to police forces in Central America was resumed, but it focused on increased professionalism and reduction of human rights abuses.

4. George C. McGhee, "The American Ambassador Today." Fourth Graduation Exercises of the Senior Seminar in Foreign Policy, The Foreign Service Institute, U.S. Department of State, June 8, 1962.

5. The Near East region, of course, includes both Egypt and Israel, by far the greatest beneficiaries of U.S. foreign aid since the signing of the Camp David accords in 1978. The United States transferred $23 billion in economic assistance to Israel through 1994 and an additional $37 billion in military aid. Bilateral U.S. aid to Egypt amounted to $23 and $20 billion in economic and military assistance, respectively (USAID, 1995a: 10, 13).

6. This is the primary form of economic assistance coordinated and documented by the OECD.

7. USAID missions scheduled to be closed were located in Afghanistan, Belize, Burkina Faso, Botswana, Cameroon, Cape Verde, the Caribbean regional mission, Chad, Chile, Côte d'Ivoire, Lesotho, Oman, Pakistan, the South Pacific regional office, Togo, Tunisia, and Zaire. An additional mission on the border of Argentina and Uruguay was also scheduled to close.

8. This .15 percent/GNP level was also far below the .20 percent level of the previous year and the .25 percent level registered a decade earlier by the United States.

9. It is worth emphasizing here that both military and economic aid are included in the annual aid package sent to Congress. This practice tends to give the U.S. people and the press a distorted image of both types of aid.

10. Of the $1.4 billion in 1994 U.S. economic aid to Russia, $930 million was in the form of grants, $481 million in the form of concessional loans.

11. For example, Egypt and Israel have received more than $2 billion in economic support funds every year during the 1980s and early 1990s. The other major ESF recipients—the Philippines, El Salvador, Honduras, Pakistan, Turkey, and, most recently, Panama and Nicaragua—were allocated a total of $1.4 billion in fiscal year 1990. The remaining available economic aid from all sources totaled approximately $7.2 billion.

12. Warren Christopher further enunciated the policy shift in April 1996, declaring global environmental preservation a key U.S. foreign policy goal.

13. A 1994 survey by the University of Maryland indicated the average American assumes foreign aid to cost fifteen times its existing level, a perception that prompted a majority of Americans in opinion polls to support cuts in foreign aid.

5

Japan's Emergence as a Foreign-Aid Superpower

Alan Rix

Despite a prolonged recession and political crisis, these remain exciting times for economic aid in Japan, the world's largest source of development assistance by a wide margin. The volume of Tokyo's aid has continued to grow in the 1990s, to $13.2 billion in 1994, and its outlays are expected to increase further as Japan pursues its 1993–1997 target of $70–$75 billion (OECD, 1996a: A7, A8). Since the 1970s foreign aid has come to represent Japan's global contribution to international stability, and in the post–Cold War period this role has steadily expanded. As the Japanese Ministry of Foreign Affairs (1993: 3) proclaimed, "Japan is obligated to meet the expectations placed on it by international society, and is working to increase the quantity and quality of its aid."

Japan attained the status of a foreign-aid superpower through aggressive increases in aid allocations in the 1980s and early 1990s, a time when the U.S. program reached its peak and began a precipitous decline. The Japanese government subsidized massive construction of economic infrastructure in LDCs, actively participating in the World Bank, the OECD, and regional development banks. Its aid policy not only has adjusted to meet shifting recipient needs but has also responded to broader trends in international politics since the Cold War's demise.

Japan is no longer the export-driven aid donor of the past. It is increasingly respecting recipient demands, taking on the responsibilities of an aid leader and accepting greater international scrutiny of its aid program. In the emergent post–Cold War world, Japanese foreign aid has bolstered many former Soviet bloc countries' efforts to reconstruct their economies and move toward market-oriented reforms. In this and other respects the Japanese government has carefully used foreign aid as a critical agent of global economic diplomacy.

Japan's 1994 disbursements of $13.2 billion represented an increase of nearly $2 billion from the 1993 total of $11.3 billion and were by far the largest single contribution among members of the OECD's twenty-one-member Development Assistance Committee. In addition to these transfers of official development assistance, Japan disbursed nearly $4 billion in other aid—including export credits, equities, and multilateral assistance support—to developing countries. China became the primary recipient of Japanese aid in 1994, and major increases were reported for the Philippines and Vietnam. Outside East Asia, large aid packages were approved for Brazil, India, Syria, and states within the former Soviet bloc.

Private capital flows also increased in 1994, to a record $11.8 billion in current dollars and exchange rates. These private transfers, which included $7.4 billion in direct investment, raised the total of Japanese capital flows to developing countries to $28.5 billion. (The United States was the source of $46.3 billion in private investment in 1994, making it the largest source of all capital to developing countries.)

Within these totals, important underlying trends continued: a reduced emphasis on bilateral loans as opposed to multilateral transfers; a significant increase in grants versus low-interest loans; and emphases on sustainable development and political reform (Gaimusho, 1993: 32). Japan's rise during the 1980s and early 1990s as the world's leading aid donor has done more than increase the flows of aid; it has encouraged better aid, clearer policies, and more openness. However, it has also led to controversy at home about the direction and objectives of Japan's overall foreign policy. Japan's aid flows are substantial by virtually any measure, but new types of pressures are coming to bear on the aid program from both domestic and international sources.

In this chapter I will review the background and the main issues of Japanese ODA and assess how they are affecting Japan's overall strategy and performance in world politics. I will emphasize the domestic context of Japanese foreign aid, as well as systemic influences that also have been crucial in shaping aid flows.

BECOMING AN AID SUPERPOWER

Japan quietly assumed the status of an aid donor early in the postwar period while still a rapidly developing economy and a recipient of World Bank assistance. Japan's primary concerns in the 1950s involved industrialization and long-term economic growth. In part these goals required Japan to become more active on the world stage by participating in multilateral trade and development organizations and by encouraging the growth of potential trading partners. For that reason, Japan's early forays into concessional funding (or "economic cooperation," as it was called) were mainly self-interested.[1]

Japan joined the Colombo Plan in 1954, concluded its first reparations agreement in the same year, and commenced yen loans in 1957. Since then its performance and reputation as an aid giver has fluctuated. Bilateral disbursements grew rapidly from $145 million in 1960 to ten times that amount by 1977 in real terms (Rix, 1980: 32). From this early period Japan was widely perceived as providing assistance to LDCs primarily as a means to facilitate its own economic expansion. From the 1950s through the 1970s, exports and food and resource imports were critical to Japan's domestic economic growth and were prime objectives of Japan's aid strategy. The flow of aid was closely tied to emerging Asian countries, sources of raw materials and potential markets for Tokyo.

Throughout this early period Japanese leaders were not overly concerned by the details of the international aid debate, although Japan joined the DAC as a founding member in 1961. The government openly targeted its aid priorities to meet domestic needs rather than to suit the development theories and preferences of the international aid community. Thus, Japan offered a high proportion of aid in the form of loans rather than grants— even to very poor countries. It disbursed aid to a relatively narrow band of neighboring states in East Asia, many of which had already established intimate trade ties with Tokyo, and pursued a policy of providing support for economic infrastructure more than social or governmental projects. Criticism of Japan's "aid imperialism" dogged the aid program from the outset (Halliday and McCormack, 1973).

Within the Japanese government there were, and indeed still are, fundamental differences over aid philosophy (Rix, 1993, 1980). These have led over time to complex processes of aid management, as different agencies have attempted to place their stamp on aid policy. The government frequently dispersed political responsibility for aid, confusing recipients and international organizations and reinforcing the domestic orientation of the aid program.

Through the 1970s foreign aid played a relatively minor part in Japanese foreign policy, except as a means of strengthening relations with key Asian neighbors (Olson, 1970). The amounts of aid were relatively modest, and apart from its influential position in the Asian Development Bank (an organization founded in 1965 from a Japanese initiative), Japan did not contribute greatly to international development efforts. Since the early 1980s, however, Japanese leaders have made an aggressive and largely successful attempt to use foreign aid more constructively in promoting international development. This effort has arisen in response to greater demands by other industrialized states wanting Japan to expand its "burden sharing," by LDCs seeking more aid on more favorable terms, by regional partners looking to Japan for greater leadership and initiative, and by powerful interest groups within Japan itself. As a result of this pressure, aid flows have increased rapidly under explicit funding targets and "aid-doubling" schedules established by the Japanese government in the 1980s. A greater commitment to multilateral agencies has also emerged, and the use of "strategic aid" has become an accepted feature of what had been a strictly economic policy (Yasutomo, 1986). Moreover, Japan has committed vast sums to international peacekeeping efforts and in 1991 was among the primary sources of funding for the U.S.-led Gulf War against Iraq.[2] Foreign aid in a variety of forms became a central component of Japan's foreign policy, especially given the country's heightened profile as the largest single donor to dozens of recipient states (Gaimusho, 1988).

CONTROVERSIES IN JAPANESE AID

Throughout its short history, the Japanese aid program has been contentious, both at home and abroad. These controversies originated with Japan's postwar experience of providing aid, first in the form of reparations to East Asian states it occupied in the 1930s and early 1940s, then in the country's rapid emergence as an economic superpower in the 1980s and 1990s. The ongoing disputes tell us much about the scope and features of the Japanese aid program and about the expectations of other donors, which have more strongly coordinated their aid policies through the Paris-based OECD. Japan's aid program in the 1990s has largely been directed toward fulfilling these steadily rising expectations and gaining credibility within the international community.

Let us now consider some of the nettlesome issues which Japanese leaders have confronted in recent years.

Quantity and Quality of Aid

One of the ongoing arguments about Japanese aid has focused on the quality of the aid delivered, or the degree to which it responds to human needs on a global scale. Given its explicit objective of hastening Japan's own economic revival, the aid program in its early years was widely seen as lacking in many qualitative areas. Japanese leaders sidestepped many of these issues but pledged greatly to increase net aid commitments. Rapid growth in Japanese aid resulted from the implementation of explicit five-year targets in 1978. The Japanese government, limited in other aspects of foreign policy under its postwar constitution, was determined to demonstrate its commitment to aid and publicly undertook the effort to disburse constantly higher volumes of aid. The fifth and latest such aid target specified an objective of $70–75 billion in ODA transfers over the period 1993–1997. As its overall aid quantity grew, Japan widened the range of recipients to 144 in 1992, and the number of recipients for which it was the largest donor increased to

31 in 1991 (Gaimusho, 1993).[3] Total Japanese ODA over the same period rose by more than 300 percent in real terms, with the fastest-growing functional area being technical assistance, which jumped nearly fivefold between 1981 and 1991. As a result of this rapid increase, which was greatly inflated by appreciation of the yen against the U.S. dollar, Japan became the largest donor within the OECD in 1989. Given the major cutbacks in U.S. ODA allocations in the mid-1990s, Japan has solidified this status and is likely to retain it through the millennium.

Unlike Western European donors, however, Japan paid relatively little attention to the quality of its aid. Thus, Japan languished near the bottom of the DAC in measures of development-aid quality. Japan was still performing poorly in 1993: sixteenth out of twenty-one in ODA share of GNP (0.29 percent), seventeenth in the grant element of ODA, and nineteenth in the proportion of aid allocated to LLDCs.

More than other qualitative measures, the continuing low grant element brought accusations that Japan was still using aid more to serve domestic purposes than to assist recipient development. Coupled with a large loan program and an espoused emphasis on recipient "self-help" and "reciprocal cooperation," Japan has retained a reputation for being self-serving even in the midst of widely publicized reforms. The origins of Japan's aid in reparations and export-development programs of the 1950s and a traditional belief that aid should provide a "return" to its donor underpinned these trends.

Likewise, the restricted geographical concentration of Japanese aid flows has been a consistent pattern since the early years of the aid program (see Table 5.1).[4] In 1994 nearly 70 percent of Japan's bilateral ODA was

Table 5.1   Top Ten Recipients of Japanese Development Assistance, 1970–1994

1970–1971	1980–1981	1993–1994
Indonesia	Indonesia	China
South Korea	South Korea	Indonesia
India	Thailand	Egypt
Pakistan	Bangladesh	Philippines
Philippines	Philippines	India
Myanmar	Myanmar	Thailand
Thailand	Pakistan	Pakistan
Taiwan	Egypt	Bangladesh
Iran	Malaysia	Sri Lanka
Sri Lanka	India	Syria

Source: OECD (1996a: A75–A76)

directed toward Asian LDCs, particularly those in East Asia (48 percent) and South Asia (17 percent). China, Indonesia, and the Philippines accounted for about one-third of Japanese development aid in the early 1990s. Meanwhile, sub-Saharan Africa (10 percent) and Latin America (9 percent) received much smaller shares, and the once substantial aid volumes disbursed to the Middle East (20 percent in 1991) fell in 1993 to 3.5 percent.

Japan's emphasis on East Asia has been criticized by multilateral development agencies and the leaders of many LLDCs, but national officials have steadfastly defended the policy by noting that Japan has close cultural, geographic, and economic affinities with these recipients. Given their persistence in this regard, it is unlikely that Japan's geographical concentration on East Asia will diminish significantly in the late 1990s.

Aid Administration

Another controversial and complex aspect of Japan's aid program involves its administrative structure for managing aid policy. Japan's aid bureaucracy is the by-product of several factors: four decades of incremental growth in aid; entrenched institutional interests within the Japanese government; weak political leadership in the aid area; and a lack (until the early 1990s) of clear definition of the goals and purposes of Japanese aid. These are formidable barriers to effective policy management, and many of the problems of Japanese aid derive from them.

The system operating today is little different from that of the 1970s. It still features a multiplicity of bureaucratic actors and political masters, two main implementing agencies (both referred to as "Japan's aid agency"), a disaggregated budget, and no clear line of cabinet responsibility. There are, in fact, four main agencies involved: the Ministry of Foreign Affairs; the Ministry of International Trade and Industry (MITI); the Ministry of Agriculture, Forestry and Fisheries; and the ministry-level Economic Planning Agency. None is preeminent, and although the Ministry of Foreign Affairs generally receives the largest share of the aid budget, it is not a major force in domestic bureaucratic politics.

Alongside these four, some fourteen other ministries and agencies have aid programs and accompanying budgets, and their ministers also have a measure of political oversight of aid policy. The two aid-implementing agencies are the Overseas Economic Cooperation Fund (the OECF, established in 1961), responsible for bilateral loans, and the Japan International Cooperation Agency (JICA, established in 1974), responsible for managing technical aid and grants. The Export-Import Bank of Japan is also involved in the aid program as cofinancier with the OECF on projects, but its loans do not qualify as ODA. The Japanese government announced plans in 1995 to merge the OECF and the Export-Import Bank, which if enacted would create "one of the largest financial institutions in the world" (OECD, 1996a: 110).

A chronic difficulty with such a decentralized institutional structure has been the complexity of its procedures, a feature widely discussed and criticized, most recently by the Japanese government's Administrative Management Agency (Rix, 1993). With such cumbersome procedures have come problems of inefficiency, mismanagement, corruption, and recipient dissatisfaction. Efficiency has been undermined by the severe understaffing of the Japanese aid organizations and by the inability of political leaders to meaningfully reform the system despite the growing importance attached to aid within Japanese foreign relations (Orr, 1990: 51). These problems are serious impediments to making aid flows more transparent and responsive to recipient needs.

Links to the Private Sector

A third central issue regarding Japan's aid program has concerned the links between aid and the Japanese private sector. These ties were strong in the early years of Japan's aid giving because of explicit export-promotion objectives and the fact that most of Japan's aid was tied to the purchase of Japanese exports. The Japanese government (quoted in Hanabusa, 1991: 90–91) has openly acknowledged that "the private sector of the donor nation should be involved in the aid process. The donor government should not hesitate to create opportunities for its business community to participate in aid programs, as long as such activities are conducive to the recipient's steady economic development."

Japanese leaders throughout the postwar era have promoted a broad-based cooperative process between government and business, currently termed "comprehensive economic cooperation." Government and private-sector flows have been used to deal with LDC debt problems and to build infrastructure deemed essential for long-term economic expansion within recipient states (Rix, 1990: 31–34). Ideas about how the private sector could be involved in Japanese aid widened in the early 1990s, as a growing network of NGOs became not only financially viable but increasingly vital as a means of delivering Japanese aid.

Private industries—including the largest Tokyo-based multinational corporations—and financial institutions continue to be an essential element of the aid system, and they provide an important measure of dynamism and innovation in aid policy. Private contractors are often closest to and most familiar with recipient conditions and needs and may maintain close contacts with recipient governments. Such connections remain necessary to the implementation of bilateral aid programs, which are ultimately based upon individual project management, but the role of foreign aid in abetting Japan's "MITI economy" remains controversial.

Foreign aid remains a subject of intense debate in Japan not only among decisionmakers but also in the public arena. Aid policy is now widely recognized as an integral feature of Japan's international profile and thus has emerged as a favorite target of media scrutiny. This has not always been the case. Only since Japan has become one of the world's top aid donors has public interest grown, spurred on by often sensational press reports of aid mismanagement. Alongside greater media attention have come demands from interest groups, notably those associated with the NGO movement and, more recently, the environmental lobby. But Japan's aid success has also excited interest in political circles, and opposition parties have increasingly pushed to reform the aid system.

As people in other major Western donor countries grew weary of aid in the early 1990s, Japanese interest boomed, which helped political leaders convince voters of the need to devote continued high shares of the budget to foreign aid. The successful marketing of aid as a concrete symbol of Japan's greater international responsibility and global contribution has been one of the major outcomes of the aid debate in Japan.[5]

In addition to solidifying Japanese-LDC relations, foreign aid has served in the 1990s as a central component of Japan's ties with other industrialized states. It has served as a practical and visible means of reassuring the United States of Japan's sincerity about its commitment to global burden sharing in the post–Cold War era. Japanese aid flows during the Cold War lay at the margins of the superpower conflict; their support of market-oriented economies was seen in Washington as compatible with U.S. geopolitical interests along the Pacific Rim, a front line in the containment effort, and they certainly were preferable to military transfers and alliances in the region.

One of the difficult questions for Japan in the late 1990s is how to implement its recently espoused reforms of aid management in the transformed environment of the post–Cold War—indeed, how Japan's foreign policy making is to accommodate shifting guidelines that govern diplomatic contacts and economic relations with many of Japan's partners. These issues will be discussed in detail below.

REFORMS IN JAPANESE AID

The controversies that have surrounded Japan's aid program for several decades have not vanished, but Japan's policies today very much reflect the nation's status as an aid superpower. Although the aid system in Japan is as complex as ever, the Foreign Ministry has led the way in developing new approaches to aid and in securing their broad acceptance. The Ministry of Finance has continued to control Japan's international financial contributions and its participation in multilateral aid organizations. This agency remains financially conservative but nonetheless seeks to gain international recognition for Japan's aid. Although political leadership remains weak in this area, in recent years there have been significant innovations in the articulation and delivery of Japanese foreign aid.

Historically Japan's aid philosophy has not been clearly articulated, but the government approved and released a formal statement of government principles on aid in June 1992 (Overseas Economic Cooperation Fund, 1993: 9). The Aid Charter identified priority regions and sectors and cited the promotion of environmental protection as a central focus of aid decisionmaking. Similarly, it restated Japan's "traditional basic thinking on ODA—the idea of humanitarian consideration and recognition of mutual reliance as well as promotion and support of the self-help efforts of recipient countries."

But the charter went further, stating that aid programs should foster "an effective and just distribution of resources in [developing] countries, and the preservation of 'good governance'" (Gaimusho, 1993: 365). In implementing aid, Japan has declared that it will consider the link between growth and environmental protection, avoid the use of aid for military purposes, and assess recipients' military expenditures and weapons exports and development, particularly vis-à-vis weapons of mass destruction. Along with other major donors in the post–Cold War aid regime, Japanese leaders have promised to consider recipient progress toward democratization, respect for human rights, and other political reforms.

The charter served as an unambiguous and ambitious statement of aid policy, a commitment to new principles yet a strong defense of the traditional tenet of self-help. It effectively responded to criticism at home and abroad, but it created a longer-term problem: Japan must now try to uphold the new standards. Officials in the Foreign Ministry argued that it was relatively easy to make decisions on the status of actual and prospective recipients with respect to these standards; the director of the Economic Cooperation Bureau cited Vietnam, Mongolia, El Salvador, and several Central Asian states as being in alignment with the Aid Charter; and Sudan and Zaire, among others, as pursuing policies incompatible with Japan's new aid standards.

Problems arose when countries of strategic importance to Japan, such as China, India, and Pakistan, did not fulfill the conditions. In such cases Japanese leaders encouraged the recipients to undertake political or economic reforms. "It is not the case," the bureau's director (Hirabayashi, 1993:

29) observed, "that if one item doesn't fit the Charter, we can't give aid." Ultimately, it was made clear that Japanese foreign policy would not be determined by the Aid Charter alone.

Japan's continued attainment of its aid targets despite a prolonged slump in its own economy and amid a political upheaval in Japanese politics (which in the early 1990s witnessed the disruption of the Liberal Democratic Party's longtime hold on power) is further evidence of Japan's commitment to maintaining its current high profile in aid. The national budget for FY 1994 increased the ODA budget by 4.8 percent. ODA increased more than any other expenditure item except national debt repayments, but this was still the lowest annual hike since 1976 and the fourth consecutive year in which the increase was lower than the previous year's. This budget treatment still retains ODA in a special category, as fiscal restraint has forced other budgets to be cut dramatically. Expansion of aid programs in the late 1990s consequently faced strong opposition in many parts of the bureaucracy as pressure mounted to give priority to other spending programs, such as reconstruction costs following the Kobe earthquake.

Another important aspect of the Aid Charter was its explicit acknowledgment of the need to deal with the qualitative aspects of Japan's aid. Although overall measures of Japan's ODA quality have not shown remarkable improvement, at the program level a range of reforms was undertaken in the mid-1990s. Some resulted from internal administrative changes, whereas others were genuine responses to criticism of Japan's aid.

The untying of Japan's aid is one example of Japanese reaction to outside opinion. Since 1978 Japan has generally not made ODA loans contingent on purchase of Japanese exports, partly because of long-standing criticism of Japanese aid as commercial in orientation and geared to the support of private Japanese firms. Japan's ODA in 1991 was 80 percent untied, behind only New Zealand and Sweden among the twenty-one DAC members. Grant aid was still tied, but 97 percent of Japan's loans in 1993 were "general untied," the rest "LDC untied." As a result, the rate at which Japanese firms gained contracts on Japanese ODA projects fell to 29 percent in 1992, compared to 53 percent for contractors in LDCs and 18 percent for those in other OECD countries. There is also a much greater level of transparency in Japanese loan and grant procedures and far more receptiveness to the involvement of overseas contractors in Japanese surveys and other aid projects. Japan has also greatly increased the flexibility of its loan program. Loans (versus grants) still form a greater share of ODA in Japan than in other donor countries, but new types of loans allow for more flexible delivery and more favorable terms.[6]

In grant aid, too, changes are clearly visible. Although Japan's total share of grants in ODA remains low by comparison with other donors, the volume amounts are large. The proportion of Japanese grants going to low-income countries (LICs) and LLDCs rose in the early 1990s to nearly three-quarters of the total. Other reforms include increased nonproject grant aid and a well-financed small-grants scheme that bypasses the lengthy decisionmaking process required for major bilateral grants. The program received a 50 percent funding increase in 1994 budget despite cutbacks in other aid budgets.

Multilateral aid has always been an important part of Japan's ODA program. Japan has long been a major contributor to the United Nations, the World Bank, and regional development banks. It has also been at the forefront of multilateral efforts to assist the rebuilding of Eastern Europe, Russia, and the former Soviet republics. Japan's influence in multilateral banks and financial institutions remains strong, but there are barriers to Japan's enhanced role in such agencies, including lack of qualified personnel and differences in employment systems (Islam, 1991: 178–179).

In environmental aid Japan has become a leading contributor of funds to facilitate global initiatives. The major statement of this commitment came at the 1989 Paris Summit of Western leaders and was renewed and elaborated at the 1992 United Nations Conference on the Environment and Development. All areas of Japan's aid administration expanded their environmental programs such that in 1993 environmental aid as a distinct funding category constituted 12.8 percent of Japan's total ODA.

Despite this boosted environmental aid, criticism of Japan's environmental record continues, and doubts remain regarding just how carefully Japan weighs environmental-impact studies of its aid projects. The OECF rhetorically follows environmental guidelines, but there is little study of the environmental impact of Japanese aid projects. By the mid-1990s much remains to be done to ensure that environmental impact became a major criterion in assessing aid requests to demonstrate that Japan's environmental aid actually has some effect in alleviating environmental destruction.

JAPANESE AID TOWARD THE MILLENNIUM

The transformed post–Cold War period has provided Japanese leaders with unexpected challenges and opportunities in their foreign relations. In an era of geoeconomics, in which Japan has played a leading role, foreign aid has been thrust onto the center stage of Japanese diplomacy. Given that current conditions require creative and generous responses by all major industrial powers, expectations for Japan to assist in the process of political and economic readjustment in Eastern Europe and across the former Soviet Union have been extraordinarily high. The wave of UN peacekeeping missions and regional military crisis—including the Gulf War and the Balkan conflict—have heightened such expectations.

Remarkable changes have taken place in the Japanese aid program as this process of systemic adaptation has continued. The passage of the Aid Charter, for example, was a clear statement of the country's commitment to widely accepted norms of aid giving, despite the obvious problems in implementing these new standards and procedures (Arase, 1993). Though expectations of what Japan can do are perhaps overstated, Japan itself identified the "strengthening of Japanese leadership" as one of the three pillars of ODA activity in 1994 (Kitajima, 1994: 118).

The meaning of such rhetoric is less clear. Japan's wider interests dictate that it establish global influence outside the realm of its often conflictive bilateral relationship with the United States and pursue an agenda of its own making both in Asia and in the wider global community. To achieve such goals Japan must rely heavily on foreign aid, not only through close bilateral aid relations with LDCs (especially in cases where Japan is the largest donor) but also through Japan's work at the multilateral level.

As an arm of national policy, foreign aid has been used flexibly and selectively by Japanese leaders, with considerable success. It has helped Japan to attain a position of economic and political prominence in East Asia, a status the nation may soon enjoy in the South Pacific and, perhaps, South Asia. Aid has helped ease bilateral tensions with the United States (and may yet do more), provided Japan with a leading position in regional banks and multilateral development organizations, and given Japan leverage in dealing with countries of the Middle East, Latin America, and Africa. Japan has not yet used aid extensively as a means of political bargaining or diplomatic coercion, but the Aid Charter gives the necessary policy support for such moves.

Japan's more active promotion of its aid interests is already evident. The PRC remains a favored recipient of bilateral loans, but Japan is reassessing its policy of pledges in advance. More money is being promised to assist the development of Vietnam, in line with Japan's leading role in international efforts to support market-driven economic development in Indochina—efforts that contributed to renewed diplomatic relations between Vietnam and the United States in 1994. Japan made yen loans to Vietnam of $480 million in the early 1990s, becoming that nation's largest aid donor and giving Japan a significant interest in the long-term economic future of the region. The prospect that yen loans to Cambodia may resume reinforces that interest. The five former Soviet republics of Central Asia have been targeted for aid as part of Japan's policy of supporting democratization, an objective also applied to Japan's assistance to Mongolia and Cambodia (Gaimusho, 1993: 7–8).

Achieving a balance between expanding influence and implementing the potentially restrictive Aid Charter will be difficult in the late 1990s and into the next millennium. "Cutting off aid should be the last resort," the

Foreign Ministry (quoted in Kawakami, 1993: 15) stated. "When a government fails to understand that peace, human rights, and democracy are indispensable to development, we must try to change its attitude through dialogue first." The Japanese government froze aid to Haiti after the 1991 coup d'état and has made clear to the government of Pakistan its views about weapons expenditure and the need for economic responsibility. How far these principles can consistently be put into practice in aid to the PRC, Indonesia, Vietnam, or Myanmar will be the real test of the Aid Charter in the years to come.

Although there are pressures in Japan for some budgetary restraint on aid, notably from the Finance Ministry (which wants to refocus on aid quality and limit the ongoing increases in aid quantity), Japan's renewal of its aid targets through 1997 reflected a desire to stay at the forefront of DAC contributions. Japan's effort to ensure continued high levels of aid was reflected in its opposition to proposals within the DAC to trim the list of eligible aid recipients. Japan has successfully urged the addition of the five Central Asian republics to the DAC list and the removal of other states, such as Singapore and Brunei. Japan's interests undoubtedly lie in having more rather than fewer eligible recipients in order to maximize disbursements and in having Asian nations remain eligible to maximize its opportunities for continued leverage in Asian economic development. Whereas other donors are most concerned about the overall levels of their aid flows and often prefer to concentrate on aiding selected developing countries in line with DAC standards, Japan's future influence and international position depend on its having a wider client base and maximizing its "market share" in aid over the long term.

A broader issue yet to be resolved concerns Japan's long-term capacity to take on the burden of supporting global development. Japan's society and economy are changing rapidly, as the political crisis of the early 1990s made clear. Its population is aging, and the corresponding demands on welfare, the labor force, the tax base, and the social infrastructure are enormous. The cutbacks announced in 1994 demonstrated that foreign aid will have to exercise some of the restraint being forced on the economy in general. In an era of unstable parliamentary coalitions in Japan, however, fiscal reform is still a long way off.

Similarly, the problems of Japan's aid administration remain. Despite some improvements, there is still no attempt to resolve basic policy issues, including the absence of a free-standing foreign-aid ministry and the divided political responsibility for what is now regarded as Japan's most flexible international policy measure. Given that foreign aid serves as a microcosm of Japan's broader approach to foreign economic policy, these administrative concerns involving the aid program may be viewed as symptoms of more serious problems.

The difficulties in maintaining purpose and direction in Japan's aid program are caused by its diffuse administration and compounded by the fact that the domestic stakeholders in Japan's aid are now more numerous and vocal. In years past, the ministries and a limited range of contractors (specialized engineering consultants and larger construction and trading companies) were the main groups interested in aid. With more aid, more recipients, greater media attention, and more transparency, the aid "industry" in Japan has expanded. New business participants, different pressure groups (including public-interest, human-rights, environmental, and women's groups), and a rapidly growing number of NGOs have become involved in the aid system. In addition, foreign participants are now taking part, as firms from industrialized countries compete for development projects subsidized by Japanese aid—and are encouraged to do so by the Japanese government. These factors make for a complex policy mix, throwing the Japanese aid program under greater pressure both at home and abroad.

Becoming a permanent aid leader in the next millennium and gaining respect among industrialized and developing countries alike will not be easy. The Japanese government has been able to manage major decisions on aid policy—setting quantitative targets, accommodating the business sector, establishing the Aid Charter—but the political complications of this huge program, with its growing spin-offs at both domestic and international levels, makes the need for reform of the aid system in Japan both urgent and unavoidable.

Foreign aid gives Japan enormous opportunities to influence both economic and political events in a great many of the world's poor countries, and the new Aid Charter gives Japanese diplomats a formidable lever with which to exact agreement from recipient governments on human rights, military expenditure, environmental regulation, economic policy, and governance. Yet Japan, in contrast with many other donors, has been wary of using this leverage, and its resort to such methods is likely to be limited in the coming years. Pressure is difficult to sustain without political stability and policy commitment at home. Unfortunately, Japan in the mid-1990s has endured heightened economic uncertainty and political and social upheaval.

Despite these constraints, Japan undoubtedly will remain a major player in international aid, commercial lending, and private industrial investment. Based on its progress to date and its declared intentions, it will continue to lead in assisting the newly industrialized countries of the Pacific Rim and in propelling economic development throughout East Asia. If the recently proclaimed objectives are translated into practice, Japan will remain one of the top contributors to international financial institutions. Given Japan's heightened role in an era of geoeconomics, its voice will undoubtedly be heard. As in the past, its diplomacy will continue to be premised on a desire to establish itself as an influential actor in world affairs, independent of other major powers, including the United States.

The framework for such leadership is in place after many years of determined effort by the Japanese government, NGOs, commercial interests, regional financial institutions, and global development agencies. And the resources appear to be readily available, even under the austere conditions faced by Japan in the late 1990s. Thus, it apparently will be the resolution of domestic issues, both political and administrative, that largely determines how Japan exploits its new-found prominence as a foreign-aid superpower.

NOTES

1. For elaborations on this widely held view, see Brooks and Orr (1985) or Yanagihara and Emig (1991).

2. These efforts have been as close as Japan has come to using foreign aid for security purposes. Given the constitutional restrictions on Japan's foreign policy, and given that country's sensitive relations with the United States, Japanese aid has otherwise been disbursed exclusively in economic rather than military form.

3. These numbers decreased slightly in the mid-1990s but were expected to remain high given the long-term outlook for Japanese aid and the widespread cutbacks in aid programs from other donors, particularly the United States.

4. Other than Egypt, the primary African recipient of Japanese ODA—Kenya—ranked fourteenth on this list, and the leading Latin American recipient, Mexico, ranked twelfth (OECD, 1996a: A76).

5. Aid often cemented Japanese ties with LDCs, although often in a fairly crude fashion, as was the case with the Philippines under the dictatorial regime of Ferdinand Marcos (Takahashi, 1993).

6. Nonproject loans are about 40 percent of the total, with structural-adjustment loans the major part. Loans for sector programs, project rehabilitation, and local-cost financing are also provided. The share of loans going to traditional economic infrastructure areas fell in the early 1990s, with increased amounts devoted to social and political infrastructure (OECF, 1993).

6

Cross-Pressures in Western European Foreign Aid

M. Leann Brown & Joanne M. O'Connor

Western European governments have sustained close and multifaceted relations with developing countries since completing their recovery from World War II. These relations have evolved from imperial domination to more nuanced political, economic, and cultural interactions that have included, on both bilateral and multilateral levels, the large-scale transfer of foreign aid.

During the Cold War, many Western European aid programs were designed in part to complement the U.S. effort to contain communism and the appeal of Marxism-Leninism and, more broadly, to maintain influence within LDCs, which were moving from colonial rule to political independence. In the wake of the Cold War, these rationales have yielded to myriad new objectives that reflect the traditional interests of the donor states, the collective interests of European Union (EU) members, and global problems as advanced by the United Nations, the Paris-based OECD, and international financial institutions.[1]

As we will argue in this chapter, the purposes, modalities, and scale of Western European foreign aid mirror predominant long- and short-term international trends. Most official developmental assistance from Western European donors is allocated to recipient governments with the purpose of achieving specified foreign-policy goals. However, despite the resilience of state-centrism, Western European states increasingly rely upon multilateral aid instruments, including those of the EU and the OECD, in pursuit of transnational objectives. As in the case of other regions, then, aid from Western Europe serves as a microcosm of broader trends in world politics between the Cold War and the millennium, a period in which the cross-pressures of integration and fragmentation have driven the foreign policies of rich and poor states alike.

The outlines of current and future international trends are already discernible in Western European ODA policies. The triumph of liberal economic and political models, the dissolution of the Soviet bloc, enhanced

Western European economic integration, efforts to promote sustainable development, and other events have all had profound effects on European aid policies.

Foreign aid, however, constitutes a relatively modest portion of the foreign economic relations of the major Western European countries. Private investment and bank lending have grown to comparable or greater volumes in the 1990s, as they have in the case of worldwide capital flows. Further, the effectiveness of aid in facilitating the political stability and economic development of LDCs has been shown to be marginal in many instances (see Chapter 2). Yet Western European aid represents a large share of global economic aid flows—about 45 percent in 1993—and continues to reflect the broader foreign-policy objectives of these donors. As their objectives have changed in the post–Cold War period, so have the direction, volume, and terms of their foreign aid.

STATE CENTRISM AND BILATERAL AID

Although no single causal explanation is sufficient to explain the cluster of purposes behind the foreign aid of Western European governments, most aid flows remain bilateral and attributable to relatively transparent national interests. Motivations dating back to the colonial era have become intertwined with contemporary political, economic, and cultural objectives. Their rhetoric notwithstanding, European donors commonly regard foreign aid as an instrument of foreign policy.

During the Cold War many aid programs were seen as useful weapons against communist encroachment in the developing world. Economic assistance was seen as a way to maintain recipients' allegiance to the Western alliance or, at a minimum, to preserve their neutrality. Aid provided leverage to guarantee recipients' voting support in international organizations, particularly the United Nations, and in the context of regional politics. European aid has further been considered an effective means to promote trade by enhancing the economic prospects and import capacity of recipients and guaranteeing donor access to raw materials and export markets. These assumptions have expressed themselves most directly in donors' granting preferential access to their markets for goods from LDCs and in the tying of aid packages to procurement from donor-country firms.

Western European governments have generally operated under the notion that mutual benefits are achieved by closer involvement between their advanced industrial economies and the raw material–producing nations of the developing world, many of which are among their former colonies. Of course, the extent to which aid actually conveys economic benefits to the donor economy is difficult to assess. Certainly, allocating funds in the form of aid to LDCs is not a particularly efficient means of enhancing domestic economic growth. Because foreign aid does not dominate the agenda of national policymakers or citizens in industrialized states, it is easier to mobilize popular support for or acquiescence to aid allocations if politicians are able to demonstrate that domestic benefits derive from aid policy (Malik, 1991: 2). Thus, the politics of self-interest intermingle with the presumably altruistic bases of development aid to create a volatile and controversial dimension of Western European foreign policy. As we will find, bilateral and multilateral aid flows coexist, often uneasily, pursuing divergent goals and reflecting general contradictions in the foreign economic policies of Western European states.

Let us briefly review the performance of the three Western European states sending the largest volumes of financial resources to developing countries—France, Great Britain, and the Federal Republic of Germany—before turning to the multilateral sources of the region's foreign aid flows and other aspects of Western European aid.

French Foreign Aid

Traditionally the major donor among Western European states, France initially used aid as a means to retain its colonies and assimilate them into a "greater France" (see Chapter 11). This assimilation strategy gave France stronger ties with its former colonies than other colonial powers achieved, especially given the influence of the French language, culture, and military policy and the economic orientation of the former colonies toward Paris.[2] Additionally, France retains a significant number of small islands and territories as overseas departments and territories (DOM/TOM), and these receive substantial subsidies that France classifies as foreign aid but that other donors consider internal subventions.[3]

In the early 1960s, more than 90 percent of French aid went to former colonies. This percentage fell sharply later in the decade, however, reaching 73 percent by 1970 before growing again in the 1980s. By 1994 French aid to Africa and Oceania, home to most of its former colonies and ongoing overseas possessions, accounted for more than 80 percent of its bilateral ODA, the most common form of economic aid (OECD, 1996a: A73). France remains the primary source of bilateral funding and a major source of total economic revenues for a large number of African countries both north and south of the Sahara Desert.

Congruent with France's assimilative approach to colonialism, its early aid policy was strongly influenced by the belief that French culture and civilization should be bestowed as a part of development—and as a much-needed alternative to superpower hegemony (Hewitt, 1989). As Charles de Gaulle (quoted in Hugon, 1984: 200) observed, "I resolved to clear away the obligations... imposed on her by her empire. But in order to avoid a foreign (American or Soviet) influence replacing that of France, so that the African peoples should speak our language and share our culture, we should help them."

Because of the strong politicocultural component in its aid rationale, France's ODA maintains a strong emphasis on education and public administration (Berthelot, 1973: 37). More than one-third of total French ODA disbursements continue to support technical cooperation in these areas, making France the largest contributor among advanced industrial countries in this functional category. As many analysts (see Hook, 1995) have observed, this type of aid facilitated the French government's self-proclaimed *mission civilisatrice* in the developing world.

During the Cold War, French leaders frequently justified their traditional preference for Africa by noting that French aid helped ameliorate superpower tensions and offered a "third way" for nonaligned states in the francophone region. Providing a counterpoise to Soviet and U.S. influence was seen as vital to French interests. Development assistance to African countries lent credibility to France's self-described "world vocation" and often guaranteed the voting support of aid recipients for France's policy positions in the United Nations (Magnard and Tenzer, 1988: 156–195). In this respect, Hugon (1984: 189) found that French aid policy has existed within the

> geopolitical framework of defense of the French language and culture, of France's military presence and policing role in francophone Africa, of the region's integration in the French monetary zone, of France's quest for security and for supplies of raw materials, but also of assistance and development in francophone Africa.

The Cold War's demise lessened France's appeal to LDCs by depriving Paris of its previous status as an alternative to the superpowers. But aggregate French aid flows have continued to rank third, behind those of the United States and Japan. Disbursements amounted to $8.5 billion in 1994, an increase of 8 percent over the 1993 total of $7.9 billion in current dollars (OECD, 1996a: A7, A8). Despite its increasing allotments of aid to Eastern Europe and the former Soviet Union—more than $1 billion between 1992 and 1994—one pattern remain unchanged: eight of the top ten recipients in 1994 were either French overseas territories or former colonies in francophone Africa.

British Foreign Aid

In the immediate post–World War II period, Britain's foreign aid policies reflected a desire to establish beneficial economic relationships with its former colonies as officials worked to establish the Commonwealth system. The proportion of bilateral aid going to Commonwealth countries remained approximately 90 percent throughout the 1960s; by 1970 most recipients had achieved independence, and since 1975 the Commonwealth proportion has remained at about 65 percent.

British bilateral aid flowed to dozens of LDCs in 1993–1994, with the largest amounts of ODA going to India, states of the former Yugoslavia, Bangladesh, Zambia, Uganda, and Kenya (OECD, 1996a: A81, A82). India, formerly the crown jewel of the British Empire, has consistently been its primary aid recipient, and Pakistan and Bangladesh have consistently received large amounts of aid. Yet when all of the country's aid flows are considered, states in sub-Saharan Africa received 43 percent of British aid, those in South and East Asia an additional 32 percent.

Aid from Great Britain was also affected by Cold War considerations, often dictated by the United States, and by the desire to support political stability within anglophone states. As late as the 1980s, Nicaragua and Cambodia were excluded from British assistance on the basis of Cold War concerns. Support for aid waned during the 1980s, as Prime Minister Margaret Thatcher's Conservative government decreased British foreign aid by more than one-third. Her government reversed Britain's long-standing aid policy, stating that future transfers would emphasize Great Britain's political, industrial, and commercial interests along with the recipients' developmental needs (Lumsdaine, 1993: 85, 249). By 1990 more than 80 percent of British ODA was tied to the purchase of British goods and services, a larger percentage than that registered by all but three other major donors. The multilateral portion of British aid increased in the 1970s and 1980s, however, often reaching 50 percent of the total.

British ODA flows totaled $3.2 billion in 1994, below the peak levels recorded in the early 1980s. Aid as a percentage of British GNP remained stable at .31 percent, less than half the .7 percent advocated by the OECD. But if the growing volume of private capital is included ($6.7 billion in 1994), the percentage of Britain's GNP directed toward LDCs rose to nearly 1 percent during the period. This pattern became increasingly common during the 1990s among other Western European states, along with the United States and Japan, which reduced aid levels in real terms while serving as the source of rapidly growing transnational bank loans and foreign investments in developing countries.

German Foreign Aid

Unlike Britain and France, the Federal Republic of Germany has not been saddled with the legacies of colonialism and has exhibited a more globalist,

development-oriented approach to foreign aid.[4] Despite this global orientation, Germany has given several countries disproportionate amounts of aid
for special political reasons. For example, Israel and Yugoslavia received
significant sums of assistance as compensation for German atrocities during
World War II.

But Germany, like other Western European states, has had other motivations. German aid policy was initially regarded as a foreign-policy instrument for "containing the influence of the Soviet Union in the Third World
and more particularly for preventing diplomatic recognition of the German
Democratic Republic (GDR) by the increasing number of newly independent countries" (Hofmeier and Schultz, 1984: 206). For many years, the
West German government refused to extend concessional loans or grants to
recipients that recognized the GDR. This Cold War orientation, of course,
changed abruptly with the collapse of the Berlin Wall in 1989. Not only
would a reunited Germany find its efforts directed toward reviving its former adversary in Moscow, it would discover how costly the absorption of
the GDR would be. As Chancellor Helmut Kohl pursued this difficult task
in the face of growing internal dissension in Germany, the expansive scope
of its aid program remained intact.

Reflecting its global nature, German bilateral aid averaged about $7 bil-
lion and extended to more than 100 recipients in the early 1990s. Its primary recipients in 1994 included Indonesia, the states of the former Yugoslavia,
China, Egypt, and India (OECD, 1996a: A74). German ODA as a percentage of GNP fell from a level of nearly .50 percent in the early 1980s to .34
percent by 1994, when much of its resources were redirected toward domestic priorities. Recipients in sub-Saharan Africa received the largest share of
1994 German ODA (27 percent); those in East Asia received 20 percent.

These ODA flows did not reflect the large volumes of German aid to
former Soviet bloc states, which amounted to nearly $6 billion between
1992 and 1994, approximately 35 percent of all aid from DAC states
(OECD, 1996a: 109).[5] Nor did they reflect the equally large volumes of private loans and investments from Germany—$12.6 billion in 1994 alone—
which collectively made Germany the strongest economic force in the
developing world among Western European states.

About 40 percent of German bilateral aid was tied to procurement in
Germany in the 1980s and early 1990s, half of it designated as technical
cooperation. In this respect, Germany could be considered rather liberal
compared to other donor countries. Because of the competitive advantages
of many German industries, however, contracts were often awarded to
German firms even without the government's tying large proportions of the
aid. In the 1980s, as the effects of structural change slowed economic
growth, increasing pressure arose from the business community to tie more
aid to procurement from German sources. In justifying aid policies, the gov-

ernment often stressed that aid to LDCs helped create and preserve German jobs (Hofmeier and Schultz, 1984: 211).

German bilateral assistance underwent immediate changes in the wake of unification and the transformation taking place in Eastern Europe and the former Soviet Union. Large-scale German assistance was assured before the Soviet Union collapsed late in 1991. Kohl had offered to extend such aid, along with security guarantees along the eastern frontier, to facilitate Mikhail Gorbachev's acceptance of German unification on Western terms. More generally, given its location, Germany had particular interests in the success of economic and political reforms across the former Soviet bloc. It was widely believed that economic development from market reforms in this region would generate long-term benefits for Germany's economy—and it was equally apparent that a collapse of the Eastern European reform movement would imperil Germany (Ling, 1992: 19).

Under this lingering assumption, the government and German people have struggled through several years of recession and high interest rates, which have in turn stimulated nationalist uprisings and social unrest in some areas. Kohl remained determined to maintain this revised version of *ostpolitik*, however, and warned that the failure of the former Soviet bloc's market transition would ultimately prove far more costly to German citizens than the continued extension of economic aid.

Other Western European Aid Flows

An exhaustive review of all Western European aid flows is beyond the scope of this chapter, but it is worth reviewing briefly the role of other major regional actors. Italy, the Netherlands, and Spain will be highlighted.

Among these donors, Italy has maintained the largest aid program, which in many years was larger in volume than that of Great Britain. Italian ODA flows in the early 1990s peaked at about $3.5 billion before falling to $2.7 billion in 1994 (OECD, 1996a: A7, A8). Its primary recipients during this period included Egypt, Tanzania, China, Mozambique, and Argentina. The largest percentage of Italian aid was transferred to sub-Saharan Africa in the early 1990s, although a growing share was transferred to recipients in southern Europe, the Middle East, and North Africa. The Italian government devoted about .27 percent of GNP to official development assistance during the early 1990s, the lowest level since the early 1980s. After heated debate, the Italian government approved legislation in 1995 to align its aid program more closely with that of the European Union, a further sign of the growing integration and foreign-policy cooperation among EU members.

The experience of the Netherlands provides further evidence of the tension between the self-interests of Western European aid donors and the collective interests of aid donors and LDCs. The Dutch government, which had maintained one of the highest-quality aid programs throughout the post–World War II period, struggled in the early 1990s to maintain its qualitative standards in the face of growing economic austerity. Aid flows declined to $2.5 billion in 1994, and aid as a percentage of Dutch GNP fell to .76 percent, far below the levels of nearly 1 percent reached in the 1980s (OECD, 1996a: A7, A8). Both bilateral and multilateral aid levels declined, reflecting a general trend among mid-level Western European donors.

The Spanish government, by contrast to the other Western European donors, has only recently emerged from being a net recipient of foreign aid. By 1994 Spain disbursed more than $1.3 billion in ODA, with its primary recipients including Mexico, China, Indonesia, Morocco, and Ecuador (OECD, 1996a: A80). Spanish ODA as a percentage of GNP averaged about .28 percent in the early 1990s, far below the DAC standard of .70 percent. Other qualitative aspects of Spanish aid flows, such as the proportion of grant share (.25 percent GNP) and the share of aid devoted to LLDCs (.03 percent), ranked among the lowest of OECD donors. For these reasons, Spanish leaders were urged by the DAC in 1994 to improve aid quality and to improve the internal administration of Spanish aid.

The emphasis on state-centric political and economic motives as the primary determinants of Western European ODA does not imply that such factors as altruism and a sense of social responsibility do not influence aid policies. Public opinion polls confirm that Western European citizens share a sense of moral responsibility for the fate of foreign countries, particularly those they directly or indirectly dominated in the past. Many influential political parties have embraced humanist precepts and have proclaimed solidarity with LDCs. It must be emphasized, however, that when the fiscal costs of foreign aid are debated in European parliaments, state-centric interests are most commonly cited as justification for bilateral aid programs.

INTERDEPENDENCE AND MULTILATERAL AID

If, as we have argued, political and economic self-interests and Cold War considerations were determining factors in the allocation of bilateral aid during the Cold War, a growing recognition of transnational interdependence resulted in increased emphasis on multilateralism in the aid programs of Western European donors (see Malik, 1991).

Aid from the European Community (EC, predecessor of the EU) provided a means of burden sharing for its member states. With Belgian support and mostly over German and Dutch objections, many elements of the French colonial philosophy of "associationism" were incorporated into the 1957

Treaty of Rome. Part IV of the treaty established free-trade areas among the six original EC members and more than twenty-two countries and territories, most of which were former African colonies of Belgium, France, and Italy. The Treaty of Rome also established the first European Development Fund (EDF), the nucleus of collective aid policy. Thus, from the outset the integrating states of postwar Western Europe included foreign aid in the center of their regional agenda.

In the late 1990s the EDF is administered by the European Union but financed by direct contributions from member states; non-EDF aid is funded out of the EU budget. Accounting for about 5.5 percent of the EU's overall budget, about half of this aid is used to provide financial assistance to non-African, Caribbean, and Pacific countries, with the remaining portion allocated for food aid. The trade aspects of aid policy are primarily the EU's responsibility, whereas the member states have taken a lead role in development assistance.[6]

As time passed and African colonies achieved independence, associationism evolved into a vehicle whereby European states played an active collective role in postcolonial African economic development. In July 1963, EC members and eighteen newly independent African states signed a convention of association in Yaoundé, Cameroon. Partially in response to international initiatives, the Generalized System of Preferences (GSP) was enacted to favor trade in manufactures from LDCs.[7] The plan allowed LDCs to export industrial products to the EC without paying tariffs. Many agricultural goods were also granted duty-free access. Not all countries or commodities were included, nor was the plan income-graduated to favor the poorest countries. Associated countries continued to receive greater preferences relative to other LDCs, and textiles and clothing, though particularly important exports for many LDCs, were exempted from the program (Grilli, 1993: 23).

When Great Britain joined the EC in 1973, bringing with it obligations and institutional arrangements with its former colonies, forty-six African, Caribbean and Pacific countries were "associated" within the GSP framework. A new convention, Lomé I (in reference to the capital of Togo, where the negotiations occurred between 1975 and 1980), was signed in February 1975 and came into force in April 1976. Subsequent Lomé Conventions— Lomé IV went into force in January 1990—and their accompanying development funds have since persisted as the primary EC instruments of development aid through four incarnations.

Lomé I recognized for the first time the considerable stakes Western Europe had in the economic fortunes of developing countries. Included among its provisions was the System for the Stabilization of Export Earnings (STABEX) to compensate aid recipients during periods of fiscal instability deriving from shortfalls in export earnings from single commodities regardless of fluctuations in export revenues.[8] Least developed countries were exempt from repayments, and repayable STABEX credit did not carry interest charges. STABEX allowed some EC resources to be allocated automatically on the basis of recipient needs rather than donor self-interests.

EC aid accounted for a growing share of total aid transfers to sub-Saharan Africa in the 1960s and 1970s. French influence may be seen in the fact that EC aid allocated to the Sahel and francophone West Africa was on average four times higher than that sent to anglophone Africa.[9] The distribution of bilateral and multilateral EC aid only partially overlapped at the national level, suggesting that coordination between members' bilateral contributions and EC assistance was not complete even with regard to associated countries.

European associationism was a defensive strategy from the beginning. It served first to protect European countries from the negative effects of decolonization, one of which was the threat of disruption of their regular supply of industrial raw materials. From this perspective, a minimum level of political stability and economic development in the newly independent African states served crucial EC interests. Associationism also represented an attempt to retain for Europe a measure of political influence in a world dominated by the United States and the Soviet Union, whose Cold War rivalry affected virtually every aspect of the global ODA regime and North-South relations in general.

Some analysts portray these associative relationships as important because the institutional arrangements between aid donors and recipients are built around the formal principle of parity; aid goals and amounts are negotiated with recipients and administered in association with them. Others stress the positive effects of long-term EU aid commitments. Although efficient disbursement has always been a problem of EU aid, multilateral aid in general is of superior quality. In its current form, EU aid remains relatively free of explicit commercial ties; recipient countries must procure goods and services within the EU market, but given its size the economic costs of this requirement are inconsequential (Grilli, 1993).[10]

Among European donors, Germany has most overtly embraced the language of interdependence and multilateralism. The election of the Social Democrat–Liberal government of Willy Brandt in 1969 led to a deemphasis on foreign-policy considerations and the emergence of ODA policy that stressed the

> protection of human rights, furthering of democratic behavior and reduction of military expenditure in the developing countries. [This consensus ensured that] the provision of aid is expected to be on the principles of social progress and justice for the poorest population groups. The fight against absolute poverty is confirmed as the overriding aim of German development policy (quoted in Hofmeier and Schultz, 1984: 214).[11]

Aid interdependence increasingly extended to institutional linkages in aid efforts. Although the EU has prided itself on preserving a "partnership" with LDCs in determining the kind and volumes of assistance proffered, EU hard-liners insisted in the mid-1990s that explicit conditions be attached to aid commitments. In their view, such conditions should coincide with those of the major international lending organizations—which had loosely grouped the conditions around the concept of sustainable development—or at least be implemented in close coordination with the World Bank and the IMF. British and Dutch leaders were particularly supportive of adopting these regime criteria for aid, a step also taken by many donors in their bilateral aid allocations (Hewitt, 1989: 295–296).

THE TRIUMPH OF LIBERAL ORTHODOXY

Neoclassical economic and liberal political ideologies were hallmarks of the 1980s and persist in Western European foreign economic policies in the late 1990s. Within the global aid regime, this approach most often reveals itself in conditionalities that require recipients to undertake structural adjustments to make their national economies more compatible with the norms of the LIEO. The concurrent pressure for political liberalization, drawing impetus and affirmation from the collapse of the Soviet bloc, seeks to encourage not only economic growth but also democratic reform, the rule of law, and the protection of human rights in recipient countries, all central tenets of sustainable development. This trend is exemplified by World Bank and IMF demands for changes in the social as well as economic policies of recipient governments (see Chapter 2). The World Bank led the way by initiating structural-adjustment programs that required recipients to improve education and judicial systems, trim state bureaucracies, open markets, reduce population growth, and subsidize environmental protections (Malik, 1991; Hewitt, 1989: 295–296).

Following the French-African summit in June 1990, French officials reported on new aid policies directed toward its "ambit" countries and stressed the need for economic and political reforms. They stated that the rule of law would be an essential condition for economic and democratic development. However, France retained its focus on its overseas territories and former colonies in francophone Africa, along with its programmatic concentration on political infrastructure and state building on the French model. France remained the nucleus of economic integration among many of these LDCs in the "franc zone," which relied upon Paris as a central bank and as a lender of last resort.[12]

As noted, under the monetarist leadership of Margaret Thatcher the

British government was dubious about the utility of ODA as an agent of global economic development. In its surviving aid programs, however, Britain continued to fund the privatization of state-owned enterprises in LDCs, and British leaders became vocal advocates of conditionality requirements in both bilateral and multilateral aid.[13] In 1990 John Major, in his capacity as chancellor of the Exchequer, warned LDCs they must undertake sweeping political and social reforms if they wished to qualify for further British aid (Burnell, 1991: 6–9). As prime minister, Major maintained these policies, endorsing British ODA transfers only after being persuaded that recipients had adopted widely accepted standards of "good governance."

This trend was also evident in October 1991 when Germany's minister of economic cooperation, Karl-Dieter Spranger, announced that particular attention would be given to the political and economic systems of aid recipients. Specifically, the new policy identified human rights, constitutionalism, political participation, and "pro-market" economic development in LDCs. To implement these policies, the German government devised a complicated index to assess the aid-worthiness of potential recipients. Indicators included the proportion of military expenses to total government spending; the ratio of military spending to cultural, educational, and health-care spending; and the ratio of arms trade to total foreign trade (Ling, 1992: 33).

Priding itself on its position of political neutrality and respect for the autonomy of ODA recipients, the EU has exhibited mixed tendencies with regard to such political conditionalities. In the late 1970s, however, EC aid to Uganda and Equatorial Guinea was suspended during the peak of political and human-rights abuses perpetrated by the Idi Amin and Macias Nguema regimes. Negotiations for a cooperation agreement with the Andean Pact were halted in July 1980 after a coup d'état in Bolivia. Economic cooperation with the PRC was frozen after the Tiananmen Square massacre, and aid to Haiti was cut off after the military thwarted election results and assumed power in the early 1990s. Yet the EU has often continued aid programs to repressive states despite declarations by members that they had become unsuitable for their own bilateral transfers. Lomé IV places greater emphasis on human rights, gender equality, environmental protection, regional economic integration, and the need for comprehensive, self-reliant, and sustainable development (Dinan, 1994: 458). In the wake of the Cold War, as security rationales for ODA programs have disappeared and as a consensus has emerged within the UN and the OECD over the political prerequisites of aid, the EU has become more consistent in targeting aid to moderate states.

In the 1990s the *economic* conditionality of aid from the reconstituted EU has also been more greatly emphasized, a reflection of the new paradigm of development assistance proclaimed by the OECD (see Chapter 1). It made its first formal appearance in the Lomé IV specification that a portion of the aid be designated for structural adjustment in recipient countries. It has appeared much more forcefully in aid transferred to Eastern Europe, where funds have been explicitly designed to hasten democratic and market reforms.

REDIRECTING AID TO EASTERN EUROPE

In the late 1980s, the Western European response to the democratic revolutions in the former communist bloc assumed three dimensions. First, Western European leaders addressed the most urgent needs of the Eastern European countries as they undertook the difficult transition to market-driven economies. Second, complementary trade policies were established to improve the access of Eastern European exports to EU markets. Finally, institutional arrangements were put into place with unprecedented speed to facilitate long-term economic and political ties between Western and Eastern European states.

The heads of European governments first discussed a concerted response at the Rhodes summit in December 1988, when the fissure of the Iron Curtain was becoming increasingly likely. At the July 1989 Paris summit of twenty-four industrialized countries (the Group of 24, or G-24), the European Commission agreed to assume responsibility for coordinating Western aid to Poland and Hungary (see Commission of the European Communities, 1990). At this meeting these states launched a joint effort known as "Poland-Hungary: Assistance for Restructuring of the Economy" (PHARE).[14] The EU is an autonomous party to PHARE but also coordinates its activities, which include food deliveries, credit and investment guarantees, technical assistance grants, and official debt relief measures. In particular, bridge loans and a stabilization fund were put into place for Poland. G-24 assistance has been extended from the short to the medium term and integrated into IMF and World Bank programs (see Chapter 9).

The EC played a prominent role in the establishment of the European Bank for Reconstruction and Development (EBRD), which French president François Mitterrand proposed at an extraordinary meeting of the European Council in Paris in November 1989. Other G-24 countries soon endorsed the proposal; the bank was institutionalized in May 1990 and began operating in London in April 1991. The EC, the Commission, and the European Development Bank contributed 51 percent of the new bank's start-up capital (Dinan, 1994: 475).

Outside PHARE, Western European states organized to provide assistance to the Soviet Union during its final year and subsequently to Russia and the members of the CIS. The trade component of EU assistance to Eastern European countries consisted of liberalizing trade with all states, including the former Soviet Union, and granting most-favored-nation status to Bulgaria, Hungary, and Romania while bringing Bulgaria, Czechoslovakia, Hungary, and Poland under the Generalized System of Preferences (Grilli, 1993: 310–311).

As might be expected, the pressing new aid obligations in the former Soviet bloc created a dilemma among EU policymakers. The case for significantly revamping aid priorities to favor Eastern Europe was persuasive. Though not fully articulated, fears of massive migrations of economic refugees added urgency to the EU policy response. Yet would these new responsibilities be undertaken at the expense of long-standing recipient states in Africa and South Asia? Concerns persisted that the EU would be unable to meet both old and new assistance objectives.

A final development with implications for Western European ODA was the consolidation of the single market envisioned by the 1987 Single European Act and the 1993 Maastricht Treaty. Little consensus exists among analysts as to the likely consequences of this transformation for EU aid programs. On the one hand, a positive projection holds that LDCs will find the more integrated and liberalized European market a larger and more congenial destination for their exports. The counterpoint to this argument, however, is that the enhanced market may translate into higher barriers to LDCs' exports. In effect, they may be effectively closed out of the single market.

The Maastricht Treaty incorporated general principles of development cooperation into the EU's structure. One important article stated that the EU's overall aid activity would "be complementary to the policies pursued by the Member States" and would foster the "smooth and gradual integration of the developing countries" into the international economy, democratization in LDCs, and greater respect for human rights. Promulgation of a common foreign policy was a central component of the treaty. Prospects for close cooperation in this area remained dubious, however, especially as the Balkan crisis failed to elicit a cohesive response from Western Europe. But, perversely, because the members' vital national interests were not at stake in the area of development aid, it provided a potential basis upon which a coherent European foreign policy might expand.

CONCLUSION

A striking feature that emerges from this comparative examination of Western European aid is the constancy of the individual countries' aid purposes and programs despite the passage of time and changes in governmental party control. But broad international forces and events have prodded national governments to produce meaningful adjustments in their foreign aid programs.

Foreign aid from the major Western European countries has reflected long- and short-term international trends. Thus, the global context of foreign aid has always been critical. The post–World War II era was characterized by a nation-state-centric system engaged in bipolar Cold War competition. Western European aid was largely directed to assist the U.S.-led effort to contain Soviet influence in the developing world, and later to subsidize the process of decolonization.

By 1970 many new states had achieved political independence and appealed in international fora for economic assistance. The ensuing decade was one of extreme economic dislocation, however, with OPEC-induced stagflation and persistent unemployment plaguing advanced industrial countries in Western Europe and elsewhere. These and other factors gradually interjected the language of interdependence into aid policies, and donors increasingly turned to multilateral channels as instruments of burden sharing. Development assistance was provided for in the Treaty of Rome, which established the European Economic Community, but the multilateral component of Western European aid became extensive only in the 1970s. For most of its history, the EC prided itself in honoring the sovereignty of LDCs through noninterference in their political affairs. Aid from the EC was concentrated in grant form, generally untied to donor goods and services, of long-term duration, and relatively stable over time.

Many of these aspects of noninterference were later called into question by the ascendant neoclassical economic and liberal political ideologies of the 1980s. As distress persisted in Western European economies, governments increasingly embraced free-market solutions, which were not always congruent with the declared developmental aspirations of the aid programs. Beginning with the conditionality requirements of World Bank and IMF programs, donor states sought to impose structural-adjustment and sustainable-development requirements on recipients. With the collapse of the Soviet Union in 1989, bilateral and EC aid programs stepped in to sustain and reward progress toward market and democratic reforms across the former Soviet bloc.

It appears in the mid-1990s that European foreign aid has come full circle. As an area outside of vital state interests, Western European bilateral aid may be amenable to further consolidation as part of the Common Foreign and Security Policy (CFSP) envisioned in the Maastricht Treaty. Given the recent trends outlined above, we may safely predict that bilateral and multilateral ODA from Western Europe will continue to reflect predominant but often clashing international trends. As the tension between the perceived national interests of each donor state and the collective interests of the EU unfold into the next millennium, these cross-pressures will undoubtedly guide aid flows for years to come.

NOTES

1. The ratification of the Maastricht agreements in November 1993 created the European Union, encompassing the former European Community and establishing the basis for expanded cooperation in foreign and monetary policies.

2. The economies of these francophone states are coordinated through the Paris-based Union Monetaire Ouest Africaine.

3. Overseas departments include Guadeloupe, Guyana, Martinique, Mayotte, Réunion, and St. Pierre et Miquelon. Overseas territories include New Caledonia, New Hebrides, Polynesia, and Wallis and Futuna. DOM/TOM subsidies represented nearly half of total French aid into the mid-1990s; if this aid is discounted, France may be classified as a middle-range donor (Lumsdaine, 1993: 85, 303).

4. The Federal Republic of Germany in this discussion refers to West Germany prior to October 1990 and the unified Germany thereafter. Information presented in this study pertinent to Germany's ODA does not include aid provided by the former German Democratic Republic (GDR).

5. The multilateral component of Germany's ODA has been about 30 percent since the mid-1970s (Deutsche Bundesbank, 1990: 37).

6. As of the early 1990s, EU financial aid represented about 15 percent of the combined efforts of the member states.

7. The idea of tariff preferences granted unilaterally on a nonreciprocal basis was devised within the United Nations Conference on Trade and Development in 1970 to promote industrialization in LDCs. The system consisted of customs duty reductions or exemptions accompanied by quotas on finished or semifinished industrial and processed agricultural products. Beginning in July 1971, the EC was the first multilateral organization to apply the GSP to members of the Group of 77 within UNCTAD and to the overseas countries and territories of the member states. By 1990 the system covered 131 countries and states.

8. These funds were more accessible to beneficiaries than the IMF's Compensatory Financing Facility (CFF), which operated only when export receipts fell below a specified level. Whereas the CFF imposed interest charges and expected repayment of resources drawn from the facility, Lomé provided for a partial conversion of STABEX payments into grants when export receipts from a primary commodity did not return to preexisting levels.

9. Even when the figures are adjusted for Nigeria among anglophone countries, aid to francophone Africa remained 30 percent higher than aid to anglophone recipients.

10. These programs have not been without controversy. Critics charged that Lomé aid and trade provisions confined recipient countries to the role of primary commodity exporters. Other detractors argued that EU preferences lost their worth for recipients because LDCs had increased their involvement in multilateral negotiations and benefited from the liberalization of tariffs engendered by successive rounds of the General Agreement on Tariffs and Trade (Grilli, 1993: 342).

11. Brandt chaired an international group that yielded the Brandt Commission Report, the basis for a comprehensive reformulation of German and global aid policy (see Brandt Commission, 1983 and 1980). Brandt's view of interdependence

comingled donors' "enlightened" self-interest with recipient needs: "What is right just also happens to be what is expedient as well" (Lumsdaine, 1993: 171).

12. Relations within the franc zone were strained in 1994 after the French government devalued its currency, but the long-term basis of economic coordination remained intact (see Chapter 11).

13. Technical-cooperation projects performing these tasks expanded greatly in the early 1990s and accounted for about 40 percent of British bilateral aid in 1995.

14. The EC countries, members of the European Free Trade Area, Australia, Canada, Japan, New Zealand, Turkey, and the United States constituted the G-24 members of PHARE. G-24 assistance was extended to Bulgaria, Czechoslovakia, and Yugoslavia in July 1990. The GDR was included until its reunification with West Germany in October of that year. Finally, the Baltic states were included in PHARE in October 1991.

7

The Disillusionment of Nordic Aid

Katie Verlin Laatikainen

With a combined population of 23 million, the Nordic states—Denmark, Finland, Norway, and Sweden—hold an anomalous position among the world's leading donors of foreign aid.[1] "Progressive," "moral," "benevolent," "altruistic," even "sanctimonious" are terms used to characterize their approach toward developing countries (Ohlin, 1973).

Although foreign aid involves a voluntary transfer of resources from affluent to impoverished states, reciprocal conditions that primarily serve donor interests are often attached to such transfers. This is a central reality of foreign aid—both contemporary and throughout history—and an underlying theme of this volume. The relative dearth of such linkages in the case of Nordic aid serves as an important exception to this rule. The receptiveness of Nordic leaders to initiatives such as the NIEO and their support for developing countries in the United Nations, World Bank, and OECD have made them widely regarded as the "darlings" of the Third World (Rudebeck, 1982).

This perception is supported by many empirical measures. Although they account for only about 3.2 percent of the total population of OECD countries, for example, the Nordic share of OECD aid in 1990 was 7.9 percent (OECD, 1991a: 59). Thus, the Nordic donors have played a role within the global aid regime greater than their size would call for, and they have accentuated their influence through high-profile engagement in regional and international development organizations.

One may speak of a Nordic aid "model" because of the consensus Nordic donors maintain with respect to the ends and means of foreign assistance and because of their extensive coordination in this area. Nordic finance ministers meet annually for consultations and hold informal discussions on aid issues routinely. Ongoing policy coordination contributes to a relatively united front in development policy. This is not to say that all Nordic aid programs are identical; indeed, the many substantive differences are detailed throughout this chapter. However, the Nordic aid programs share enough common history, normative presumptions, and institutional features to constitute a distinctive approach to foreign assistance.

This approach has been frequently termed "neutralist" for these donors' independent stance vis-à-vis the United States and Soviet Union during the Cold War, a posture that reflected their broader foreign-policy orientations. The Nordic states, though members of the First World, were known for aid policies that were generally free from superpower interference and that championed the interests of the Third World. But this neutralist description, which persists in the post–Cold War era under very different geopolitical circumstances, is misleading for two reasons. First, neutralism does not adequately reflect the posture of all the Nordic states: Both Denmark and Norway are members of the North Atlantic Treaty Organization (NATO), whereas Finland and Sweden have remained outside the alliance. Denmark, a member of the European Community/Union since 1972, was joined in 1995 by Finland and Sweden, but voters in Norway narrowly rejected EU membership in a national referendum.

More critically, the neutralist label suggests that Nordic aid policies have, in their own way, been primarily dictated by the Cold War rivalry. However, the Cold War and its passing have had little impact on Nordic donors, in contrast with other OECD members. Their aid policies are better understood as an externalization of domestic political structures and the projection of Nordic social democracy (Holmberg, 1989; Jinadu, 1984; Beckman, 1979). Nordic aid is in this view a consequence of internal pressures and an expression of cultural values rather than the result of external opportunities and constraints. The strength of social-democratic ideals largely accounts for the uniformity of Nordic aid policies despite the varied positions and postures of the Nordic states in the international system.

The Nordic states share several development priorities in addition to poverty alleviation. These include environmental protection, public health and education, and the promotion of human rights and democracy. A related concern is "securing for women a central and fully integrated position in the development process" (Danish International Development Agency [DANIDA], 1993b: 61).[2] Democracy and human rights are in the Nordic perspective "essential prerequisites for development" (Norwegian Ministry of Foreign Affairs [NMFA], 1993: 12). Since the 1992 UN Conference on Environment and Development—the Earth Summit—sustainable development has been an integral element of Nordic development strategies.

Among the facets of Nordic aid that render the individual donors distinct from one another, bilateral aid flows are directed toward varying sectoral categories that reflect the expertise and interests of each donor state. Danish aid projects, for example, emphasize rural development and increased food production.[3] Finland, by contrast, concentrates on those policy sectors in which its international competitiveness is greatest: forestry, water and fisheries, social development, and economic infrastructure (Vesa, 1979: 114; see also Kiljunen, 1983). The Norwegian government has been relatively vague with respect to sectoral priorities, although family planning and children's rights have been consistently emphasized. Swedish sectoral priorities are also ambiguous. After disappointing large-scale industrial and infrastructure projects in Vietnam and India, Sweden has since emphasized nutrition programs, health care, and small-scale rural industry (Holtsberg, 1986: 157; see also Andreen, 1986).

Despite the limited influence of the Cold War in the articulation and implementation of Nordic aid, these policies are undergoing considerable change in the period between the Cold War and the millennium. This change is less a result of the Cold War's passing than a reflection of the changes and challenges facing the domestic Nordic model of social democracy. Fundamental shifts in Nordic aid and challenges to the Nordic aid model have occurred since the 1980s. These shifts, to be reviewed below, have been propelled by broader changes in the international political and economic system during the post–Cold War period.

THE HISTORICAL CONTEXT OF NORDIC AID

Aside from Denmark, which holds overseas territories (the Faeroe Islands and Greenland), the Nordic states do not have a contemporary imperial heritage. With Sweden and Finland as neutrals and Denmark and Norway as members of NATO, the strategic interests of these countries have been largely limited to the European, Baltic, and Arctic regions. Economically, these are small industrialized states with generally open markets that are dependent upon investment and exports to the industrialized world. (Though exports to LDCs are growing, they remain a relatively minor element of Nordic trade.)

The precursor of Nordic foreign assistance was the long involvement in eastern and southern Africa of independent church missions, whose efforts included not only spiritual relief but also education and medical assistance (Stokke, 1985). Humanitarian concern for the living standards of mass populations in newly decolonized states provided the impetus for contemporary Nordic aid (Heppling, 1986). There was "surprisingly little debate and criticism concerning the appropriateness of or need for this new activity. Idealistic motives were thought to be highly realistic" (Andrén, 1981: 694).

This early Nordic aid, which preceded the Cold War and the decolonization period, engendered the widespread Nordic perception that foreign assistance should flow in a "recipient-oriented" manner, with representatives of LDCs directly involved in decisionmaking and implementation of aid-funded projects. Nordic development legislation codified this approach.

The Norwegian Development Agency (1993), for example, proclaimed that aid "must be provided on a general humanitarian basis and should not be based upon economic, political, or religious particularistic interests. . . . Norwegian development cooperation is not guided by economic or military interests; it is based on the principle of solidarity."

The moral tone of Swedish aid policy has often been implicit rather than explicit, and tangible returns to Swedish taxpayers have rarely been included in aid legislation. As Ohlin (1966: 56) observes, "Aid has never been seen as an enterprise in which Sweden herself could have any legitimate self-interest beyond that of her stake in global peace and survival." Strategic interests in extending foreign aid were limited to the promotion of collective security as defined by the Swedish government.

A strong "multilateralist ethic" (Beckman, 1979) and support for international organizations provided additional motivation for Nordic development cooperation. The United Nations, like the League of Nations before it, has received strong Nordic support and encouragement to promote equity in a world of great-power politics. Nordic states were small and middle powers; caught in the cross fire of a burgeoning superpower rivalry, they recognized the benefits the UN could confer not only to themselves but also to vulnerable LDCs. The desire to strengthen the UN was particularly critical for Finland, whose foreign-policy options were constrained by its "special relationship" with the Soviet Union.[4] Consequently, the development policy of Finland has been "based more on a follow-up of actions taken by other Scandinavian countries" (Antola, 1978: 233).

A primary goal of Nordic aid has been to promote social as well as economic development in recipient states. Norwegian legislation passed in 1962 declared, "Development cooperation should be based on a combination of social welfare and growth, and the aspects of a fair distribution of income and general welfare should be given more prominence." In Sweden's Government Bill 100, also adopted in 1962, the goals of official development assistance were identified as economic growth, economic and social equity, political autonomy, and democratic development in recipient states. Early Danish ODA (cited in Holm, 1979: 95) was designed to "further economic growth, create social progress, and enable political independence. . . . Denmark perceives growth and development as inseparable elements, because growth is a precondition for political independence." Finnish legislation passed in 1963 promoted active involvement in UN development activities and expanded cooperation in North-South initiatives.[5]

Early efforts were channeled largely through the UN because of the donors' desire to support multilateral organizations and because their own aid bureaucracies were in their infancy. By 1970 concerns over the effectiveness of multilateral development aid and the establishment of national aid agencies had prompted the Nordic states to expand their bilateral programs. These agencies included the Danish International Development Agency (DANIDA), the Finnish International Development Agency (FINNIDA), the Norwegian Development Agency (NORAD), and the Swedish International Development Agency (SIDA).[6]

During the 1960s, the UN's first "development decade," aid donors targeted bilateral ODA contributions of at least .7 percent of GNP. This goal was embraced by all the Nordic states, and all but Finland have consistently surpassed this target, in some cases exceeding a full 1 percent of GNP in aid allocations. By 1990 the Swedish ODA budget consumed nearly 87 percent of the total Foreign Ministry budget (Swedish Ministry of Foreign Affairs, 1993), and within other donor states a comparable portion of foreign-policy expenditures were allocated to development assistance.

Unlike many other aid donors, the Nordic states have eschewed project-oriented aid in favor of "country programming," which has involved ongoing Nordic efforts in southern Africa and the Indian subcontinent. Rather than extending aid to large numbers of LDCs on the basis of aggregate calculations of relative need, aid transfers under the country-programming effort are limited to a handful of LDCs so that the recipient "becomes the project" (Edgren, 1986). Sweden and Norway introduced country programs in the 1960s, and Finland followed suit in the mid-1970s. In order to maximize the effectiveness of Finnish aid, government leaders targeted several LLDCs and further required that program countries' development strategies be consistent with those espoused by the United Nations (Antola, 1978: 235). The Danish government has moved increasingly in this direction in the 1990s, concentrating its aid packages on fewer than twenty-five carefully selected recipients.[7]

Program countries, once selected on the basis of development plans submitted to Nordic development authorities, negotiate multiyear assistance agreements. In the 1970s, during the early stages of country programming, Nordic donors gave a large degree of autonomy to recipients and exercised little oversight as to the utilization of aid transfers. The rationale was to show respect to the recipients of aid and to encourage them to find self-sufficient paths to development. Consequently, the most crucial step for the Nordic donors was in the *selection* of recipient states; once selected, the relationship would be long-term and involve considerable resources. Selection of a development partner indicated a large degree of Nordic confidence in the recipient country.

QUANTITY AND QUALITY OF NORDIC AID

As Table 7.1 demonstrates, the volume of Nordic aid varied widely during the first three years of the post–Cold War era, ranging from $1.3 billion dis-

Table 7.1   Nordic Development-Aid Flows, 1992–1994

Donor	1992–1994 Total ODA Disbursements	Percentage ODA/GNP (DAC average)	1994 Aid to LLDCs/GNP (DAC average)	1993–1994 Primary Recipients
Denmark	$4,178[a]	1.03 (.32)	.36 (.07)	Tanzania Uganda Vietnam
Finland	$1,289	.46	.12	Tanzania Nicaragua Zambia
Norway	$3,424	1.06	.44	Mozambique Ex-Yugoslavia Tanzania
Sweden	$6,048	.99	.31	Ex-Yugoslavia India Mozambique

Source: OECD (1996a)
Note:
a. ODA disbursements in millions of current U.S. dollars.

bursed by Finland in 1993 to $6 billion spent by Sweden (OECD, 1996a: A7, A8). These aid levels were at least twice those recorded in the early 1980s in constant dollars, reflecting widespread increases not only by Nordic states but by other industrialized states as well. Aid volumes peaked in all four cases in the mid-1990s before leveling off or declining in both bilateral and multilateral categories. This trend reflected broader trends among aid donors, which responded to growing domestic pressures by curtailing aid flows (see Chapter 1).

Unlike other industrialized countries, most Nordic states during the early 1990s did not report significant increases in *private* financial flows to the developing world. Only Sweden reported an increase of private financial flows, although the 1993 volume of $584 million remained below the 1990 peak of $660 million (OECD, 1995a: H27). As other chapters in this volume have elaborated, on a global scale cutbacks in foreign aid were accompanied by net increases in the flows of private capital, which often outweighed the aid reductions in terms of total volume.

Although their absolute levels of aid flows are not as large as those of many other OECD members, the Nordic states have long emphasized the *quality* of their aid programs. Within the DAC, the terms of aid flows are often as important as their aggregate volume. Thus, the DAC annually reports on several closely watched indicators of aid quality that reflect the relative sacrifice of ODA donors and the obligations they confer upon recipients. Unlike the United States and Japan, the donors of the largest but qualitatively poorest aid programs, the Nordic states are distinctive in that their relatively small aggregate volumes of ODA achieve qualitative standards that are among the world's highest. Given the importance attached to this aspect of Nordic aid, it is worth reviewing some of these categories in detail.

Aid as a Share of GNP

As noted above, this closely watched measure of aid quality reflects the degree to which industrialized countries, regardless of their aggregate economic output, are committed to aiding less affluent peoples in the developing world. Among members of the DAC, the average ODA/GNP level in the early 1990s was .32 percent (see Table 7.1). Sweden committed itself as early as 1962 to allocating 1 percent of GNP for development assistance. It achieved that target in 1992 but has since fallen below the 1 percent level in the face of growing economic strains. Norway committed to the 1 percent target in 1970 and has met or surpassed it since 1982; its ODA/GNP level peaked at 1.16 percent in 1992 before falling to 1.05 in 1994.[8]

In a major governmental review of foreign aid in 1989, the Danish Plan of Action reaffirmed Denmark's commitment to attaining the 1 percent level. This target was reached in 1992, and despite a decline in the aggregate amount of Danish aid in 1993 its ODA/GNP level actually increased from 1.02 to 1.03 percent. The Finnish government in 1980 pledged to disburse .7 percent of GNP and consequently averaged a 15 percent annual increase in aid appropriations throughout the 1980s (OECD, 1991a: 138). After attaining a disbursement level of .8 percent/GNP in 1991, Finland temporarily abandoned this target because of a severe recession accompanied by an unemployment level of nearly 20 percent. During the next two years its ODA/GNP level fell considerably, to .64 percent in 1992 and to .31 percent in 1993. Finnish leaders pledged to regain the .7 percent benchmark by the year 2000 (FINNIDA, 1993a).

Per Capita Aid Flows

The quality of Nordic aid is further reflected in ODA disbursements per capita, a category of aid quality that demonstrates to what degree the aid commitment imposes burdens upon and is accepted by the overall population. Whereas the DAC average was $67 per capita aid in 1990, the figures for the Nordic donors ranged from $143 in the case of Finland to $232 in that of Norway (the figures for Denmark and Sweden were $185 and $205, respectively). Per capita aid flows increased in real terms for all Nordic states during the ten-year period between 1983 and 1993, although some reductions in these levels were reported in the mid-1990s.

The burden that citizens of these states carried with respect to ODA were by far the largest among the DAC members, and even the like-minded Netherlands only attained the Finnish level in 1990. The United States, by contrast, allocated $38 in foreign aid per citizen in 1993; Japan, whose aid flows exceeded net U.S. outlays by this time, provided $94 in per capita aid. Thus, in this and other areas the Nordic states compensated for their lower aggregate aid disbursements.

The "Tying" of Development Aid

Another litmus test for the quality of aid programs involves the use of tied aid. In this area, the Nordic states are more similar to other OECD members. Though much Nordic aid is extended in grant form, it is often tied to the procurement of donor goods or services. The Danish Plan of Action required that about 50 percent of its bilateral assistance be spent on Danish goods and services, "although there is room for some local cost and third-country procurement to be financed from this tied aid" (OECD, 1991a: 136).

More than any of its neighbors, Finland requires donor procurement for bilateral assistance. Purchasing goods and services for development activities from Finland "increases contacts between Finland and developing countries and reduces the inevitable negative effects of development cooperation on our balance of payments" (FINNIDA, 1993a: 32). Tying aid to procurement has allowed Finland to expand its aid program dramatically into the 1990s and to maintain public support for aid activities. About one-third of Norway's bilateral assistance is extended in tied form, half in the form of technical cooperation.[9] The Swedish government has traditionally pursued a policy that separates commercial interests and aid delivery (Holmberg 1989; Beckman, 1979). Nonetheless, by the end of the 1980s, 35 percent of its bilateral aid was tied to domestic resources.

Multilateral Aid

Denmark, Finland, Norway, and Sweden collectively transfer about 30 percent of their ODA funds through multilateral agencies, well above the DAC average of 24 percent (OECD, 1995a). Sweden annually has provided the most multilateral assistance, but this represented just 28 percent of overall Swedish ODA in 1993. (The shares for Denmark, Finland, and Norway were 35, 20, and 38 percent, respectively.) All these donors have supported multilateral assistance for its presumably apolitical nature; when industrialized states allow their aid funds to be channelled through intermediaries, their political and economic self-interests are presumably subsumed by collective goals. For this reason, the degree to which donors provide aid multilaterally is one of the most closely monitored indicators of aid quality.

The Nordic countries have acted collectively in a number of instances, although combined Nordic aid remains a marginal part of the countries' respective ODA budgets. This regional assistance, provided largely on a project basis, is administered by national aid agencies; cooperative projects occur only in areas where there is overlap with the bilateral programs. Many of these initiatives involve the region-to-region cooperative project known as the Southern African Development Cooperation (SADEC), established in 1984.[10] There are also Nordic working groups promoting democratization in Central America, Namibian independence, women in development, and sustainable development (Nordic Council of Ministers, 1990). These regional activities are modest compared to the extensive Nordic cooperation and strong financial support for UN development activities. This is exemplified by the Nordic states' commitment to the United Nations Development Programme. In 1989, Nordic contributions accounted for 33 percent of the entire UNDP budget, and in the early 1990s they accounted for about 40 percent of the UNICEF budget. Though multilateral shares of total ODA have decreased over the past three decades, they remain a substantial part of the development budgets of Nordic states.

There is a decided preference among the Nordic states for using UN channels rather than international financial institutions such as the World Bank Group. The United Nations and its associated organs and agencies have consistently received the lion's share of Nordic multilateral assistance. These channels are preferred for several reasons: They are insulated from political and commercial pressures, they have universal representation, they generally allow LDCs to participate in decisionmaking, and they serve as central repositories of development experience. In many cases, actions by single donors do not sufficiently address socioeconomic problems that face the least developed countries. Programs administered by the UN are more often organized through donor-recipient dialogue and are thus generally segregated from donors' political agendas. Traditionally, UN bodies have most closely reflected Nordic development priorities—poverty alleviation and good governance that empowers large segments of LDC populations.

The long-standing practice of supporting NGOs in the development process continues to expand in all Nordic aid programs. In 1992 development funds channeled through NGOs ranged from about 5 percent of total ODA in Denmark to more than 10 percent of Norwegian ODA. These groups, particularly churches, have for many years been utilized to distribute humanitarian and disaster relief. Secular NGOs such as industrial and agricultural cooperatives are often employed in transferring technical assistance. Support for NGOs as development agents serves dual purposes. First,

NGOs act "below the governmental level" to deliver assistance to the poorest strata in developing countries. Grassroots activities by NGOs can target populations such as rural women, children, and minorities, that are often ignored by the political authorities in developing states. Second, these organizations involve broader sections of donor-nation populations, mobilizing large numbers of individuals and groups interested in improving living conditions in the developing world.

CHALLENGES TO THE NORDIC AID MODEL

In response to the well-documented shortcomings of many aid programs and to growing domestic strains, Nordic leaders have become more realistic in managing aid policy in the 1990s. Their new practices have included monitoring the effectiveness of aid flows and imposing explicit conditions for replenishments based on political, economic, and social reforms. What was labeled "concerned participation" in Sweden and "partnership" in Norway became a general trend in Nordic country programming. Recipients were subject to stringent rules regarding government spending, currency valuation, and macroeconomic policy in general.

This trend, part of a global pattern in the 1990s, has allowed many donor priorities to creep into the aid relationship. Concerned participation allows the Nordic states to pursue their priorities, such as environmental sustainability, women's rights, human rights, and democratization. Denmark and Finland have gone further and have made a formal linkage between aid disbursement and a functioning policy of structural adjustment (Holm, 1979). In contrast to the IMF and World Bank, Finland and Denmark have stressed "measures related not only to growth but also to greater distribution of well-being, together with the alleviation of the adverse effects that inevitably accompany structural adjustment" (FINNIDA, 1993: 18). Norway and Sweden generally abstain from overt macroeconomic conditionality in their aid programs, but concerned participation has allowed them to introduce sociopolitical dialogue into their aid relationships and therefore to deviate from their earlier, purely recipient-oriented aid profile. Although neither donor explicitly conditions aid disbursement upon adherence to a prescribed macroeconomic policy, each reserves the right to monitor recipient behavior and to expect aid transfers to be used productively (OECD, 1991a: 149).

A more serious challenge to the Nordic reputation for supplying "pure" aid is the growing influence of commercial interests in aid policy. This trend began, innocently enough, when LDCs requested that their economic interactions with the industrialized world extend beyond aid relationships. This external demand converged with growing domestic pressures from industrial and business leaders who sought to become involved in the aid programs. The resulting policies thus reflected donor interests (such as promoting exports), challenging the recipient-oriented development objective of poverty alleviation in the Third World.

The most prominent growth of commercial interests has occurred in Sweden, traditionally a "champion of free and fair trade as well as of pure and untied aid" (Jacoby, 1986: 97; see also Holmberg, 1989; Beckman, 1979). The separation of ODA from commercial interests has been at the heart of the Swedish self-identity as a benevolent aid donor. Indeed, the volume of Swedish aid was not to be diminished even in times of recession. In response, business and industrial interests "turned to proving their efficiency as a means of effective fulfillment of the prescribed development objectives" (Jacoby, 1986: 87). LDCs's demands for "trade, not aid" were answered in Sweden with the concept of "broader cooperation."[11]

In 1978 the Swedish Fund for Industrial Cooperation with Developing Countries (SWEDFUND) was established after a long domestic political struggle. Similar programs in Norway and Finland followed in 1979. These national funds have promoted private investment and joint ventures in LDCs in the form of equity loans and investment guarantees.[12] In Norway such financing can only be used for investment in partner countries, and projects must adhere to established development priorities. By 1992, Finland's comparable program had invested in nine projects in six LDCs, then began extending its activities to Eastern European recipients.

"Associated financing" has become an increasingly common instrument of aid in the Nordic countries. Among the most prominent examples, the Swedish Agency for International Technical and Economic Cooperation (BITS) was established in 1979. BITS's mandate was to broaden and strengthen Sweden's relationship with LDCs in areas where it could offer expertise, competitive products, or services. The program's operational aspects included technical assistance (e.g., consulting, training, and personnel exchanges). More substantially, BITS provided mixed credits for investment projects. By 1987, BITS accounted for 8.6 percent of Sweden's development-aid budget, SWEDFUND less than 3 percent. The Finnish Export Credit Corporation, meanwhile, has been most closely involved in mixed credits and associated financing to medium-income developing countries. These activities were expected to reach 5 percent of Finnish ODA by the mid-1990s. Of more direct interest to Norwegian business and industry were the arrangements for promotion of Norwegian exports. An interest-rate support facility was established in 1976 to facilitate or directly subsidize exports of capital goods to LDCs, with a grant element to up to 25 percent. In contrast to its Nordic neighbors, Norway funded these development instruments outside the ODA budget.

Unlike Sweden and Norway, Denmark has never insisted upon a separation between aid and commercial economic interests. Since the 1970s its foreign ministry has greatly expanded its services to the industrial sector (Holm, 1979: 99). Among the Danish instruments is the Industrialization Fund for Developing Countries, which is designed to assist private enterprises in the developing world with capital investments and technical expertise.[13] Under the Danish Investment Guarantee Scheme, established in 1966, Danish companies were protected against losses incurred in connection with direct investment in LDCs.[14] In 1990 these guarantees covered twenty-eight investments in twenty LDCs and totaled $29.2 million.

There has been a concomitant growth of such instruments on the regional level as well. The Nordic Investment Bank, established by the five Nordic states (including Iceland), provided financing for investment projects involving businesses from more than one Nordic country. Much of this funding has gone to middle-income recipients and is not financed from ODA budgets. In 1989 the Nordic Development Fund (NDF) began functioning with the aim of promoting economic and social development in LLDCs. The NDF provided long-term credits on highly concessional terms (forty years, ten-year grace period, interest-free) as part of cofinancing with other international institutions.

Domestic commercial pressures for return flow have obscured what was previously a general preference for separation of aid and private economic interests. Many of the new forms of assistance are delivered to middle-income countries and impose obligations that in some cases approach market rates. Gone are the days of Nordic contrition for the structural impediments to development in the South, which were reflected during the 1970s in Nordic support for the NIEO. Though they still acknowledge systemic pressures, Nordic leaders in the post–Cold War period have placed stronger emphasis on the responsibility of recipients in making development efforts successful. Though this type of interaction may be beneficial for market-friendly development, its divergence from the "pure" Nordic model has been widely acknowledged and often criticized. But leaders in each Nordic state, who must respond to a widening array of domestic economic problems, have viewed the inclusion of such economically driven aid programs as a prerequisite for the extension of more traditional programs.

The growth of commercial interests in Nordic aid is not only a result of domestic pressures and the economic burden of extending such generous amounts of aid. These trends reflect a fundamental reassessment of the Nordic approach to development assistance. The spectacular dynamism of the "Asian Tigers" stands in stark contrast to the abject poverty that continues to characterize LDCs in Nordic priority areas of South Asia and southern Africa. This contrast has shaken the Nordic states' confidence in their own models of development.

The Norwegian government has been particularly explicit in placing responsibility for the lack of economic growth upon LDCs: "The fact that many countries have not succeeded in achieving lasting social and economic progress is often due to internal problems caused by inappropriate policies and the misuse of power" (Norwegian Development Agency, 1993: 11).[15] Finnish leaders emphasize that the donor's role is secondary to the conduct of the recipient, citing the latter's "will to develop" as a critical requirement for success.

In these respects the Nordic states have taken a page from the OECD manual for ODA and have begun to underscore economic factors of development (see Hook, 1995). Economic growth, previously a marginal aid objective, has assumed a central position in the Nordic approach, and the social aspects of development appear in some cases to have taken a back seat in funding calculations. To create conditions for long-term development and recipient responsibility in the 1990s, for example, "NORAD will be placing great emphasis on developing the productive sector in partner countries with a view toward creating employment opportunities and stimulating the growth that is essential to the reduction of poverty and the development of welfare programs for the population at large" (NORAD, 1993: 7). A related objective is to build LDCs' capacity to sustain growth after outside assistance has been withdrawn. Leaders of FINNIDA (1993b: 10) suggested this new, pragmatic approach may result in "a change in the scale of development funding in the future, assuming that the same goals can also be reached by means other than development cooperation."

In a broader context, the more business-oriented nature of Nordic aid is a manifestation of the new paradigm in global development that has emerged in the Cold War's wake (see Chapter 1). The emergence of this new approach is most visible in Scandinavia because it contrasts so sharply with the region's traditional emphasis on aid quality and its responsiveness to the needs of the world's most impoverished populations.

NORDIC AID TOWARD THE MILLENNIUM

Given the changes outlined above, the Nordic aid approach has become less distinguishable from that of other OECD donors. The news media and scholarly literature have heralded the death of the Nordic model. The early 1990s witnessed the ascension of conservative governments across the region whose objectives included dismantling much of the Nordic welfare state and promoting market-driven economic policies. Obituaries for the Nordic model of social welfare may be premature, but there clearly has been a fundamental reassessment of the Nordic identity, culminating in the Finnish and Swedish decisions in late 1994 to join the European Union.

Norway's electorate voted to remain outside the EU. Tellingly, this Nordic state retains the most characteristically Nordic aid profile: Norwegian flows are the highest in the region as a percentage of GNP, their terms remain very favorable for recipients, and funding for commercial instruments is still separate from the ODA budget. The relative continuity of the Nordic aid approach in Norway reflects the continued strength of social-democratic ideals and solidarity in that country (see Nordic Development Fund, 1992; see also Nordic UN Project, 1991, 1990).

What does EU membership and a divided Nordic region portend for the Nordic development approach? How will EU and Nordic aid cohere? It is instructive that the EU has pioneered many of the instruments, most notably trading privileges and general preferences, that integrate LDCs into trade relationships with the industrialized North. The Lomé Conventions offer nearly seventy African, Pacific, and Caribbean states stable and guaranteed access to EU markets (see Chapter 6), and the ALAMED (Asia, Latin America, and Mediterranean) agreements provide a number of instruments for joint ventures and licensing projects in many middle-income states. Though EU members maintain their own bilateral and UN aid programs, collective EU aid has been commercially oriented, as social concerns have been promoted through other channels.

Under the provisions of the Maastricht Treaty, EU members pledged to coordinate a Common Foreign and Security Policy that includes provisions for ODA. Still unresolved is whether such coordination will involve a cen-tralized European development policy or whether coordination will remain fragmented among the fifteen member states. Coordination rather than amalgamation is the Nordic tradition and preference, although the European Commission has expressed support for a supranational European develop-ment policy. Regardless of the eventual structure, areas of agreement in the emerging CFSP are apparent. In 1993 the European Commission detailed priority areas for development, including democracy, human rights, health, education and training, food security, poverty alleviation, and external financing and debt. These objectives were roughly consistent with those mandated by the UN in its sustainable-development campaigns of the mid-1990s.

The most obvious impact of EU membership on Nordic foreign aid is that it will no longer be definitively considered Nordic in nature. Now a divided region with Norway remaining outside the EU, the practice of joint Nordic statements in the UN and other multilateral fora is proscribed by membership in the union. While informal consultation among the Nordic states will no doubt continue, and the general priority of social equity remains, the existence of a cohesive Nordic position in many international organizations is likely a thing of the past. The extent to which a European aid policy replaces bilateral and regional programs will become clearer as the millennium approaches, but the common Nordic platform, influential beyond the size of these small states, will likely be a casualty of the EU.

However, Nordic EU members gain an opportunity to extend to a larger arena the social principles they have traditionally espoused. Other members of the EU, notably the Netherlands and Belgium, have shared many of the social and development priorities of Nordic states. Cooperation with these like-minded members may allow the Nordic states to introduce their vision of development into the larger EU setting. Thus, the distinctive aspects of Nordic aid may contribute to, rather than be subsumed by, the aid policies of the EU.

Ultimately, the Nordic and European development approaches may interact synergistically to create a new model with its own character. The EU approach, which generally focuses upon trade and investment relationships, will extend Nordic development cooperation beyond acts of charity, whereas the Nordic emphasis on the social aspects of development can enrich the EU's more businesslike approach. The point is not whose vision is morally superior but how effectively industrialized states foster balanced growth and representative government in the developing world. Combining different orientations, ideas, and experiences may produce renewed vigor and innovation in the development dialogue, which throughout the Cold War was hamstrung by ideological posturing and superpower hegemony.

Beyond the issue of EU membership, the Nordic approach to foreign aid will continue its adaptation to the post–Cold War development climate. The Nordic approach epitomized altruism and unselfishness in the 1960s and 1970s, a time of high esteem for the social-democratic model, which paired economic growth and social equity. Today the Nordic model of development is less influential as it confronts ongoing criticism both internally and from overseas (see Laatikainen, 1995). As the Nordic states determine what it means to be Nordic in the next millennium, they must also redefine their relationship with the impoverished peoples of the world. Their new outlook will have an impact on global development that transcends the states' individual roles, economic capabilities, and political influence.

NOTES

1. Iceland is part of the Nordic cultural group, but its aid activities are minimal, and its government does not participate in the OECD's Development Assistance Committee. Consequently, Iceland is not included in this chapter.

2. Their persistence in this area was instrumental in shaping the agenda of the UN conference on women's rights held in 1995 the People's Republic of China.

3. Denmark benefits from the aid objective of eliminating poverty in least developed countries: "Besides the humanitarian reason one could add that the poor

countries are also the countries where agricultural production is the most important and where Danish expertise in agro-industry has a potential market" (Holm, 1979: 96).

4. Finland joined the United Nations in 1955 and was a net recipient of World Bank assistance until 1967.

5. Although he studied only the Swedish case, Hook (1995) identified the value orientations central to Nordic and particularly Swedish aid. These orientations include social democracy, equality, pacifism, and neutrality.

6. The five Swedish agencies with a role in foreign aid were merged into SIDA in 1995 as part of the government's plan to make the aid program more efficient.

7. Among program countries, Tanzania has been the primary recipient of Nordic aid through much of the 1980s and 1990s; other major recipients have included India, Bangladesh, Mozambique, and the former Yugoslavia.

8. The Norwegian government in 1977 and again in 1981 debated the idea of committing to a 1.3 percent level but declined to make it an official target.

9. Although most of Norway's capital project assistance is untied, the bulk of commodity assistance is tied to procurement in Norway as long as costs are internationally competitive.

10. The SADEC includes Angola, Botswana, Lesotho, Malawi, Mozambique, Swaziland, Tanzania, Zambia, and Zimbabwe.

11. The growing influence of Swedish industry in foreign aid was echoed in other Nordic countries; Denmark, an exception to this pattern, had for many years utilized its industrial sector in development assistance (Stokke, 1985; Holm, 1979).

12. SWEDFUND has supported more than twenty-five industrial projects and is funded through Sweden's official aid budget.

13. This program supported 167 projects in 54 countries and in 1990 totaled $21 million covering 12 new as well as ongoing projects.

14. This protection was limited to $400,000 in losses associated with political instability in developing countries and did not cover commercial risk.

15. Norway underscores the importance of preventing aid dependency among recipients. "The policies, choices, and priorities of the recipient country are suitable for promoting development (only if they) are responsible for their own share of development cooperation activities" (NORAD, 1993: 8).

8

The Rise and Fall of OPEC Aid

Timothy Luke

The very formation of OPEC was in itself a minor "revolution" and the first example of raw-material-producing countries joining together in collective strength to negotiate their legitimate rights with the international companies which then dominated all aspects of oil producing and pricing in OPEC countries. The "revolt" of OPEC's five Founding Members . . . was a reaction against the injustice and humiliation caused for them by these powerful multinational corporations.—OPEC ministers, September 1981

The Organization of Petroleum Exporting Countries operates in the late 1990s under a shadow that still lingers from a quarter-century earlier, when the cartel burst onto the world stage as a powerful economic and political actor. In provoking the first of two global energy crises, OPEC demonstrated how the coordinated manipulation of the oil supply could play havoc with the economic fortunes of the world's wealthiest states and promote OPEC's social and political agenda.

The OPEC states, flush with seemingly bottomless reserves of cash, gained the attention of rich and poor countries alike. Upon achieving this stature, they began disbursing foreign economic assistance as a key instrument in their collective foreign policy. Arab oil princes were ready to shower whole hosts of overseas beneficiaries with economic assistance wherever the interests of prospective recipients converged with their own.

Emboldened OPEC ministers stood before leaders of other LDCs as exemplars of organized defiance against the Western economic superpowers. Their cartel would "promote a spirit of global interdependence. In this case relationships between OPEC and the rest of the Third World have a privileged place" (Jaidah, 1983: 42). For several years after its formation, OPEC served as a potential role model for LDCs that relied upon other commodity exports—such as coffee, cocoa, and seafood—as a primary source of income.[1] As Blake and Walters (1987: 179) observed regarding the precedent set by OPEC:

> If less-developed countries possessing the major sources of a particular
> mineral resource could maintain a common front vis-à-vis all the major
> multinationals in that industry, none of these states could be relegated to
> the position of a supplier of last resort. Collectively, they would still be
> able to exert considerable weight in international distribution and sales.
> This is, of course, the strategy that was employed so successfully by oil-
> producing states between 1973 and 1979.

OPEC's massive oil profits were seen as potential engines for growth among the Group of 77 (G-77) states with which the cartel was rhetorically aligned. OPEC's founding coincided with the decolonization of Africa and state-building efforts across the developing world, giving LDCs a numerical superiority in the UN's General Assembly and many specialized agencies. Given its newfound wealth and its proven ability to create havoc with industrialized economies, the cartel portrayed itself as a fitting advocate for the interests of LDCs in the emerging North-South dialogue. OPEC ministers (1984: 144) proclaimed in December 1976 their "full harmony and solidarity with the efforts of developing countries to attain the objectives of the new international economic order."

Among the by-products of OPEC's rapid rise to economic power was its creation of large-scale programs of foreign assistance. From 1973 to 1992, OPEC members disbursed more than $100 billion in economic aid to LDCs worldwide. Of these funds, 63 percent was disbursed as part of multilateral aid packages, and just 37 percent flowed bilaterally from OPEC states to recipient governments (Faquih, 1993: 12–13). OPEC leaders promised to maintain high aid levels indefinitely, describing their manipulation of the world oil market as a retaliatory measure against Western elites who had previously called the shots in all aspects of global economic activity—agriculture, and industry, trade and monetary policy, multinational corporations, the World Bank and IMF—were viewed as colluding with powerful states to control the world economy.

This charge was particularly applicable to the oil industry, which had for decades been dominated by a handful of Western oil conglomerates. As demand for petroleum escalated in an increasingly interdependent world, the energy sector suddenly appeared in the early 1970s as the linchpin of the global economy. Recognizing this, OPEC leaders defended their supply restrictions and price increases as part of a broader and overdue effort to redistribute global wealth from rich to poor. Encouraged by their early success, OPEC ministers (1984: 112) in 1973 warned that any concerted action undertaken by industrialized-importing countries aimed at undermining OPEC's legitimate aspirations would only hamper the stable relationships that have normally existed between these and OPEC members countries. . . . (T)o seek a direct confrontation with OPEC may have a damaging effect on the world economy.

OPEC's policy, which included raising the per-barrel price of crude oil from $1.30 in 1970 to $10.72 in 1975, was enormously successful, producing "one of the most massive transfers of wealth in history" (Pool and Stamos, 1989: 9). Oil exporters watched their revenues leap from $23 billion in 1972 to $140 billion in 1977 while they reduced output and assumed control of the industry's pricing structure (Yergin, 1991: 634). The OPEC embargo not only produced much higher gasoline prices, it prompted price increases in virtually every economic sector, caused high unemployment and balance-of-payment deficits in wealthy states, and exposed the industrial world's overall reliance on steady and affordable supplies of fuel.[2] Many Americans still remember the gas lines that extended for blocks, and they remember the strenuous efforts by the Ford and Carter administrations to promote energy conservation in U.S. homes and businesses and to support the development of alternative energy sources.[3]

This unusual cartelization of the oil industry—accomplished by public rather than private actors—was hailed by many leaders in developing countries and within several agencies of the United Nations as a crucial part of the ongoing effort to create a new international economic order. A majority of states within the UN General Assembly, with strong OPEC backing, reaffirmed their support for the NIEO in the 1974 Charter of Economic Rights and Duties of States. The United States opposed many provisions of the NIEO, particularly those calling for a more central state role in economic development and for higher levels of U.S. foreign aid and other means of global economic redistribution.

Not only did OPEC represent a unique commodity cartel, its members emerged as unusual foreign-aid donors. After all, they remained officially classified as developing countries themselves, apart from other donors, which drew most of their wealth from the manufacturing sector. In addition, OPEC's aid funds were almost literally skimmed off the top of its oil exports, minimizing the impact on taxpayers in OPEC states. For many years, Gause (1994: 43) observed, "The central question for the rulers of these states has been how to spend money, not how to extract it from society, as the overwhelming share of OPEC revenues came from external sources such as oil revenues, investment income, and other kinds of direct payments."

Since OPEC's explosive arrival on the world scene, however, its great expectations have diminished along with the cartel's oil revenues, its share of global petroleum production, and the inflation-adjusted world price of oil. New sources of non-OPEC oil on the supply side, and demand-side energy savings induced by oil conservation, profoundly changed the existing patterns of world consumption. In turn, OPEC's capacity to serve as a vital foreign-aid source slipped in the 1980s as the United States, Japan, and members of the European Community (now the European Union) dominated the global aid regime.

Few during the 1970s anticipated the oil glut that ensued a decade later, when oil production rebounded, conservation efforts took hold, and a prolonged economic recession in the West eroded its demand for oil. Led by Japanese manufacturers, the global automobile industry produced smaller and more fuel-efficient vehicles. The U.S. government, otherwise slow to respond to Japan's rapid ascension in the auto industry, set minimum levels of fuel efficiency for U.S. cars in the late 1970s. Within fifteen years General Motors, Ford, and Chrysler had regained their profitability, if not their previously dominant market shares.[4] Demand for petroleum was further reduced as nuclear energy, natural gas, and renewable energy sources became more widely utilized. As long as significant supplies of non-OPEC oil were available from Alaska, Mexico, Russia, the North Sea, and other sources, as was generally true after 1980, OPEC's ability to control supply and price levels in the global oil market was greatly impaired.

Even in their peak years, the flows of most OPEC aid were limited to a sharply defined set of special recipients: first, to other Arab countries such as Jordan and Syria; second, to non-Arab Islamic countries such as Turkey and Pakistan; and, last, to a few LLDCs in sub-Saharan Africa and elsewhere. In this respect the self-interested foundations of OPEC aid were exposed—as was the oil nations' failure to achieve their stated objective of serving as a torchbearer for the world's poor and politically disenfranchised.

OPEC thus provides another example of the central role of foreign aid since it became an important part of North-South relations after World War II. As other chapters in this volume have described, aid flows have varied widely over time and across geographical regions, reflecting prevailing political relations and the constantly shifting economic conditions of rich and poor states. However, whereas other donors increased their aid commitments through the end of the Cold War, the near collapse of OPEC aid represents a glaring exception to this trend. The rise and fall of OPEC foreign aid demonstrates vividly how the self-interests of donor states have prevailed both over those of impoverished aid recipients and over declared collective interests; it also shows how fragile solidarity among wealthy states can be when the imperatives of economic self-interest prevail. Finally, OPEC's foreign-aid experience illustrates how ephemeral this policy instrument may be, given its dependence on not only the willingness but also the continuing economic prosperity of donor states. Given that the development of poor states is an inherently complex, long-term process, the volatility and caprice of aid flows as exhibited in the OPEC case is especially problematic.

THE RISE OF OPEC FOREIGN AID

Founded in Baghdad in September 1960, OPEC was designed to protect the mutual interests of its member states against the cohesive bloc of transnational oil companies. "Members can no longer remain indifferent to the attitude heretofore adopted by the Oil Companies in effecting price modifications," the cartel's ministers (OPEC, 1984: 1) proclaimed at their first conference. The original five members of OPEC—Iran, Iraq, Kuwait, Saudi Arabia, and Venezuela—collectively exported 80 percent of the world's crude oil and hoped to reverse a trend in the late 1950s by which oil prices had remained stagnant and actually fell in some years. At first OPEC was ineffective against the combined power of the "seven sisters" in the oil industry: British Petroleum, Chevron, Exxon, Mobil, Shell, Standard Oil of California, and Texaco (Blair, 1976).[5] But macroeconomic trends, new limits on production, and coordinated leadership exercised in the late 1960s and early 1970s made OPEC a force to be reckoned with in the oil industry.

As more oil-exporting regions were discovered in the developing world, OPEC grew in membership to include Algeria, Ecuador (until 1993), Gabon, Indonesia, Libya, Nigeria, Qatar, and the United Arab Emirates. But the five original members continued to play leading political roles in the organization, and the Gulf region, the home of each of all the founding members except Venezuela, became a global power center (Schneider, 1983; Blair, 1976). With its secretariat in Vienna, OPEC asserted itself from the early 1970s through the 1980s on a wide range of issues, many of which had little to do with oil or global energy policy.

The assertiveness of the OPEC states was sparked by the proliferation of private oil producers, including a growing number of independent companies such as Marathon and Getty, which established oil concessions in several OPEC states and challenged the oligopolistic control of the Seven Sisters. After the Libyan government, led by Muammar Qaddafi, demanded that the price of oil pumped on its territory be raised and that Tripoli receive higher earnings from the concessions, a precedent was set by which the governments of oil-producing states dictated to the private producers the volumes and prices of their oil output. OPEC solidarity crystalized in late 1973 after the Yom Kippur War in the Middle East, when its members agreed to withhold oil supplies to supporters of Israel, primarily the United States. The result of this boycott was a surge in global oil prices and vast profits for both the oil companies and the OPEC governments.

With such large amounts of cash on hand, the OPEC states become major donors of foreign aid in the late 1970s and early 1980s. OPEC donors funded an elaborate network of multilateral and bilateral development institutions to channel aid to a variety of clients (Le Vine and Luke, 1979). OPEC aid, which doubled between 1973 and 1974 to $4.5 billion, peaked in 1980 at $9.6 billion. As a percentage of the donors' GNP, a closely watched measure of aid quality, OPEC aid during the 1970s far exceeded the OECD benchmark of .7 percent, most often ranging between 2 and 3 percent. In 1975 the Arab OPEC countries disbursed nearly 8 percent of their national output in the form of development assistance, an unprecedented level of aid commitment.

Bilateral Aid Programs

In addition to contributing to the cartel's shared aid transfers, several OPEC countries established large-scale bilateral programs, giving nearly $100 billion in aid from 1973 to 1992. The major donors were Saudi Arabia, with $64 billion in bilateral aid; Kuwait, with $18 billion; and the United Arab Emirates, with $10 billion. Most of this aid was concessional, with about 60 percent directed toward other Arab states (Faquih, 1993: 13). Libya and Iraq provided nearly $2.5 billion each, Qatar about $2 billion, and Algeria about $1.2 billion during the twenty-year period.[6]

By 1995 only three OPEC states maintained significant development-aid programs. Aid flows from Saudi Arabia, which amounted to $3.7 billion in 1990, fell to $317 million in 1994, the lowest level since 1972. Kuwaiti ODA, however, increased in the wake of the Gulf War from $203 million in 1992 to $555 million in 1994, with more than two-thirds transferred to Syria. Notably, Kuwaiti ODA equaled 2.01 percent of GNP in the latter year, a higher percentage than that of any other donor of development assistance.[7] The UAE, meanwhile, disbursed $100 million in 1994 (OECD, 1996a: 118).

The first bilateral aid institution in the OPEC states was the Kuwait Fund for Arab Economic Development, organized in 1961. For its first thirteen years it concentrated on development projects only in other Arab countries, but in 1974 it broadened its scope to include LDCs in other parts of the world. The Abu Dhabi Fund for Arab Economic Development was chartered in 1971 to give aid to other Arab states, and the Saudi Fund for Development and the Iraqi Fund for External Development both began distributing development assistance to Arab and developing countries in 1974. The Libyan government, meanwhile, began in 1972 to fund the Libyan Arab Foreign Investment Company, which was designed to subsidize private ventures in LDCs. Finally, the Venezuelan Investment Fund was created in 1974 to advance Venezuela's own industrialization as well as to make foreign investment and financial cooperation part of its broad effort to advance development abroad.

The case of bilateral Iranian foreign aid is particularly instructive. The Iran Organization, established in 1975, coordinated all of Iran's foreign investment and assistance as well as all external investment in and loans to Iran. But all along it was clear that these financial flows were centrally directed from Tehran, first by the shah and then by the revolutionary ayatollahs, to serve Iran's narrow foreign-policy interests (in both secular and sacred forms) as a would-be great power or citadel of pan-Islamic revolution. Whether to further the shah's ambitious program to become an influential middle power on the scale of France, Germany, or Japan or, later, to advance the Islamic movement's support of fundamentalism, Iran's foreign aid retained its strong measure of self-interest. Moreover, its protracted conflict with Iraq consumed large amounts of cash throughout the 1980s, undercutting the pool of available aid funds.

As noted above, the vast majority of foreign aid transferred by OPEC aid institutions has been directed to African or Asian states with major Arab and/or Islamic populations. From their inception into the early 1990s, for example, the Abu Dhabi and Iraqi funds each only aided one Latin American country, and the Kuwaiti and Saudi funds only aided two apiece. Moreover, most bilateral OPEC aid took its cue from Western programs in which aid promotes trade. Hence, primary support was given to energy-intensive development projects such as those involving the construction of transportation networks (22.5 percent of all projects funded), agricultural and agroindustrial enterprises (20.2 percent), energy development (19.3 percent), and industrial plants (15.7 percent). OPEC leaders recognized that development projects in LDCs would require petroleum or petrochemical resources that could originate within OPEC sources. Health projects, telecommunication networks, and educational initiatives, by contrast, made up less than 10 percent of all projects funded by OPEC assistance.

As sources of aid, the OPEC states have established an uneven track record. For the most part, these countries are still very much engaged in modernizing their own domestic economies and societies (Luke, 1983). None has developed its agricultural sector successfully enough to be self-sustaining in foodstuffs, however, and none has established an extensive heavy industrial base, even though Iraq and Iran have constructed some sophisticated military industries with outside technical assistance (Luke, 1985). Indeed, many of these states still receive some kind of foreign assistance themselves, and most are heavy borrowers in private capital markets. Consequently, their overall economic output, individually and as a group, is still modest compared to that of most OECD aid donors.

Multilateral Aid Programs

OPEC multilateral aid programs were initiated in 1971 with the establishment of the Arab Fund for Economic and Social Development, a regional institution dedicated to financing projects in the member states of the Arab League. In 1976 the OPEC states jointly created the OPEC Fund for International Development to direct aid to carefully selected LDCs in South Asia, Africa, and Latin America. They also established institutional linkages with the IMF and its International Fund for Agricultural Development.

Though OPEC members provided loans to a few middle-income developing countries, most of their multilateral aid transfers were highly concessional, particularly to LLDCs. Along with these programs, OPEC donors supported the Arab Authority for Agricultural Investment and Development to achieve food security in Arab countries and the Arab Bank for Economic Development in Africa to channel OPEC assistance to non-Arab African states. This bank administered the Special Arab Fund for Africa to redress short-term balance-of-payments problems in the region. OPEC countries also underwrote the Arab Fund for Technical Assistance to African and Arab Countries, which coordinated the work of technical experts in these areas; the Arab Gulf Program for United Nations Development Organizations, which invested in various projects within the forty-five-member Organization of the Islamic Conference; and the Islamic Solidarity Fund, which provided support to Islamic states worldwide for social and economic development.

These multilateral OPEC aid institutions have been augmented by national trust funds administered by the African Development Bank (ADB), the Inter-American Development Bank (IDB), and the Caribbean Development Bank (CDB). The Arab Oil Fund, established and funded by Algeria, and the Nigeria Trust Fund continued to provide economic aid to African Development Bank members in the mid-1990s. The Venezuela Fund financed development and balance-of-payment support in Latin America and the Caribbean to IDB and CDB members through those financial institutions. These programs most often provided short-term "bridge" monies to strengthen recipients' trade balances.

As we have seen, most development aid from OPEC states has been directed to assist Arab and/or Islamic states, with much smaller volumes allocated to sub-Saharan Africa, South Asia, Latin America, and the Caribbean. These patterns diverge from those of other multilateral aid organizations, which ostensibly serve apolitical objectives and emphasize socioeconomic need in recipient states rather than the interests of donors. In this respect multilateral OPEC aid has closely mirrored bilateral OPEC assistance and, more generally, the foreign-policy objectives of each donor country and the cartel itself.

THE FALL OF OPEC FOREIGN AID

The reign of OPEC, both as an economic power and as a source of foreign aid, was relatively short-lived; its decline in the 1980s and 1990s has been longer lasting.

The problems began shortly after the first oil embargo, when OPEC states began a domestic spending binge in the name of modernization. Even as oil revenues grew, the cartel's net balance of payments fell from a $678 billion surplus in 1974 to a $2 billion deficit in 1978 (Yergin, 1991: 634). Internal dissension over production ceilings and prices multiplied as the border war between Iran and Iraq—two of OPEC's founding members—decimated both economies throughout the 1980s. As Sadek Boussena (quoted in OPEC, 1990: 303), president of the cartel's 1990 conference, openly acknowledged: "Our fortunes have faded badly, prices have fallen to their lowest levels for 18 months, with the risk of bringing, once again, OPEC Member Countries' revenues and economies to the brink of collapse."

Even for the wealthiest OPEC donors, aid commitments in absolute terms and as a percentage of GNP fell rapidly into the 1990s. Aggregate aid volumes declined steadily during the late 1980s, bottoming out at $1.6 billion in 1989 before rising again in the early 1990s. Among the major sources, aid from Saudi Arabia fell from $3.7 billion in 1990 to less than $539 million in 1992, its lowest level in twenty years.[8] These cutbacks in OPEC aid occurred in both bilateral and multilateral aid programs. Concessional loans through the Saudi Fund for Development, for example, were exceeded by repayments from earlier loans. Kuwaiti aid fell from $1.3 billion in 1990 to $381 million three years later as it embarked upon a long-term recovery from the 1990–1991 Gulf War. Aid from the UAE decreased from $888 million to $236 million. Concomitantly, levels of OPEC aid as a percentage of donor GNP fell below 1 percent beginning in 1982.

Adding to OPEC's problems, the international spot market in oil became more significant in the 1980s, making it very difficult to determine which cartel members were selling how much to whom and when. Consequently, cheating by OPEC members on pricing and supply arrangements became widespread. Saudi Arabia attempted to maintain discipline by adjusting the production levels used in OPEC price-management formulas, but its efforts were nullified by the "free riding" of other oil producers. Bickering among OPEC members over production and price levels has consistently been the rule, coherent collective action the exception.

The oil price hikes of the 1970s did not *cause* the abject economic decline of much of the developing world during the 1980s and early 1990s, but they certainly contributed to the problem. As other chapters of this volume have described, many LDCs struggled with persistent socioeconomic problems after gaining their independence during the 1960s and 1970s. With low levels of economic output, little manufacturing capacity, vulnerable agricultural sectors, limited export capabilities, and ineffectual governments, these LDCs often have seen what little growth they have achieved eaten away by large population increases and mounting demands for public services. With the collapse in the early 1980s of raw-materials markets, which still had not recovered more than a decade later, the limited comparative advantage of most LDCs in global export markets has largely disappeared. Thus, their capacity to emulate the OPEC cartel, never considerable to begin with, vanished as well.

OPEC's contribution to the decline in the developing world's fortunes in the 1980s and 1990s has carried with it several ironies. First, the problems of many LDCs were accentuated when their oil-import bills soared as a result of OPEC's ceilings on energy production, causing widespread budget deficits and energy shortages in countries that desperately needed low-cost oil in their early phases of modernization. Foreign currency reserves were often drained by the increased costs of oil and other commodities and services which resulted from higher energy costs. In addition, exports fell dramatically because of reductions in demand and the resulting drop in commodity prices. As a result, many LDCs' national accounts could only stay open through massive borrowing from multilateral and bilateral organizations, creating higher foreign debts and debt-service obligations.

In another irony, the glut of OPEC petrodollars in the 1980s contributed to the developing world's debt crisis. Large volumes of these funds, deposited by OPEC members in multinational banks, were lent primarily to Latin American LDCs on market terms, not concessional terms. When these countries encountered stagnant commodity earnings and other problems and were unable to reimburse the commercial banks, the global debt crisis followed (see Gilpin, 1987). OPEC's role in abetting the debt crisis was at first denied, then acknowledged in the late 1980s, but OPEC leaders did not accept blame for the willingness of Mexico, Brazil, Argentina, and other LDCs to plunge into commercial capital markets when aid funds fell short.

Finally, major internal disruptions occurred in many LDCs as development projects stalled, governments rose and fell (often violently), and national development strategies collapsed because of slow or no growth in the economies of primary trading partners. Thus, these nations' needs became more acute, and their reliance on development aid intensified. Until the early 1990s, the volumes of foreign aid from OECD members and most other donors increased virtually every year, bringing some relief to struggling regions and making up for the reductions of OPEC aid. However, with the end of the Cold War and the emergence of new recipients of foreign aid in Eastern Europe and the Soviet Union, allocations to traditional recipients began to decline (see Chapter 1). This process coincided with OPEC's continuing aid cutbacks, which occurred for very different reasons, further hampering the flow of aid to the world's poor between the Cold War and millennium.

OPEC AID TOWARD THE MILLENNIUM

As we have seen, OPEC's financial windfall in the 1970s propelled the cartel into the forefront of international economic relations and led to the establishment of elaborate bilateral and multilateral aid programs designed to serve OPEC's social and political agenda. But these efforts have fallen victim to the transformed international system of the 1990s. The OPEC aid programs remain structurally intact, however, making possible their resurgence if political and economic conditions within the cartel stabilize.

In the late 1990s, many of the structural contradictions that led to OPEC's demise in the 1980s continue. New supplies of oil from former communist countries and other non-OPEC members have thrust excessive volumes of petroleum onto world markets. Global demand for oil remains soft because of a prolonged recession in the industrialized world and new efficiency measures. Further, internal demands and social unrest within OPEC states have generated continuing friction in the cartel over how to manage price and supply structures.[9] Pervasive tensions between the self-interests of each oil exporter and the collective interests of the cartel are far from resolved. Renewed tensions along the Iraqi-Kuwaiti border in early 1996 and the continuing aftershocks of the Gulf War, which created a makeshift Arab coalition as part of Operation Desert Storm, underscored the fragility of the cartel. Though a cyclical upswing in oil prices is within the realm of possibility, OPEC will likely never have the clout its members exploited so skillfully in the 1970s.[10]

In the late 1990s, then, foreign aid remains largely a financial sideline of the states that emerged as major figures in OPEC's heyday of the 1970s. Flat world oil markets, new pressing domestic priorities, and the costs of the Gulf War have lowered the ability of even these wealthy countries to make good on past aid commitments. The chronic internal dissension within OPEC has undermined its ability to act as a forceful player in the post–Cold War dialogue between rich and poor. OPEC aid organizations continue to channel some resources to LLDCs in Africa, Latin America, and Asia, but the vast majority of remaining OPEC aid still goes to other Arab and Islamic countries very close to home. In declining order, these recipients include Egypt, Turkey, Morocco, Syria, Bahrain, and Jordan.

Not all the evidence from the early 1990s was discouraging. The Kuwaiti government, still recovering from the Gulf War, signed twenty-seven loan agreements with twenty-one countries in 1993. These loans amounted to about $660 million, more than double the loan commitments made in 1992. Outgoing loans through the Kuwait Fund exceeded repayments in 1993 by about $100 million (OECD, 1995a: 110).[11] In addition, OPEC oil production reached levels in the early 1990s not seen since the late 1970s. Consequently, as Blake and Walters (1987: 190) observed well before the Cold War ended, emerging trends "suggest that the world is not free from a possible replay of events that gave OPEC great political-economic leverage during the 1970s. It is a mistake to assume that the oil crisis today is no more than an artifact of history."[12]

But even if global oil markets tighten again in the coming years, intra-OPEC frictions, the strategic rivalries between OPEC members and non-OPEC states and the tendency of cash-pressed members to exceed production quotas likely will constrain the effectiveness of the cartel. This lack of influence will only deepen the estrangement of OPEC from its presumed beneficiaries in the developing world, many of whom have turned to Western donors, the World Bank, and, increasingly, private capital markets and multinational corporations for economic stimulus.

In OPEC's short history its combative approach to the outside world has been exceeded only by its internal dissension, which has destroyed its founders' high hopes and caused bitter disappointment within other LDCs, though bringing relief to many political leaders and consumers in the developed world. Even if OPEC's fortunes revive in the next century, the increased costs of domestic governance, security policies, and economic development throughout the cartel will likely prevent its members from playing the almost fantastic role they once assumed as the world's most unlikely foreign-aid donors during the Cold War.

NOTES

1. Such states, which derived more than 60 percent of their export earnings from basic commodities, included in the late 1980s and early 1990s Bhutan, Burundi, Dominica, Ethiopia, French Guiana, Guadeloupe, Malawi, Maldives, Martinique, Rwanda, St. Lucia, and Seychelles (Kegley and Wittkopf, 1995: 267).

2. The United States at the time of the first oil shock depended on OPEC for about 50 percent of its petroleum imports. According to a U.S. government estimate, the embargo reduced U.S. gross national product by about $25 billion in 1974 and $28 billion in 1975.

3. The problem was widely referred to as an "energy shortage" during this period, suggesting that the global oil supply was suddenly running dry and high energy prices, long gas lines, and fundamental changes in Western living standards would be inevitable and permanent. Growing demand for petroleum by the United States indeed outpaced its own supplies, adding to the upward pressure on prices, but this

was largely due to a lack of aggressive oil exploration and a recognition that the Gulf region could easily fill the void.

4. In addition to its other efforts to reduce its dependence on OPEC oil and to promote energy conservation and the development of alternative energy sources, the U.S. government and other Western states established the International Energy Agency (IEA) in 1974 to coordinate their response to future disruptions of oil supplies.

5. Prior to OPEC's ascension, Exxon in 1970 earned the most oil revenues ($1.3 billion), followed by Texaco ($822 million), Gulf ($550 million), Mobil ($483 million), and Standard Oil of California ($455 million). See Jaidah (1983) for an elaboration.

6. Meanwhile, the labor-importing Arab countries also transferred to the Arab labor-exporting countries about $91 billion in aid from 1973 to 1990 as well as about $10 billion to other non-Arab developing countries, ranging from the Philippines, India, Pakistan, Bangladesh, North Korea, and South Korea. Among Arab recipients, most worker remittances were transferred to Egypt (46 percent), Yemen (17 percent), Jordan (10.5 percent), and Syria (6.5 percent).

7. The ODA/GNP levels for Saudi Arabia and the UAE in 1994 were .25 and .27, respectively.

8. The most recent reductions in Saudi foreign aid "reflect the changed financial situation of Saudi Arabia after the Gulf War" (OECD, 1995a: 110).

9. Contrary to widespread perceptions that linger in the late 1990s, many OPEC countries have struggled with fiscal crises ever since their aid flows peaked in the early 1980s.

10. The sluggishness in world oil markets continues to be the central threat to OPEC finances and to its foreign-aid capabilities. Saudi Arabia's foreign-capital holdings, for example, dropped from $142 billion in 1984 to about $50 billion in 1994, and the cash reserves of the Saudi Arabian Monetary Agency fell from $7.4 billion in 1993 to $4.5 billion in April 1994 (Boustany, 1994: A14).

11. Though its bilateral aid volumes increased in 1993, the Kuwaiti government continued its pattern of reducing multilateral commitments.

12. The UN-sponsored embargo of Iraqi oil exports in the wake of the Gulf War led to higher gasoline prices in 1996, when limited exports were permitted to raise funds for Iraq's growing social needs.

Part 3

Recipients of Foreign Assistance

9

Aid and Reform in the Former Second World

Janine R. Wedel

The collapse of communist governments across the Soviet bloc and the prospect of their transition to market economies and democratic rule inspired a shift in the priorities of Western foreign-aid donors. Development agencies reoriented their programs, diverting funds and personnel en masse from the Third World to the former Second World. Since 1989 the world's wealthy governments have disbursed nearly $40 billion in aid to the region and have committed to even higher aid levels well into the next millennium. Through this process the Central and Eastern European countries and the new independent states of the former Soviet Union (CEEC/NIS) have become vast laboratories for social transformation. With the ongoing presence of multiple aid programs, the region has witnessed an intense commitment on the part of donor governments, agencies, and individuals to rapid societal change.

In this chapter I will review this process of postcommunist reform, which has altered international relations in many salient ways, including the direction and volume of foreign-aid flows. I will describe how the aid community reorganized itself to accommodate these new efforts, then turn my attention to the critical issue of donor-recipient aid relations, which has often determined the success or failure of projects. Finally, I will examine the eastward expansion of the aid effort from the CEEC states to the former Soviet Union before concluding with some general lessons and recommendations.

Emphasis will be placed upon the Visegrad states of Poland, Hungary, and the former Czechoslovakia, where I have conducted extensive field research in the post–Cold War period and interviewed numerous officials on both the donor and recipient sides of the aid network. As I will describe, the planning and strategic considerations associated with foreign aid are undoubtedly important, but they are empty in the absence of effective means of *delivering* economic assistance. For it is in the delivery process that principles are put into practice, expectations are put to the test, and donor and recipient governments interact most directly.

Members of the OECD's Development Assistance Committee transferred about $28 billion to CEEC/NIS states from 1992 to 1994, a three-year period in which an elaborate multilateral effort emerged to promote economic development and democratic reforms across the region. The Federal Republic of Germany has been by far the leading aid donor to the region, providing approximately 40 percent of DAC flows, followed by the United States and France. German commitments to the former Soviet Union, part of the reunification agreement reached between Helmut Kohl and Mikhail Gorbachev, were compounded by the enormous costs the FRG incurred in assimilating East Germany and its decrepit industrial base. Austria, the fourth-largest aid donor to the region, transferred by far the largest proportion of its GNP, an average of .20 percent, in economic aid to CEEC/NIS recipients. Most of the aid to the regions was transferred bilaterally, although the European Commission provided more than $1 billion to these recipients (OECD, 1995a: 87).

The primary Eastern European recipients of official development assistance during the first two years of the organized aid effort (1993–1994) included former Yugoslav states, which received more than $1 billion in both years, and Poland, the recipient of nearly $1 billion in Western aid in 1994.[1] Other ODA flows, which were widely disbursed across the CEEC region, were much smaller in scale: $51 million to Hungary, $50 million to Bulgaria, $47 million to Romania, and $38 million to the Czech Republic (OECD, 1995c). Within the former Soviet Union, Russia and Ukraine each received more than $1 billion during the two-year period, and in February 1996 the IMF agreed to a three-year, $10 billion concessional loan to Russia (see Gordon, 1996). Other NIS aid recipients included Belarus ($656 million), Kyrgyzstan ($428 million), and Georgia ($172 million).[2]

Many priorities that the development community has brought to the region—privatization and democratization in the context of economic austerity—have in recent years become important priorities of development efforts worldwide. The general reasons for assisting the CEEC/NIS, such as promoting economic and political stability, creating markets, and helping the region become more democratic and friendly to the West, are much the same as reasons for giving aid to other developing areas. Yet Western governmental aid to the region has been treated very differently from aid to other regions. Western aid to CEEC/NIS has been accompanied by higher expectations, a greater sense of urgency, and an emphasis on technical expertise rather than capital assistance.[3]

As I will emphasize throughout this chapter, the shift in attention to the CEEC/NIS region prompted a broad change in the priorities, resources, and personnel commitments of the world's aid donors. Many aid programs to the

Southern Hemisphere were cut back and redirected to the CEEC/NIS region in the era of belt-tightening that followed the Cold War, but by any measure the transition states had massive funding needs. Following the collapse of the Soviet Union in 1991, many of the mechanisms and machinery in place across Eastern Europe were extended eastward, where they were adopted in Russia and the other former Soviet republics. When the opportunity arose, many aid practitioners active in Poland, Hungary, and other Eastern European states were transplanted to Russia, Ukraine, Kazakhstan, and other parts of the NIS.

Long before the Soviet bloc collapsed, most foreign-aid donors had in place large aid programs. To administer aid to these new recipients, with their very different histories and needs, donors added new mechanisms for aid management. For example, the European Union created wholly separate programs to manage assistance to the CEEC/NIS region. In the United Kingdom, aid to the new recipients was supervised primarily by the agency responsible for foreign affairs, the Foreign and Commonwealth Office, rather than by the agency traditionally overseeing foreign aid, the Overseas Development Agency. USAID, through which most U.S. assistance was administered, created a new body, the Bureau for Europe and the New Independent States, to manage aid transfers to these new recipients. The U.S. effort engaged some thirty-five federal agencies, including the Departments of Energy and Labor and the Environmental Protection Agency, most of which had no prior experience in foreign aid and had rarely been active overseas (U.S. General Accounting Office, 1991). To coordinate the effort, the administration of President George Bush created the Assistance Coordination Group, a body overseen by the State Department. The Office of the Coordinator for U.S. Assistance to the New Independent States was later established to handle aid to the former Soviet Union.

There are many similarities between the economic and political transformations in this region and those of Asian, African, and Latin American states (see Nelson, 1993; Killick and Stevens, 1991), and in many respects the assistance priorities of privatization and democratization are comparable. Yet donors, at least initially, have maintained higher expectations of what aid could achieve in Eastern Europe versus what could be achieved in LDCs. These expectations were reflected in the terminology employed to describe aid to the region, which was to undergo economic "reintegration," a term never utilized in reference to aid to Africa or South Asia. Donors tended to view the process as the recovery of a beleaguered economic region with which they perceived close cultural and historical bonds.

Many in the West argued in the early 1990s that there was only a small window of opportunity in which to effect change in the CEEC/NIS region. Donors spoke of the need to move quickly to fill the political-economic vacuum created by the collapse of the communist bloc. Donors also assumed that the region's leaders and citizens would readily accept political, economic, and social changes imposed from the outside. Aid to these fledgling countries would presumably demonstrate support for economic reform and, by delivering tangible results, would thwart any domestic opposition.

The different treatment afforded the CEEC/NIS region as compared with the Southern Hemisphere had consequences for every component of the aid network. For the donors, it resulted in the reorientation of aid efforts, as described above. For the recipients, the donors' elevated sense of urgency and high expectations led to promises that could not be fulfilled and to widespread frustration. Such a sequence was observable throughout the CEEC region and became evident across the former Soviet Union as the post–Cold War aid effort spread eastward.

PHASES OF AID IMPLEMENTATION

In this section I will focus on aid programs to the Visegrad countries of Poland, Hungary, the Czech Republic, and Slovakia, efforts that have been under way since 1990. Responses to the needs of these countries are instructive for two reasons. First, these states received the most donor attention in the initial stages of the democratic transition. Second, because these countries were considered the transitional states most likely to succeed, they became, in effect, models for other recipients. If the lessons of aid were not understood in the Visegrad region, the problems experienced might be repeated and even compounded in Bulgaria, Romania, the states of the former Yugoslavia, Albania, and the former Soviet Union.

Hundreds of interviews from 1991 to 1995 with aid officials in the Visegrad region along with documentary evidence shed light on the performance of foreign-aid programs. Specifically, they reveal a three-stage progression that unfolded in the initial post–Cold War period.[4]

Phase 1: Euphoria (1989–1990)

On a popular level, the East Europeans brought an idealized view of the West and had naive expectations of what foreign aid could do for them. The late Rita Klimova, former Czechoslovak ambassador to the United States, characterized her country's expectations at the time: "People imagined the United States to be a kind of rich Soviet Union." Her implication was that the Eastern European recipients anticipated a continuation of economic dependency, with the West taking the place formerly held by the Soviet Union, but that the rewards for them would be greater than during the period of Soviet hegemony (Wedel, 1992a: 132).

The expectation that the West would come to the aid of Eastern Europe was encouraged by the flood of Western visitors conveying their interest in the region and their willingness to help. Misinformation that circulated in the news media in 1990 and 1991 fueled these expectations. In Poland, word quickly spread that Western states were sending billions of dollars in aid without qualifying that this amount included export credits and loans that would have to be repaid. And many people in the region did not understand that much of the grant aid was for technical, not capital, assistance and that advisers, not money, were being sent. All of this confusion occurred in a highly charged political climate whose main actors were only beginning to confront the enormous task of converting societal aspirations into reality. The disappointment felt by elites and the general public paved the way for the difficult second phase in the aid process.

Phase 2: Frustration and Resentment (1991–1992)

The rosy scenarios of the euphoria stage succumbed to frustration and resentment after the anticipated results were not immediately forthcoming. Aid outcomes suffered not only from recipients' inflated expectations but also from donors' unfulfilled promises.

Among the first manifestations of this phase was that many people in the region began to wonder where the money went. In 1992 Polish president Lech Walesa reflected growing elite and public disenchantment when he spoke at the European Parliamentary Forum in Strasbourg: "It is you, the West, who have made good business on the Polish revolution. . . . The West was supposed to help us in arranging the economy on new principles, but in fact it largely confined its efforts to draining our domestic markets."[5]

In fact, there was a considerable gap between donor commitments and actual disbursements in the region. By 1992 only an estimated 11 percent of committed resources actually had been transferred to the CEEC states (Institute for East-West Studies, 1992). Hundreds of "first meetings" with representatives of donor states led many Polish, Hungarian, and Czechoslovak officials to conclude that the West was delivering far less than promised. The pendulum swung from an open-arms welcome to skepticism. Officials in Warsaw, Budapest, and Prague complained that their concerns were ignored despite the presence of many aid bureaus and seemingly constant fact-finding missions from the West. Polish officials were unable to obtain reliable information about how much U.S. assistance was being spent on particular projects, although USAID had an office just a few blocks away.

Early on, many Poles dubbed the consultants the "Marriott Brigade" because they tended to stay at Warsaw's pricey new five-star Marriott hotel. Polish aid official Marek Kozak went so far as to suggest that the main benefit derived from the Marriott Brigade was not the expertise it provided but the hard currency it contributed to the local economy (Wedel, 1992a: 133). Perceptions of Western arrogance were exacerbated by major donors' tendency to use commercial accounting firms to carry out their agendas in priority areas such as privatization. Especially in the early stages of aid delivery, these consultants were more likely to cause resentment than were academic specialists and public administrators, whose projects were often quietly successful and whose personal styles were seen as more sincere.

The ill will flowed in both directions. Although few U.S. officials expressed doubts in public, they sometimes denigrated the recipients in private and suggested that they were unequipped to utilize the aid effectively. When recipients perceived such attitudes, the cultural divide widened and led to the third phase of the relationship.

Phase 3: Reality Check (1993–1995)

By the mid-1990s the model countries—Poland, Hungary, and the Czech Republic—had effectively adapted to the aid programs. Follow-up interviews in these countries in 1994 and 1995 revealed a tangible progression in knowledge, experience, and expertise. Officials became more skilled at working with the donor community and more realistic about what aid could and could not do for them. In some cases they concluded that the costs of a given program in terms of time commitments and donor requirements outweighed the benefits, and they opted out.

A related development was the blurring of donor and recipient personnel. Whereas previously it was possible to detect institutional affiliations by nationality, recipient governments increasingly turned to local citizens and expatriates who spoke the national language and had an acute sense of indigenous cultural, social, and political conditions. Donors also recruited former high-level CEEC state officials, who applied their expertise in facilitating the transition to market-based development. During this phase recipient officials were more precise than before in defining their needs and making aid requests. As Salvatore Pappalardo, a U.S. consultant in Poland, observed in 1994: "There were a lot of carpetbaggers early on. . . . At this stage of the process Poles are more aware of the things they know and, most importantly, of the things they don't know. They've learned to clarify their needs."[6]

During this period the Czech government decided to utilize a minimum of foreign aid and refrained from establishing relations with the World Bank. Prime Minister Vaclav Klaus explained, "After three years of relatively successful fundamental systemic transformation of the Czech economy and society, my experience tells me that the role of external factors in this process is relatively small and that reform begins and ends at home."[7] Zdenek Drabek, aid coordinator of the former Czechoslovakia, elaborated: "Many Czechs now proudly believe that Westerners have little to teach us, to show us, to advise. . . . The attitude has been essentially that we don't need the money."[8]

Polish and Hungarian officials, meanwhile, requested more capital and less technical expertise. In the months to follow, a consistent pattern emerged. As recipients developed their own technical expertise, requests for foreign specialists diminished. Responding at least in part to political considerations following the Copenhagen summit of June 1993, the EU began to focus capital assistance on trans-European transportation projects in the form of railway lines, roads, and border infrastructure.[9] As one EU official explained, "Investment finance is more visible to the public. That's one of the reasons we're going into it. . . . [Investment] can be seen and touched."[10]

Although Poland, Hungary, and the Czech Republic appear to be adapting effectively, it is by no means certain that countries whose transitions began in later years will adjust in the same way. In these states, including Russia, the second phase may last years longer and have even greater political and social repercussions. Or the states may not move in the political, economic, or foreign-policy directions favorable to the West. As five years of aid experience in the CEEC region has shown, there is considerable potential for aid to backfire, to be misused, or to be unwisely implemented. These results are most often unintended but occur when the goals and oversight of donors clash with the expectations of those who are supposed to be the beneficiaries of aid.

EAST TO KIEV AND MOSCOW

With the dissolution of the USSR in December 1991 and the end of the Cold War, the West promised billions in aid to the republics of the former Soviet Union. The extension of aid was seen as a strategic necessity, for the failure of reforms would presumably have dire consequences that would be felt far beyond the economic sphere. Half a decade after the aid programs were initiated, however, the reform efforts in Russia, Ukraine, and Belarus are in turmoil. Entrenched bureaucratic interests have resisted being marginalized, nationalists and communists have challenged moderates, and large segments of the public have wavered in their support for market reforms.

Already, signs of the problems encountered in Central and Eastern Europe are evident in Russia, which has received the lion's share of aid to the former Soviet Union, including a $10 billion IMF loan approved in February 1996. International lending institutions and the foreign-aid community have pressed Moscow to introduce economic reforms, privatize state-owned resources, and integrate with the West. Each of these measures has been opposed by domestic interests, and the progression from high expectations to resentment has been clearly visible.

As in the CEEC states, the administration of aid in Russia is a central concern. The management of major aid programs largely has been entrusted to a small number of cliques, which have controlled vast resources and exerted great influence. Members of these cliques have long known each other and have worked together in other areas. However, their future connection with reform is at best unclear. In the aftermath of the December 1995 Duma (parliamentary) election, in which communists won some 40 percent of the seats, reform came under siege; members of several cliques were placed under investigation, and some were purged by Boris Yeltsin in response to political pressure. Yeltsin was put on the defensive and forced to appease communists and other adversaries in the months before the June 1996 presidential election, and the atmosphere of political backlash and reprisals only worsened.

The surviving reform cliques, like the previous communist ruling elites, have their fingers in many institutional pies: business, the bureaucracy, private foundations, and parliament, to name a few. Members of the cliques are considered "institutional nomads," because circumstances demand loyalty to the group but not necessarily to the formal institutions with which the group is associated (see Kaminski and Kurczewska, 1994). These institutional nomads operate outside state structures but also penetrate them, holding multiple titles, occupying multiple offices, and carrying out myriad activities, often using public resources to further their political agendas. In entrusting large sums of money to these cliques, aid donors have reinforced this system and have legitimated the cliques' relationship to the state, which is reminiscent of state-socialist organization. The cliques' control renders claims of the depoliticization of aid hardly credible and undermines attempts to build independent institutions, ostensibly a major goal of the aid community.

Internal political rivalries are not the only source of antagonism. Two-thirds of the Russian people, according to one survey, believed in the mid-1990s that the United States had a calculated anti-Russian foreign policy. Not surprisingly, reformers and the foreign advisers associated with them have been the subject of periodic press investigations. Even before the December 1995 parliamentary elections, Richard Miles, deputy chief of mission at the U.S. embassy in Moscow, worried that aid flows had been too narrowly focused upon a small group of reformers at the expense of broader institution building.[11]

Indeed, though donors claim to promote structural changes in the Russian system, their dependence on entrenched cliques often works against this objective. Aid enhances the ability of specific elite cliques to control resources and exert influence. It thereby reinforces the interdependence between political and economic spheres—the very interdependence that characterized communist systems—because the aid supports groups that are involved in both spheres. Donors are faced with a catch-22: Although working through indigenous structures may be the only way to achieve success in the eyes of the aid community, such "success" may undercut attempts at progressive institution building.

Similar potential for disenchantment and resentment is present in Ukraine. The aid effort to Ukraine began later than that to Russia and was stepped up in 1994 and 1995 following positive press treatments in the West about President Leonid Kuchma's economic reforms. This diversion occurred because aid to Ukraine aid was seen as an alternative to aid to Russia, which was threatened following that country's assault on Chechnya and its suspected sales of nuclear technology to Iran. Ukraine has become the favorite kid on the NIS block among many Western aid donors. Disbursements of technical and humanitarian assistance to Ukraine increased to $410 million in 1992 and $468 million in 1993, and future increases were tentatively approved (United Nations Development Program, 1994: 11). Following Germany, the United States was the second-largest bilateral donor to Ukraine in the mid-1990s.[12]

Although donors naturally assume aid will be welcomed by recipients, in Ukraine, as elsewhere, aid has evoked mixed reactions—first hope, then disappointment and resentment. For example, because of perceived problems with technical assistance, Ukraine's Ministry of the Economy created a separate agency to advise the government on aid issues and to analyze the source and destination of technical assistance. According to Mykola Horkusha of the aid ministry, Ukrainian leaders quickly concluded that the aid packages were bureaucratically top-heavy. "About 80 percent of this [technical assistance] goes for consultants. . . . During the 1993–1995 period we came to the conclusion that we don't need more consultants."[13] According to Alexander Paskhaver, an adviser on economic policy, "Western consultants need to be here for at least three months to be effective. Between 1990 and 1993 a lot of consultants came in for short periods. It was absolutely useless and expensive. The money could be better used."[14]

Yet as long as Ukraine outshines its rival to the north, and as long as its prospects for long-term economic reform and integration remain relatively bright, Ukraine stands to receive continuing infusions of aid from the West. Given the fact that many past aid transfers to the NIS region are commonly viewed as investments that await future returns, it is unlikely that Western donors will suspend their efforts even in the face of formidable threats to reform.

The tenuous nature of aid to the former Soviet Union was made clear by the massive IMF aid package approved for Russia, conspicuously timed to provide Yeltsin with nearly $4 billion in funding to spend domestically just before the presidential elections. After the three-year loan agreement was signed in February 1996, IMF managing director Michel Camdessus "put the Russian electorate on notice that the IMF would cut off the funding if the Communists came to power and abandoned the reforms" (Gordon, 1996: 1A). The transparently political basis of this agreement was openly acknowledged, illustrating the urgency with which Western governments viewed the Russian elections.

AID FROM PRINCIPLE TO PRACTICE

The impact of any aid program depends on how the donor designs and implements it and how the recipient puts the aid to use. The success of aid to the CEEC region has largely depended on how recipients respond to demands for democracy and good governance and how fledgling institutions interact with Western aid agencies, which have been as unprepared for the task as their counterparts.

This section of the chapter concentrates on grants rather than export credits, concessional loans, stabilization assistance, and other forms of foreign aid. Of all the aid committed by the major Western donors since the Cold War's demise, about half has been in the form of direct grants (U.S. Department of State, 1994b: 278). Like other types of foreign aid, grant aid requires effective administration, a fact that is of particular relevance in the fragile political context of Eastern Europe and the former Soviet Union. These administrative issues and lessons will be detailed below.

Long-term Versus Short-term Support

All donors engage advisers to provide expertise to aid recipients, but long-term advisers generally are better received by recipient governments. "Fly-in, fly-out" advisers often are viewed as inadequately trained, superfluous, a burden on overextended recipient bureaucrats, and sometimes even agents of industrial espionage. However well intentioned the experts, it is not difficult to understand the recipients' point of view. Numerous advisers from international lending institutions and bilateral aid programs have often descended on recipient government ministries simultaneously. Staff members, often political appointees or employees of a fledgling civil service, soon become overwhelmed. Only a few staff members have the information sought by the consultants and the language skills necessary to communicate with them. As a result, a few officials become responsible for meeting negotiating with the many visiting delegations and consultants.

By contrast, long-term "resident advisers" who work in the host country for several years on specific topics requested by the recipient generally have been well received. These advisers frequently are chosen more selectively than those brought in for short-term projects and tend to be more knowledgeable about and sensitive to conditions within the recipient states. They are better able to engender relations of mutual trust and confidence with recipients and, consequently, to manage the implementation of aid programs effectively. Thus, donors have turned increasingly to long-term aid commitments led by consultants who are sensitive to local conditions.

Locus of Decisionmaking

The extent to which input from field representatives is integrated into critical decisions at donor headquarters is another crucial factor in aid to the CEEC/NIS region. In the case of U.S. assistance, many problems have been created by the centralization of decisionmaking, coordination, and implementation in Washington (Wedel, 1992c). According to one U.S. General Accounting Office (1992: 33–34) report,

> A U.S. official in Poland told us that decision makers in Washington did not seek advice on projects from in-country staff, even though these staff members have first-hand knowledge of the country's conditions and monitor U.S. assistance efforts. In some cases, decision makers in Washington have ignored recommended actions from in-country staff.

Although the number of USAID field representatives in the region has since grown, they still do not have the same authority as field missions that have been established for aid in the Southern Hemisphere. In response to this and other similar reports, Washington-based management changed somewhat in early 1993, with Congress mandating that authority be delegated to the field in Eastern Europe.

In two additional respects, recipient input has been an important factor. The first is the recipient's ability to influence and guide the development of aid programs. The second is the extent to which the donors exchange information with the recipient parties before and during the assistance process. U.S. programs that come under USAID contracting procedures are often seen as less effective than EU programs because the U.S. programs allow recipients less leverage to set terms and select experts. By contrast, the EU's aid programs for Eastern Europe are administered through program-management units directed by recipients (for an elaboration, see Wedel, 1994: 319–320).

In the NIS, however, the EU's aid program elicits less participation from local authorities and entails less delegation to country representatives than in Europe. Michael B. Humphreys, counselor to the EU delegation in Ukraine, explains that in principle there should be increasing decentralization in the EU's aid effort but that the NIS countries first must prove themselves. In short, Brussels has less confidence in NIS countries' ability to manage their own programs than in Poland's and Hungary's, in part because the NIS recipients have only recently established themselves as autonomous states. Moreover, the NIS countries are generally much larger than those in the CEEC region and have more fundamental developmental needs.[15]

The EU's aid to Central and Eastern Europe is composed both of technical assistance (expertise) and capital flows, whereas aid to the NIS consists almost entirely of technical assistance. Although the EU has in principle accepted many Eastern European states for membership and its aid programs attempt to harmonize their laws and legislation with the EU, it has no such plans for the NIS countries.

Donor Ties to Nongovernmental Organizations

In many cases, publicly financed private groups have unusual access to the CEEC region. The United States in particular has exhibited strong support for solutions targeting assistance to the private sector, with private firms often serving as the primary delivery mechanisms. More frequently than most other donors, USAID officials have worked closely with NGOs, which have become active in aid programs of many kinds. The U.S. government has seen the emerging states' NGOs as important conduits of technical assistance and also as building blocks of civil society. Whether their ostensible purpose is social welfare, election education, or improvement of environmental conditions, NGOs are seen as furthering the transition process.

This interpretation, however, assumes that the emerging states' NGOs are similar to their Western counterparts, despite the very different conditions under which they have developed and operate. NGOs can play productive roles, but the reality is that they may not be designed to be building blocks of democracy, as the donors often envision. As in the case of governmental agencies it is difficult, if not impossible, to jump-start the creation of genuine NGOs from the outside.[16]

Many NGO-driven aid programs are structured to bypass government bureaucracies and work directly with the private sector. Although direct aid to the private sector makes sense when the goal is to promote private business, in some program areas (e.g., environmental control) relevant governmental bodies have been virtually ignored. Further, the U.S. preference for bypassing governments is clearly misplaced when the goal is to privatize state-owned enterprises (Wedel, 1992c; USGAO, 1992: 31–36). Thus, recipient governments have often lost important opportunities to align aid projects with their long-term development and state-building priorities.

Aid and the Promotion of Private Enterprise

As noted above, the privatization and restructuring of state-owned resources has been identified by donors as the most critical need and the linchpin of the entire transition process. The United States in particular has tended to look to privatization as a way to measure the progress of the transition from communism to a market economy.

This process, however, has been difficult in many respects. The privatization of large companies has been a much slower and more politically complex undertaking than anticipated. Because the state enterprises that provided jobs, housing, and medical and day care symbolized the socialist workers' state, the breakup of these enterprises has come to symbolize transition. Yet it is very difficult to give effective and neutral aid in a politicized arena, especially when the services provided through emerging market sources are at first inferior to former state-run services and inaccessible to large segments of the population.

In Russia, a public-education campaign that began with television programs explaining business to the general public turned into a mission to convince citizens of the benefits of privatization. USAID paid a Western public-relations firm to produce the campaign, but the firm ran into trouble when it sought to find and publicize success-story profiles of privatized state-owned enterprises. In many cases employees didn't know whether their enterprises had been privatized and had difficulty identifying any real changes that had been brought about by privatization. As a Moscow representative of the public-relations firm put it, "We scoured the country and found twenty-five success stories." Yet on paper there were thousands of privatization efforts under way in the mid-1990s (Wedel, 1995).

To complicate matters, suggestions of conflicts of interest repeatedly surface when foreign aid works in such a contentious arena as privatization. A host of players—political elites, government officials, factory managers, employees, international corporations, and members of the aid community itself—all have their own agendas and personal stakes in the outcome.

However, the U.S. emphasis on the private sector has produced several aid programs that recipients report to be helpful. One of these is the Enterprise Funds Program, designed to facilitate private-sector development in the CEEC region by providing loans to small and medium-sized businesses, agriculture, and joint ventures with the United States. The funds, which are operating in many countries in the region, were intended to offer a different, less regulated type of foreign aid that would encourage private enterprise mainly through loans and direct investments rather than through grants. The funds are often cited as an aid success story and are notable in that they constitute one of the few U.S. aid programs that puts money directly into recipient economies.

CONCLUSION

In providing foreign aid to the CEEC/NIS region, donors have considered their strategic interests in helping the region become more democratic, stable, and friendly to the West. To this end, it is imperative that donors demonstrate that aid, which often entails intimate involvement in a recipient's domestic affairs, is being used to establish viable democratic structures so that all can benefit.

Aid activities can either encourage the development of a more comprehensive market system or provoke resentment to it. Recipients' perceptions of assistance and their experience with external consultants help to frame their opinions of donor states. Based on the lessons reviewed above and the observable trends in aid to the CEEC/NIS region in the mid-1990s, several factors will determine whether future aid policies are likely to produce their intended outcomes.

Of central concern is the degree to which aid programs are directed toward objectives identified and clearly specified by recipients. Many aid programs have suffered from a lack of a coherence and have tried to work in too many areas. Projects that allow recipients a large degree of design input and administrative control and that ensure local and long-term support with targeted oversight by donors are most likely to be effective. Local knowledge is critical if donor intentions are to be realized.

The quality of institutional support will also greatly determine the effectiveness of aid programs. The strength of most foreign aid to the CEEC/NIS region lies in its ability to offer technical support and long-term guidance requested by host institutions. Aid programs must be specific, defined in advance, and screened both by donors and the recipients who will be working with them. Most important, aid donors must be aware of how individual aid programs are to be integrated with those of recipients and other donor states.

Finally, the evaluation of aid programs needs to be rethought. Much project evaluation is misguided because it is based on narrow accounting criteria capable of examining only part of the aid process. Given the diversity of aid programs to the CEEC/NIS region and the substantial track record they have already compiled, future aid flows can benefit greatly if the demonstrable lessons from the past are acted upon.

As they continue to pursue these objectives in the future, policymakers should maintain modest aims and make credible claims. Donors must recognize the limits of what aid can accomplish. Further, they should pay close attention to the political and social implications of aid as well as narrow economic outcomes. For example, they should be sensitive to the cultural apprehensions of reform in some republics of the former Soviet Union, where institutional crises have been pervasive and where the potential for chaos is even greater than in Central and Eastern Europe.

If we have learned anything, it is that assistance to the former Soviet bloc is more effective when it is guided by its recipients with informed and significant oversight from donors. The effectiveness of assistance above all depends on the active engagement of both donor and recipient, in particular on the long-term commitment and sensitivity of those who provide the assistance.

NOTES

1. This figure does not include multilateral assistance to the former Yugoslavia or security assistance associated with the UN peacekeeping mission and subsequent NATO intervention. Given the extraordinary nature of the aid effort to this war-ravaged region, it is not treated in detail in this analysis of development aid.

2. These figures are tentative OECD (1995c) estimates and subject to revision as new data are provided and often erratic reporting measures are modified.

3. The Western donors refer generally to those in Western Europe and Canada. Japanese flows, much lower than those from other major donors, are included in DAC totals.

4. The officials interviewed worked at the core institutions of foreign-assistance coordination and monitoring: in Poland, the Council of Ministers; in Hungary, the Ministry of International Economic Relations; in the Czech Republic, the Ministry of the Economy; and in the Slovak Republic, the Ministry of Foreign Affairs. Other aid principals interviewed included those in ministries of finance, industry, environment, and others that helped implement aid-funded projects.

5. Similarly, Hungary's aid coordinator Bela Kadar (1993: 5) stated, "The public learns from official statements that the Western world has transferred resources on the order of $40 billion to $70 billion so far, to promote transition in the post-communist countries. One has to ask, where have all these billions gone?"

6. Interview with Salvatore Pappalardo, April 13, 1994.

7. Speech by Vaclav Klaus to World Bank, October 15, 1993.

8. Interview with Zdenek Drabek, July 7, 1994.

9. Interviews with Klaus Schmidt and Andrew Rasbash of the EU delegation in Poland, April 7, 1994 and April 22, 1994, respectively; and interviews with John Kjaer and Pierre Mirel of the program for Eastern Europe in Brussels, May 4, 1994.

10. Interview with Klaus Schmidt of the EU delegation in Poland, April 7, 1994.

11. Interview with Richard Miles, July 25, 1995.

12. As in Central and Eastern Europe and Russia, technical assistance in such areas as privatization and economic restructuring was the main type of aid trans-

ferred to Kiev, accounting for 51 percent of the 1993 total (United Nations Development Program, 1994b: 12).

13. Interview with Mykola Horkusha, deputy chair of the Department for Business Support, Ministry of the Economy, August 22, 1995.

14. Interview with Alexander Paskhaver, August 18, 1995.

15. Interview with Michael B. Humphreys, August 22, 1995.

16. For a more detailed analysis of the operations of NGOs in Eastern Europe, see Wedel (1994: 327–330).

10

The Fragmentation of Foreign Aid to South Asia

David I. Steinberg

To give money away is an easy matter, but to decide to whom to give it, and how large a sum, and when, and for what purposes, and how, is neither in every man's power, nor an easy matter. Hence, it is that such excellence is rare and praiseworthy and noble.

—Aristotle

As recipients of the largest flows of foreign assistance during the post–World War II period, LDCs in South Asia have effectively appealed to the multiple and overlapping interests of major donor states. Located along the "containment belt" surrounding the Soviet Union, these LDCs found their strategic position during the Cold War to be worth a fortune in grants and low-income loans from Washington and Moscow. And, given their proximity to Japan, many East Asian LDCs obtained additional infusions of concessional financing from Tokyo.

In the Cold War's aftermath, the geopolitical logic underpinning many aid programs has vanished and been replaced by geoeconomic concerns (Luttwak, 1990). Regional subsystems from the Middle East to the Pacific Rim have assumed more distinctive roles in the aid regime, and their internal dynamics and tensions have in some respects been accentuated by the end of the East-West rivalry. Private capital is ever more closely integrated with government concessions, fueling the economic growth of newly industrialized countries. As they have prospered by emulating the Japanese model of export-led growth and achieving regional and global economic integration, however, other Asian LDCs have slipped further into poverty and civil unrest. These events have compounded the fragmentation of Asian foreign aid in the post–Cold War period.

Further complicating matters, foreign-aid fads have long dominated in this region, reflecting new approaches to economic development and differ-

157

ing conceptions of aid quality maintained by donor governments and inter-national organizations. Yet overall, particularly in regard to the intimate linkage between donor self-interests and the volume, direction, and terms of their aid flows, the pattern of large-scale aid to the region has remained remarkably consistent into the post–Cold War era.

My focus in this chapter will be on the eastern states of South Asia. This region is defined expansively as stretching from the Iranian-Pakistani border eastward through the Indian subcontinent across China and Indochina to the Pacific Rim states. Nearly 70 percent of the world's 5.5 million inhabitants live here, of which 2.1 billion resided in China and India alone in 1993 (World Bank, 1995a: 162).[1]

The most significant attribute uniting these recipients is the sheer magnitude of economic aid to South Asia (see Table 10.1). In 1994 more than 30 percent of the $59 billion in global ODA was directed toward this region (OECD, 1996a: A61), which had seven of the world's ten largest ODA recipients during the first three years of the post–Cold War period (1992–1994), including the People's Republic of China ($9.6 billion), India ($9.1 billion),

Table 10.1 **Major Recipients of Development Aid in South Asia, 1992–1994**

Recipient[a] (world rank in aid revenues)	1993 Population (millions)	1993 GDP (per capita)	Total Aid Commitments 1992–1994
China (2)	1,178	$425[b] ($490)	$9.6
India (3)	898	225 (300)	9.1
Indonesia (4)	187	144 (740)	7.9
Philippines (5)	65	54 (850)	4.9
Bangladesh (7)	115	24 (220)	4.7
Pakistan (8)	123	46 (430)	4.6
Thailand (9)	58	125 (2,110)	3.9

Sources: World Bank (1995a), OECD (1995c)
Notes:
a. Egypt and Israel were the first and sixth-leading ODA recipients during this period, respectively (see Table 1.2).
b. GDP and aid figures in billions of current U.S. dollars.

and Indonesia ($7.9 billion). Other major recipients during this period included the Philippines, Bangladesh, Pakistan, and Thailand.

These figures do not include military-aid transfers, primarily from the United States, which have declined considerably since the Cold War. After Soviet military aid ended, U.S. military assistance plummeted from $233 million in 1991 to just $3 billion in 1994, which was disbursed widely in the form of military training (USAID, 1996a: 117). However, weapons sales continued from the U.S., China, and Russia (as documented in Chapter 3 of this volume), a process likely to expand as the NICs take a more assertive role in ensuring their own security. Given the declining role of military assistance to the region, I will emphasize development assistance.

The application of Western development models to South Asia, often reflecting ethnocentric assumptions within donor governments, has created tensions in some aid programs, failure in others. Donors fostered this attitude during the Cold War by equating technology transfer and rapid industrial expansion with national or cultural progress. As Adas (1989: 15) observed,

> Evidence of scientific and technological superiority has often been put to questionable use by Europeans and North Americans interested in non-Western peoples and cultures . . . . The application of technological and scientific gauges of human potential has also vitally affected Western policies regarding education and technological diffusion which go far to explain the varying levels of underdevelopment in the Third World today.[2]

Despite protestations to the contrary, most foreign development aid to South Asia has been donor- rather than recipient-driven. Thus, when there are calls for a Marshall Plan for Asian states, the basic dichotomy between the original model and the Asian effort is ignored, with important consequences for both expectations and success. In many cases, however, a confluence of donor and recipient interests has emerged, especially when elites in LDCs have sought foreign aid to enhance their own political power in the face of internal challenges. Throughout the Cold War major U.S. and Western European aid packages—both military and economic—sought to preserve friendly regimes in Iran, Pakistan, Thailand, Vietnam, the Philippines, and Indonesia, whereas Soviet and Chinese aid was directed toward strategic allies in Egypt, Syria, Iraq, India, Myanmar, and postwar Vietnam. As ideological rivalries have faded in the post–Cold War era, this trend has subsided to the degree that the People's Republic of China in 1994 became Japan's primary bilateral aid recipient.

East Asia has been witness to a new phenomenon—what has been called "graduation" from concessional assistance, which results when a specified level of economic development is reached and commercial lending becomes more appropriate. Japan was the first instance in 1962; Taiwan

effectively graduated in 1965, South Korea in 1992. In some cases, illustrated most vividly by Japan, aid recipients have graduated to the status of
aid donors, a trend expected to accelerate as income levels continue to rise
along the Pacific Rim. But alongside the success stories are the many
LLDCs of South Asia, with per capita incomes less than $1,000. These
include Afghanistan, Bangladesh, Cambodia, Laos, Myanmar, and Nepal
(World Bank, 1995a: 162–163). These states, along with the most impoverished, heavily populated regions of China and India, have lagged behind,
and it is their experience that will be considered most thoroughly in the
pages to follow.

THE COLD WAR ORIGINS OF ASIAN AID

The Cold War orientation to Asian aid was clearly established in the early
1950s, when the U.S. government sent consulting teams throughout the
region to determine foreign-aid needs in the aftermath of the Korean War
and amid fears resulting from the communist takeover in the PRC. Under
the 1951 Mutual Security Act, U.S. aid flows generally shifted from the
economic orientation under the Marshall Plan to a security orientation.
Enormous commitments were made to perceived strategic allies in Iran,
Japan, and South Korea, among other states. For the U.S. government it mat-
tered less that these were often repressive regimes than that they were contributing to the containment perimeter around the Soviet Union and the
PRC.

Concern with communism was not only a U.S. phenomenon. The
Colombo Plan in the early 1950s provided the United Kingdom and its
Commonwealth members with an institutional means to achieve the same
results, although this effort was more a type of clearinghouse enabling individual Commonwealth donors to pursue bilateral programs than a comprehensive, coordinated approach to development. Because it was ostensibly
multilateral, this assistance was more acceptable to nonaligned states. In
addition, the World Bank and the Asian Development Bank first excluded,
then tried to reform centrally planned economies in the region.

These essentially geopolitical factors were quite separate from the issue
of the effectiveness of the individual assistance proffered, although the mere
existence of such assistance affected the recipients' political and economic
fortunes. Fluctuations in the levels of bilateral assistance from the United
States would, in the words of State Department officials, send signals of
approval or disapproval. Withdrawal of assistance was intended to be seen
as a call for regime change in recipient states. Moreover, levels sometimes
had to be balanced, as between Pakistan and Bangladesh or between Israel

and Egypt. Paradoxically, this process resulted in some consistency and pre-dictability in the U.S. aid program.

Transfers of military weaponry, munitions, hardware, and expertise flowed mostly from the United States but also in large volumes from the Soviet Union and China. Military aid from the United States to the Near East amounted to about $50 billion between 1946 and 1990, more than half of all U.S. aid to the region; other Asian LDCs received an additional $43 billion in U.S. military transfers during this period, almost all of it during the Cold War (USAID, 1996a: 7, 117). This form of support, inadequately studied for its economic impacts, was the most overt and public of the efforts to bolster regimes considered friendly to the superpowers. But infusions of sophisti-cated military equipment had profound consequences for the region, strengthening autocratic rulers, changing state-society relations, and distort-ing broader developmental objectives.

Economic assistance, of course, was also used for security purposes. This was not only true in war-torn states such as South Korea, Vietnam, and Cambodia but also in threatened states such as Taiwan and in countries with which the U.S. military had an especially close relationship—such as Thailand, because of treaty relationships; the Philippines, because of base rights; and Pakistan, because of its early role as the base for U.S. surveil-lance flights over the Soviet Union. In the United States, supporting assis-tance, economic support funds (ESF), and other mechanisms were employed to designate economic aid with political and military objectives, blurring the distinction between the two and raising the inevitable question of aid fungi-bility (see Zimmerman, 1993; Montgomery, 1967).

It was thus not by accident that bilateral economic and military aid packages in the United States were included together in congressional debates as well as in public and press campaigns. Presidential administra-tions consistently believed that security assistance would attract more pop-ular and congressional support than would purely economic aid. Russian and Chinese military assistance was used to support revolutionary movements in several LDCs, thus serving clear strategic objectives and eliciting little domestic opposition. As noted above, this side of the foreign-aid coin has all but vanished in the post–Cold War period, although cash sales of arms have continued and indigenous arms industries have emerged in the name of South Asian self-sufficiency.

AID AND ECONOMIC DEVELOPMENT

Promoting economic development has been the ostensible purpose of most foreign aid to Asia. The goal of raising living standards and protecting human rights in LDCs involves a complex range of donor motivations and expectations. Economic development is in a sense doubly defined: by content and by process. Criteria for aid vary, shifting from aggregate economic growth and industrial output to per capita income, basic human needs, and what has become known as "growth with equity." The latter signals concern for the overall well-being of recipients—their access to social services (such as health and education), decisionmaking, and private economic markets.

Economic development, however, has been significantly defined by the donors' self-interests. Early Japanese reparations programs were in part designed to rebuild Japanese industry in the mid-1950s. The formation of the Asian Development Bank by the Japanese and the more recent, smaller-scale South Korean aid programs contributed further to this process. Since Japan's emergence as a major aid donor, three-quarters of its bilateral assistance has been to regional neighbors in East Asia—particularly the PRC, Indonesia, and the Philippines—with which the Japanese government has established parallel trade and investment ties (see Chapter 5). Gaining access to raw materials, potential markets, and cheap labor has helped drive the Japanese program—as well as French and U.S. aid relationships with Indochina and the Philippines, respectively—and enhanced Tokyo's international image as a responsible member of the global aid regime.

Even as they recognized this central motivation underlying aid flows, recipients have frequently complained about "overpriced" foreign aid. U.S. shipments of surplus wheat, for example, were said by Sri Lankan leaders to cost more than Australian wheat because of the mandated use of U.S. shipping. Burmese and Filipino recipients earlier complained about the excessive costs of material under the Japanese reparations programs. Many recipients balked at the foreign consultants and high overhead charges that accompanied development projects, a pattern observed more recently in the Central and Eastern European countries and the new independent states of the former Soviet Union (see Chapter 9). Despite such complaints, however, the enormous transfers of bilateral and multilateral aid to the region continued to rise, along with the volumes of trade and private investments.

The frequent shifts in emphasis based on changing regional conditions, innovations in development theory, and short-term self-interest undermined the credibility of aid within recipient states and their home governments. Further, important differences have existed beneath the veneer of donor unity, so mixed signals have been sent to aid recipients. The United States and Japan, for example, disagree in the World Bank on the role of the state in industrial policy, the former calling for less state intervention, the latter recognizing its importance for the economic development of recipients and for Japan's own growth.

During the Cold War, foreign aid to South Asia commonly supported such capital-intensive areas as energy, transportation, agriculture, and heavy industry.[3] Because efficacy was often measured by the net volume of financial contributions, larger expenditures for infrastructure in the above fields were stressed over smaller, labor-intensive projects having more direct impacts on living standards. Such support often directly influenced the administrative structure of recipient governments, largely because in foreign aid, as in architecture, form follows function.

Although policy reform has always been important to donors, it has loomed larger in the wake of the Cold War. Political and economic reforms have been prompted by World Bank structural-adjustment programs involving large amounts of funds required to manage debt, reform bureaucracies, privatize industries, and meet short-term liquidity shortfalls (see Chapter 2). In addition, recipients are increasingly obligated to conform to UN standards of sustainable development and good governance if they are to receive continuing aid flows from OECD donors. It is difficult, however, for aid donors and international organizations to enforce many of these conditionalities in South Asia, where the volume of aid and the accumulation of debt is so large that the recipients often call the shots.[4]

In Washington, USAID has in the 1990s been determined to use more effectively its diminishing aid programs in South Asia, setting more explicit conditions for future development aid. The Japanese government in the past stayed aloof from overt policy guidance, in part because of potential political repercussions and in part because it did not develop any detailed country strategies in South Asia until 1986. Its first and largely unpublicized Asian intervention into economic policy reform occurred in March 1988, when it warned the government of Myanmar that significant economic reforms were needed or Japan would reconsider its economic relationships with that nation.

The lessons of developmental assistance to South Asia must be sufficiently broad to withstand the region's vast cultural differences and the multifaceted interests of the major aid donors if they are to be of use elsewhere. With these caveats in mind, some common and general lessons may be advanced.

LESSONS FROM THE ASIAN EXPERIENCE

Those who win wars write history, so it is said; similarly, those donors who help states succeed write developmental success stories. It is a form of expression to which donors are prone, for the donors' sponsors or top management must demonstrate their effectiveness. There is no better way to do so than by citing developmental success stories at a national or a project level. Because economists largely control the development literature, and because sound economic policies are obviously critical (but, I will argue, not sufficient) for sustained economic growth, purely economic policy discussions predominate, often to the exclusion of other important factors.

A prominent example from the literature is a 1993 World Bank report entitled *The East Asian Economic Miracle,* which stressed the economic conditions and policies under which rapid industrial growth was achieved in East Asia. It noted the importance of the state in forming public policies conducive to growth, including an export-led approach, a competent bureaucracy, a market-friendly trade stance, investment in human capital, and increasing savings and investment. It treated delicately the prevalence of industrial policy (government coordination) in the region but emphasized the need for such strategies to be supplemented by market orientations and competitiveness.

Yet the shift toward export-led growth and away from import-substitution strategies does not explain why so many states in South Asia have failed to achieve the levels of growth that have been prevalent in East Asia. The broad lessons drawn by the World Bank from East Asia are certainly applicable as a set of general theorems, but they are less valuable when applied to individual states. South Korea, in its developmental push, went against the prevailing donor wisdom by heavily subsidizing all sectors of the economy, thus manipulating the market, dictating sectoral growth, subverting democratic tendencies, suppressing labor, and fostering multinational corporations at the expense of small businesses through rigid controls over credit. Its heavy industries expanded most rapidly in response to defense needs and a perceived retraction of the U.S. military umbrella, not primarily development rationales.

Negative lessons from South Asia are also apparent in other respects. Donor agencies too often neglected social and cultural factors that ultimately affected the efficacy of foreign aid. As a result, donors today increasingly stress good governance and human rights with staffs not familiar with or trained to consider such subjects. This chronic lack of cultural sensitivity has led in some cases to ineffective structural-adjustment efforts in which political realities have been ignored. The massive Mahaweli River hydroelectric and irrigation projects in Sri Lanka, for example, were sold to donors as "ethnically neutral." In fact, however, they were perceived by the Tamil population as a threat to their control over regions of the country they regarded as traditionally theirs and by some Singhalese as a means to expand their influence.

The general experience of donors across Asia is that their policy advice is often taken when it is seen to further the explicit economic or political aims of those in power; it is ignored, however, when such advice would advocate the redistribution or diminution of such power. Technical assistance has often been assiduously accepted when it is perceived to further state interests. The United States for decades advocated the dissolution of South Korea's state-dominated agricultural cooperative movement, which did not consist of cooperatives in the normal sense of the term. The South Korean government resisted diminishing its iron grip over the rural sector through that organization; such control only collapsed after political liberalization in 1987, an event that had little relationship to foreign pressure.

Another lesson from East Asian success is that, however sound development projects may be on paper, effective implementation is critical. Implementation is, however, a local responsibility and not responsive over any extended period to donor supervision. Early aid efforts to administer policies or projects were rarely successful. When aid projects are not only donor-driven but dominated by donor personnel at the project level, resentment from local populations and ineffective aid projects is the result (see Chapter 9).

Other lessons are more ambiguous. If the South Korean experience teaches us that big business has been effective in development, Taiwan instructs us that smaller businesses can be efficient means for growth. If export orientation seems an obvious platform for donor support, import substitution can exist parallel to it in the same country in different sectors— industrial exports and rice policy in Japan and South Korea, for example. Some general lessons from Asia are applicable elsewhere. One criterion of foreign aid success in South Asia has been sustainability, the continuation of project activity after foreign support is withdrawn. The end of assistance justified on security grounds, however, led to the evaporation of vast amounts of funds for projects that could not be sustained with local resources. If sustainability of projects is a donor concern, too much assistance of the wrong sort may be as deleterious as too little.

FUTURE DIRECTIONS OF ASIAN AID

Although the global aid regime, particularly the U.S. aid program, remains in a state of profound flux, there is a basis for reasoned speculation about the future of foreign aid in South Asia.

The first and perhaps most obvious conclusion is that despite containing about half the world's population, South Asia will receive a decreasing percentage of global aid resources both on an aggregate and per capita basis. This decrease will take place because of heightened demands from former Soviet states, Eastern Europe, the Middle East, and other priority areas, and increasing opposition to conventional forms of development aid within many Western governments.[5] As noted above, the U.S. government has undertaken a major restructuring of its aid programs, resulting in severe cutbacks of assistance to South Asia, including the planned closing of the Thailand and South Pacific offices as well as reduced overseas staffing (see Chapter 4). With the end of the Cold War, U.S. aid to Pakistan has diminished greatly, despite the fact that its population continues to earn a per capita income of less than $500 (OECD, 1996a: A88). It is likely, however, that large-scale U.S. aid to the Middle East, India, Bangladesh, and the Philippines will continue.

The military component of this aid will remain as small as it is in the mid-1990s, but this is not guaranteed. The PRC's growing military budget, its intentions in the South China Sea, and its relations with Taiwan have aggravated regional tensions and revived U.S. presence.

Japan, where public acceptance of foreign aid is still remarkably high, will be under continuing pressure to redistribute its massive foreign aid flows more equitably around the world and to concentrate less on Asia, especially Southeast Asia and the Pacific Rim. But it is unlikely that there will be a major redirection of Japan's aid. To the contrary, Japanese aid to the PRC has increased greatly, and Vietnam has emerged as a primary market for both aid and trade. As detailed in Chapter 5, foreign aid has served a central role in Japan's foreign economic policy since World War II and will continue to do so indefinitely.

South Korea, scheduled to join the OECD in 1996, and other NICs in the region will become important donors of aid to South Asia, and the political and diplomatic consequences will extend beyond the aid relationships. As the governments of China and India become more prosperous, as is generally expected, they are likely to establish large aid programs, while concurrently receiving development aid from Japan, the United States, and other major donors.

Among recipients, the PRC will likely continue to command major World Bank, Asian Development Bank, and Japanese assistance, as will India, given its new, liberalizing economic reforms. But the potential for greatly expanded aid flows to these and other recipients will be constrained by the massive Western commitments of aid to the former Soviet bloc. The IMF's approval in February 1996 of a $10 billion concessional loan to Russia demonstrated the importance of the former Second World to aid donors (Gordon, 1996). Given the cutbacks in many overall aid budgets and the increasing concentration on a small number of key recipients, the prospects for increased funding for strategically marginal LDCs in the region are dubious. In this respect a growing intraregional income gap will further divide the LDCs and LLDCs of South Asia, a pattern that will be aggravated, not eased, by aid flows.

Economic objectives are likely to take on growing importance in U.S. programs now that Cold War preoccupations have disappeared. This approach will likely include explicit subsidization of U.S. businesses through mixed credits—those provided by commercial and state sources, a practice about which the United States severely criticized Japan in previous years—investment guarantees, and policy advice on privatization and economic competitiveness. However, direct donor intervention in private business increases the danger of corruption involving donors as well as recipients, as has already been evident from scandals in Japan and South Korea.

Democratization is a loosely defined term, eroding in specificity and coherence the further it travels. Yet the growth of political pluralism (perhaps a more meaningful term) is likely to be of continuing interest to the major donors in South Asia, where the democratization wave that has swept across Latin America and, to a lesser extent, sub-Saharan Africa in the 1990s has lagged by comparison. In 1993 none of the thirteen South Asian LDCs identified earlier in this chapter was considered "free" by Freedom House (1994) in its worldwide survey. Four states—Afghanistan, China, Laos, and Myanmar—were defined as "not free," and the others were considered "partly free," in many cases a sign of gradual political reform.

The United States and Japan have both given such considerations major weight in their foreign aid policies, although their hortatory expressions have often been subverted by their more immediate self-interests. Furthermore, the suggested causal link between plural economic and political systems, a central tenet of UN and OECD democratization campaigns, has been based upon Western models that are not universally applicable. Economic growth occurred under strong authoritarian regimes of varying types in South Korea, Thailand, Taiwan, the PRC, Singapore, the Philippines, Indonesia, and Malaysia. Japan thrived under a one-party government that only recently has been effectively challenged. Undoubtedly, advances in communications and transportation, higher education, increased incomes, and other developments will place pressures for political change on even the most rigid societies; the question is not whether such pressures will exist but over what period of time democratic reforms can be expected to take hold. In South Korea the process occurred between 1961 and 1987; in Taiwan, between 1950 and 1991.

Donor governments and international development agencies should be warned of the dangers of hyperbole in Asia concerning the efficacy of democratic development. Crucial distinctions are often made between "procedural" as opposed to "substantive" democracy or between "liberalization" and "democratization." The former defines change within the system (e.g., the lessening of state regulation of the press, reforming the civil service, or expanding voting registration, etc.) and presumably may be addressed by donors. The latter, by contrast, refers to core values concerning power, authority, confrontation, and the role of the state, issues that are historically impervious to foreign manipulation. Human rights and democratization, which many LDCs have declared to be universal, were consistently subordinated to stability and development—often with the tacit consent of major donors during the Cold War. Similarly, delegates to the UN's 1993 human-rights conference in Vienna drew the distinction between "legal systems," the physical construction of law enforcement and court buildings, and "legal culture," which must reject outside pressure and reflect indigenous social norms.

In the case of the United States and Japan, a continuing tension exists between human rights issues and trade. Compromises on human rights are routinely made in light of how donors define progress toward democracy. In some cases, most glaringly the expansion of Sino-U.S. trade relationship despite China's blatant repression of human rights in many areas, this linkage is severed altogether. In the end, trade and investment will likely continue to prevail over human rights.

The successful industrial policies of Japan, where state officials and corporate directors collaborate in many areas of macroeconomic policy, have been replicated elsewhere in East Asia and thus have amplified the policy debate between free-market advocates and "neomercantilists." In this light we may expect continued policy pressure from the United States for open markets and continued resistance by East Asian NICs to the diminution of the state role in economic development. There may well be a recognition that industrial policies combined with market mechanisms may be efficacious in the future, a central finding of *The East Asian Economic Miracle*. It should be noted, however, that the political impact of market transitions is extremely tenuous and destabilizing if minorities, often with external sources of financial support, are seen to have benefited unduly.

Environmental issues in foreign aid are already important components of most major donor programs in South Asia, both multilateral and bilateral. These are likely to increase and intensify as populations and urbanization increase, water pollution worsens, industries expand, wildlife is threatened, and natural resources are exploited for short-term gain. We may expect growing pressures against large dam construction, highway construction, and other major infrastructure projects because of unknown environmental consequences. When donors refuse to provide support because of potential environmental effects, as with the Three Gorges Dam across the Yangtze River in the PRC, states may fund such projects themselves regardless of the financial or environmental costs.

Paradoxically, in this respect there will be continuing urgency among Western states to supply more energy resources, already in short supply in a number of South Asian states. Energy-sector investments by development banks and bilateral donors, especially Japan, are likely to remain extensive. In this area the clash between industrial expansion, which is commonly linked to population control and higher living standards, and environmental protection is likely to be conspicuous.

The World Bank is expected to expand its environmental lending in the late 1990s. Noting the "fundamental market and policy failures concerning natural resources and environment that have received little corrective action," a 1992 World Bank study called for a new framework for improving environmental management. Its recommendations for policy reforms including pricing, tax, and market measures; provisions for public disclosure and environmental litigation; the strengthening of public institutions; increasing public- and private-sector investments in the environment; and improved means of technology transfer. Given that pollution extends across state boundaries, environmental issues cannot be viewed as state-specific. Increased soft coal use in China, among other prominent examples, has major deleterious effects in South Korea and Japan, and indeed around the world.[6]

There are growing indigenous voluntary and advocacy organizations in most of the Asian states concerned with these issues, and many are assisted by foreign-aid organizations. Nongovernmental organizations have traditionally played important roles in foreign aid, especially humanitarian assistance and medical relief. They have proven to be important constituencies for the U.S. aid program, and they are increasingly used in Japan. It is likely that expatriate national and international NGOs will assume significant roles implementing the environmental regulations of Asian states in the next century.

Although traditional security considerations have faded, we may well witness the rise of a different set of security-related concerns that could involve donor activities that are national or regional, rather than global, in scope. These include programs designed to mitigate the rise of nationalism, ameliorate internal economic disparities, and increase attention to religious minorities, which could provoke separatist uprisings. These problems have been apparent in the past (e.g., northeast or southern Thailand, southern Philippines) and remain serious today (East Timor and Acheh in Indonesia, Tibet, the eastern states of India, and the Tamil issue in Sri Lanka, among others). The March 1996 military standoff in the Taiwan Straits, reminiscent of the 1950s, was of concern not only to the United States but to Japan, Russia, and other major powers.

Other security concerns may take the form of intense donor concern over regional instability—India and Pakistan over Kashmir, for example—where foreign aid may mitigate conflict or encourage conciliation of ethnic unrest. Concessional financing likely will continue to be employed to move North Korea away from its nuclear proclivities, an issue that reached crisis proportions in 1994, or to settle the Japanese-Russian dispute over the Kuril Islands. The role of foreign aid as a lubricant for the Middle East peace process is perhaps an obvious precedent, further highlighting the versatility of aid in the post–Cold War environment.

CONCLUSION

It would be too simple to claim that South Asia is changing or is at one of the many crossroads that observers have postulated and public officials have invoked over the years. The corollary is that foreign aid in the region has changed or must change. The simple reality is that all major societies and institutions constantly adapt to external as well as internal pressures. So what is new, and what is Asian?

Foreign specialists and policymakers have been forced to reassess the role of foreign assistance in improving living conditions and promoting economic growth in South Asia. Considered "hard states" because of their strong bureaucratic traditions, these LDCs were once seen as traditional or outmoded, backward- rather than forward-looking and embracing a developmentally restrictive ideology. Scholars have since discarded their misconceptions amid the rapid economic rise of many NICs, and we would do well to discard other stereotypes. Any effort to find unidimensional Asian configurations or policies is doomed to failure.

The diverse countries of South Asia will inevitably find their own development models and will continue to shape foreign assistance to their interests, however donors package their aid programs. Western efforts to support good governance and sustainable development will influence the volume, direction, and terms of foreign aid but ultimately must be rendered compatible with recipients' needs, prerogatives, and long-term interests. As states in South Asia follow their own lead within the international economy, we are likely to witness the development of indigenous forms of management and the amalgamation of competitive industries and macroeconomic policies that recognize and allow for unique expressions of culture. The Japanese government has already made this transition, as has South Korea's. Thailand, Malaysia, and Indonesia all have distinctive systems in which industrial development, propelled by the availability of low-cost labor, has transformed living conditions yet preserved vital cultural traditions.

The explosive growth of private investment in South Asia and the development of major Asian multinational corporations have pushed the need for donor assistance in fields such as international and commercial law. The World Bank and USAID have both recognized that requirement in Indonesia. This concern is likely to be increasingly important in the next decade. But laws and legal institutions that do not reflect social norms are unlikely to be capable of influence.

Given the diversity of aid sources to South Asia, development planning has been notoriously uneven. An urgent need exists not merely to improve collaborative planning between recipient and donor but to conduct regional-level planning, which is generally ignored at World Bank meetings.

Regional alliances, although important fora for high-level discussions of economic issues, have yet to be effective. Yet donors will increasingly have to pay attention to regional planning within these formal structures. There are, however, political limits that all donors will have to recognize, for donor advice on the distribution of assets within recipient states will continue to be interpreted as imperialistic intrusion by the industrialized world.

As Asians themselves become prominent aid donors, one may expect them to display greater sensitivity to local conditions because of what they have endured as LDCs and recipients of foreign aid. However, this has yet to be demonstrated. Japanese aid has been particularly insensitive, with Tokyo frequently dominating the process, and South Korea, adopting the Japanese administrative model, is likely to follow suit if its past role in industrial policy toward the Pacific Rim is any indication. Donors, whether Asian or Western, have been more guided by their own designs than by those suggested by beneficiaries. It is here that there may be hope for foreign aid in the region—Asian aid becoming more sensitive to other Asian concerns. But it has yet to happen.

The Cold War's demise contributed greatly to the expanded Middle East peace process, and the multinational coalition formed to reverse the Iraqi invasion of Kuwait in 1990 and 1991 would not have been thinkable in the context of superpower rivalry. Yet continuing tensions along the border of India and Pakistan have persisted, and new hostilities have emerged within the Korean peninsula and between the PRC and Taiwan. Widespread concern has been raised over the PRC's conduct at home and ambitions abroad, and resolution of the religious and ethnic dispute in Sri Lanka remains elusive. Anti-U.S. sentiments in the Philippines and Japan, magnified by the removal of U.S. forces from Okinawa, have cast doubts over the role of the United States in these and other areas. Thus, in some respects the end of the Cold War has indirectly fueled resurgent regional tensions, threatening economic development in many areas and establishing a basis for remilitarization. President Clinton's April 1996 tour of East Asia focused on these security issues, but it also underscored the fragile security climate of the post–Cold War era.

How much can one attribute Asian developmental successes to foreign aid? We will never accurately know. Aid likely had less impact than the donors believe but more than the recipients may wish to admit. Internal politics in both cases affect analysis as much as the aid programs themselves.

How much will foreign aid affect South Asia in the future? If current trends continue, it is likely that concessional funds will become less salient as private investments and bank lending assume a more prominent role in the region's political economy and as more NICs attain self-sufficiency both in economic and security areas. Yet past aid flows have clearly proven their worth—in promoting the "green revolution," which transformed India's agricultural sector, in building utilities and roads so that industries could flourish, and, most important, in mitigating the impoverishment of desperate populations in such places as Bangladesh and Cambodia. For these reasons foreign aid to South Asia will remain a central facet of regional development well into the next millennium.

NOTES

1. This conception mirrors that of the OECD (1996a: H8), which includes the following thirteen recipients in the Asian region: China, Indonesia, India, Philippines, Bangladesh, Pakistan, Thailand, Sri Lanka, Vietnam, Nepal, Cambodia, Afghanistan, and Laos.

2. See Bellah (1991) for an elaboration.

3. In the three decades from 1961–1991, Japan through its concessional loan program—the Overseas Economic Cooperation Fund—provided 20 percent of its loans and equity investments in electrical power and gas, 24 percent in transportation, 6 percent in telecommunications, 10 percent in mining and manufacturing, and 21 percent in commodity loans (OECF, 1993).

4. This may be said to be a variant of the popular expression, "If I owe the bank $1,000 I am in trouble. If I owe the bank $1,000,000 the bank is in trouble."

5. This was a primary reason behind the creation of the OECD–World Bank Task Force on Concessional Flows (Cassen and Associates, 1986).

6. Chinese coal produces 50 percent of sulphur ion emissions causing acid rain in Japan, and South Korean industry further contributes to the problem.

11

Foreign-Aid Posturing in Francophone Africa

Peter J. Schraeder

In October 1884 German chancellor Otto von Bismarck invited the major European colonial powers to Berlin to regulate escalating imperial conflict by defining the boundaries of colonial possessions.[1] The Berlin Conference consecrated the emerging European empires and spheres of interest throughout Africa. Except for Ethiopia and Liberia, independent Africa ultimately ceased to exist.

After World War II and the subsequent decolonization of most of Africa in the 1960s, France was the only former colonial power to maintain and expand its presence on the continent, most notably in what is currently referred to as francophone Africa—those former French and Belgian colonies where French serves as an "official language of administration and education."[2] Indeed, French leaders from the conservative Charles de Gaulle to the socialist François Mitterrand consistently have claimed that historical links and geographical proximity justified placing francophone Africa within France's sphere of influence.[3] "According to this French version of the Monroe Doctrine," explained Martin (1995: 168), "francophone Africa is seen as constituting a natural French preserve."

The belief that francophone Africa constitutes a natural French preserve explains why some Africa specialists within the French policymaking establishment cautiously greeted the collapse of communism in Eastern Europe and the former Soviet Union. In sharp contrast to the Cold War era, when Western (especially U.S.) leaders sought to strengthen and enhance France's privileged role in francophone Africa as a bulwark against communism, the end of the Cold War has heightened economic and political competition among the Western powers. As a result, French policymakers increasingly claim that the United States and Japan, and to a lesser degree Germany and Canada, pose potential economic and political threats to French interests in francophone Africa. According to correspondent Stephen Smith (1994), such statements on the part of French policymakers are indicative of a growing duel between Washington and Paris over Africa.

This competition over great-power influence in Africa has been manifested since World War II in several areas of foreign policy, including that of foreign assistance. In this chapter I offer some perspective on this phenomenon by contrasting the ODA policies of France and its two greatest perceived challengers in the post–Cold War era, the United States and Japan.[4]

French aid flows to the region ($3 billion in 1992) have remained dominant throughout the period, amounting to nearly three-fourths of overall francophone aid; its bilateral packages to Cameroon, Côte d'Ivoire, Djibouti, Morocco, Senegal, Togo, and Tunisia have annually exceeded $100 million for many years. The United States has provided the second-largest share of francophone aid, although its disbursements peaked at $702 million in 1991 and have fallen significantly in the mid-1990s. This has in part opened the door for Japan, the world's leading donor of ODA to all regions, which has doubled its share of francophone aid since 1982 (OECD, 1981–1995a).

FRENCH AID TO ITS FORMER EMPIRE

In the midst of the decolonization process, France established a large and powerful aid program in francophone Africa during the Cold War era, and it became a keystone of French foreign policy (Morse, 1973: 163). The program's goal was to reassert France's historical position in the front rank of global powers, a status the country lost during a seventy-five-year span stretching from the Franco-Prussian War to World War II (Cerny, 1980). Former Secretary of State Henry Kissinger (quoted in Hook, 1995: 66) captured the essence of why francophone Africa fits so well within French aspirations to international leadership:

> France's penchant for associating with countries ready to accept its leadership has been a constant factor in French foreign policy since the Crimean War. Unable to dominate an alliance with Great Britain, Germany, Russia, or the United States, and considering junior status incompatible with its notions of national grandeur and its messianic role in the world, France has sought leadership in pacts with lesser powers.

The evolution of French ODA toward francophone Africa during the Cold War era was driven by cultural, economic, and security interests. First, French assistance was designed to promote the *rayonnement* (radiation) of French cultural values, particularly "exceptional" values such as the French language, intellectual traditions, and way of living (Kolodziej, 1974: 479).

Also referred to as the promotion of French "cultural nationalism" (Grosser, 1965: 61) or the cultivation of *la francophonie* (a greater French-speaking community), such a policy ensured that a large portion of foreign assistance would be directed to former French colonies in Africa and to other countries (such as the former Belgian colonies of Burundi, Rwanda, and Zaire) in which French constituted one of the national languages. As explained by de Gaulle (quoted in Grosser, 1965: 205), French leaders have considered it their "historic vocation" to assist in the "ascension of all peoples to modern civilization."

The extent to which French cultural nationalism shaped foreign policy is illustrated by ODA flows during the 1980s.[5] During the transition year of 1989, which marked the fall of the Berlin Wall, the top ten African recipients of French foreign assistance—Algeria, Morocco, Côte d'Ivoire, Senegal, Cameroon, Mali, Gabon, Madagascar, Chad, and Guinea—were all former French colonies. In 1989 each of these countries except Guinea received more than $100 million in ODA, with all francophone African countries receiving more than $2.2 billion in ODA during the same year. Throughout the 1980s francophone Africa annually received about 80 percent of all French ODA allocated to Africa—close to $15 billion in aggregate ODA transfers. French ODA flows to francophone Africa surpassed the $3 billion level in 1992, as larger bilateral aid packages were approved for Cameroon ($436 million), Congo ($169 million), Côte d'Ivoire ($500 million), Morocco ($203 million), and Togo ($480 million).

France's determination to preserve and strengthen *la francophonie* is perhaps best demonstrated by the regular holding of Franco-African summits attended by the leaders of France and francophone Africa. This summit has been described as the centerpiece of Franco-African cultural relations, most notably in terms of its "familial character" and the "permanent *tête-à-tête* maintained between the French president and each of the francophone heads of state" (Martin, 1995: 170). Although the worldwide francophone summit also brings together French and African heads of state, it does not play as intimate a role as the Franco-African summit because of the attendance of powerful francophone states, most notably Canada and Belgium, that are perceived by France as cultural rivals (see Dupont, 1995).

The promotion of economic interests was perceived as integral to the furtherance of French culture and served as the second most important determinant of French ODA policies toward francophone Africa during the Cold War era. As explained by Kolodziej (1974: 479), French leaders assumed that French economic interests naturally would develop as French culture spread into the developing world. Toward this end, foreign assistance constituted "one component of a remarkably integrated system of economic relationships" that maintained and enhanced France's ties to its former colonies (Hayter, 1966: 43).

An example of this integrated system of economic relationships is the membership of thirteen former French colonies and Equatorial Guinea in the "franc zone" (Guillaumont, 1984).[6] The franc zone constitutes a supranational financial system in which France serves as a central bank and in which a common currency—the Communauté Financière Africaine (CFA) franc— is tied to the French franc and guaranteed by the French treasury. By wedding its fiscal policy to that of the franc zone, France has preserved monetary stability throughout the region. Concurrently, it has coordinated regional financial flows, regulated members' fiscal policies, provided emergency credit, subsidized private investments to franc-zone members, and offered tax breaks to French companies doing business in the region.

Whereas franc-zone member states gained financial stability, however, they lost a significant degree of autonomy over domestic macroeconomic policy. Nonetheless, scholars have demonstrated that the franc zone and its related flows of foreign assistance and investment capital have had a generally positive impact on francophone Africa. "Quantitative studies showed that until the mid-1980s, the economic performance of franc-zone countries was no worse than that of other developing economies and significantly better than the average for sub-Saharan Africa" (Ravenhill, 1995: 108).

It should be noted that cultural considerations, such as maintaining *la francophonie,* ensured the continuation and, in most cases, the expansion of ODA despite deteriorating economies and trade relationships. For example, ODA increased despite a significant decline in France's overall trade relationships with its former colonies. French products made up 58 percent of its former colonies' total imports between 1958 and 1963 but only 38 percent between 1974 and 1986. Similarly, France purchased 56 percent of its former colonies' exports between 1958 and 1963 but only 25 percent in the latter period (Moss and Ravenhill, 1989).

France's tendency to subjugate economic interests to cultural ideals was at the center of its unwillingness from 1947 to 1994 to devalue the CFA franc, despite arguments that such an action would enhance francophone Africa's economic competitiveness and promote greater trade links with France (see Guillaumont and Guillaumont, 1984). "Although most of the other countries in black Africa undertook (often massive) devaluations of their real exchange rate, the CFA [franc] appreciated in real terms," explained Ravenhill (1995: 109). "This divergence of exchange rates made it very difficult for franc zone countries to sell their export crops on world markets."

The third major determinant of French ODA policies was the promotion of security interests. Despite public pronouncements to the contrary, French ODA heavily underwrote French security interests throughout the Cold War era (see Biarnès, 1987; see also Bayart, 1984). In order to protect these security interests, French leaders signed numerous defense accords, generously provided arms and military *coopérants* for training purposes, and authorized numerous interventions by French military forces to ensure maintenance of the status quo (see Chipman, 1989; McNamara, 1989; Moose, 1985). In this regard, one can argue that French policymakers sought to spread French culture with the same ideological fervor with which U.S. policymakers sought to prevent the spread of communism. Consequently, when francophone countries attempted to renounce their special relationship with France, as Guinea did in 1958 when it voted against the creation of a revised French community of states, French retribution was swift. In the case of Guinea, all aid was cut off by de Gaulle. But as long as these countries maintained close ties with France, even authoritarian francophone leaders were unlikely to find themselves under heavy pressure from Paris to reform their governments.

THE PERVASIVE U.S. PRESENCE

As World War II drew to a close, the rise of the Cold War and superpower rivalry marked the beginning of widespread U.S. involvement in francophone Africa and other regions of the developing world. A variety of presidential doctrines—beginning with the Truman Doctrine in 1947 and culminating in the Reagan Doctrine of the 1980s—declared the self-appointed right of the United States to intervene throughout the globe (see Schraeder, 1992: 385–386). To complement U.S. security interests, especially those associated with containing the spread of communism, ODA emerged as a critical foreign-policy tool (see Chapter 4).

The reconstruction of Europe during the 1940s under the auspices of the Marshall Plan served as the centerpiece of U.S. ODA programs at the beginning of the Cold War era. The Marshall Plan indirectly aided francophone Africa, in that a portion of the nearly $3 billion in U.S. aid provided to France was diverted to its African colonies. After 1956, in the wake of the Korean War and the French defeat in Indochina, the United States, fearing communist infiltration across South Asia, shifted its aid priorities. During this period Africa was marginalized within the U.S. foreign-assistance hierarchy, receiving only 3.3 percent of all bilateral U.S. aid from 1946 to 1986 (Bandow, 1992: 79).

Throughout the Cold War the White House expected its European allies—most notably France—to take the lead in their former colonial territories (Schraeder, 1994b: 14–15). As succinctly summarized by George Ball (1968: 240), undersecretary of state in the Kennedy administration, the United States recognized Africa as a "special European responsibility," just as European nations were expected to recognize "our [U.S.] particular responsibility in Latin America." Consequently, the White House intended for its European allies to have primary responsibility for preventing communist and other "radical" powers from exploiting instability in Africa. Yet in crisis situations, when a withdrawing colonial power could not or would not maintain order, the United States took an active role. For example, Belgium's inability to manage rising conflict in Zaire led to significant long-term U.S. involvement in that country beginning with the Eisenhower administration (Gibbs, 1991; Kalb, 1982). According to U.S. policymakers, France was the only European power with both the political will and the military strength to be an active and long-term player in Africa.

Because the United States backed France as the dominant power in francophone Africa, the region only received marginal, albeit growing, levels of U.S. ODA during the Cold War. Whereas only 14 percent of total U.S. ODA to Africa in 1980 was targeted toward francophone countries, this figure increased to 22 percent in 1984 and to 26 percent in 1988. It is important to note, however, that this aid was divided among twenty-five countries and was much lower than that provided to other regions of the world. Overall figures can be misleading and must be carefully interpreted. For example, in the transition year of 1989, the United States gave francophone Africa $671 million in ODA, but nearly 40 percent of this total ($255 million) was allocated exclusively to Zaire—the primary U.S. client in the region (Schatzberg, 1991).[7]

In the mid-1990s U.S. aid allocations to francophone Africa decreased sharply from their peak of $702 million in 1991 (OECD, 1995a). Unlike the aid programs of most donors—particularly those of the Nordic states, which targeted a handful of program countries—U.S. aid flows were distributed fairly evenly among the francophone states other than Zaire.[8] These reductions resulted from the diversion of aid funds to Eastern European states and the former Soviet Union; the continued extension of massive aid to Middle Eastern recipients, including Jordan after it signed a peace treaty with Israel in 1994; and, most important, the general assault on the aid program that began in the mid-1990s, with cutbacks most often occurring in aid programs to least developed countries, many in Africa.

In its heyday U.S. ODA to francophone Africa, like U.S. policies pursued throughout the continent, was primarily driven by a combination of ideological and security interests (see Schraeder, 1994b). Ideological interests associated with the Cold War ensured that capitalist-oriented administrations, such as Senegal under Abdou Diouf and Cameroon under Paul Biya, would be treated as potential U.S. allies deserving of ODA, whereas African-Marxist administrations, such as Madagascar under Didier Ratsiraka and Benin under Mathieu Kerekou, would be isolated.[9]

As demonstrated by capitalist Côte d'Ivoire's receiving less than $20 million in U.S. ODA during the 1980s, however, shared ideological beliefs were not sufficient to attract Washington's involvement in francophone Africa. The top recipients of U.S. ODA most often were strategically important regional actors, such as Senegal and Morocco, that offered the U.S. special military access or maintained important U.S. technical facilities on their territories. As with foreign-policy relationships cultivated with other authoritarian African governments that were among the major recipients of U.S. ODA during the 1980s—most notably Liberia under Samuel K. Doe, Somalia under Siad Barre, and the Sudan under Gaafar Mohamed Nimeri—overriding preoccupations with anticommunism led Washington policymakers to overlook economic deterioration and politico-military repression in francophone Africa as long as its leaders were willing to support U.S. containment policies (Clough, 1994: 76–100).

The most notable example in this regard was the authoritarian leader of Zaire, Mobutu Sese Seko, who relied upon the Zairian armed forces and foreign assistance to consolidate his power as his popular support progressively eroded (see Kelly, 1993; see also Young and Turner, 1985). The case of Zaire, which finally lost its U.S. financial support in the mid-1990s, is instructive in shedding light on France's regional preoccupation. In Paris, U.S. support for Mobutu was perceived as an outgrowth of low-level U.S.-French competition in francophone Africa during the Cold War. French leaders, especially de Gaulle, were equally concerned about rising U.S. and communist-bloc influence in this French preserve. As a result, French policymakers viewed Mobutu as facilitating the penetration of Anglo-Saxon influence into the largest country of francophone Africa and therefore as striking a clear victory for the United States at the expense of France (Foccart and Gaillard, 1995: 310–311).

JAPAN'S GROWING AID TO AFRICA

In sharp contrast to the United States, a superpower after World War II, Japan was physically and economically ravaged at the end of the war and was a net recipient of foreign assistance for the next two decades (see Chapter 5). Prohibited from rebuilding a sizable military under its postwar constitution, Japan concentrated on internal economic reconstruction and development. After regaining full sovereignty in 1952, Japan embarked on a modest ODA program that took the form of delayed reparation payments to such regional neighbors as Burma, the Philippines, and Indonesia. Japanese ODA eventually surpassed that of any of the other industrialized democracies in 1989 and encompassed all regions of the Third World, including francophone Africa, where French policymakers noted the rising economic strength and Anglophobe proclivities of the United States's Asian protégé.

As a rising economic superpower with the world's second-largest GNP, Japan sought to use ODA in its quest for economic expansion during the Cold War (Soroos, 1988: 21).

Many analysts agree that economics constituted the overriding motivating factor of Japanese foreign-assistance policies during the Cold War. Critics charged that Japan conducted a "business foreign policy" in which governmental and corporate actors promulgated an industrial policy targeted toward enhancing exports through concessional aid. Taking it one step further, Scalapino (1992: 206) observed that Japan's protection under a U.S.-led military umbrella enabled Japanese leaders to reconstitute national security in largely economic terms. In short, the Japanese were able to pursue a neomercantilist foreign-assistance strategy that concentrated on securing Japan's regional geoeconomic interests while eschewing any political entanglements.

Economic self-interest clearly shaped Japanese ODA toward francophone Africa during the Cold War era. Specifically, Japanese policymakers consciously targeted ODA to those francophone African countries that 1) constituted important sources of raw materials—such as copper in Zaire, uranium in Niger, and chromium in Madagascar—that were vital to Japanese industry; 2) represented potential future sources of such raw materials, including oil in Gabon; 3) offered access to highly valued Japanese imports, such as fish products from Senegal; and 4) constituted important economic markets for Japanese exports (e.g., Senegal and Côte d'Ivoire were critical markets for Japanese automobiles).

In comparison to France and the United States, Japan is a newcomer in francophone Africa. It was only in 1986 that Japanese ODA to the region surpassed $200 million, and from that year aid flows rose quickly, reaching $494 million in 1989. Although approaching the level of U.S. ODA for that same year, Japanese assistance nonetheless lagged far behind the $2.26 billion in French ODA. Japanese aid to francophone Africa in the early 1990s exceeded $500 million; these levels increased in the mid-1990s in line with generally higher Japanese ODA allocations, which proved an exception to the general rule of aid reductions among most members of the OECD.

Japanese policymakers were less likely than the United States to impose ideological litmus tests as the basis for extending ODA, preferring instead to secure markets for both imports and exports (Orr, 1990: 58). During the 1980s, for example, Japan on average provided 21 percent of its ODA to socialist countries (as opposed to 6 percent by the United States). One of the most noted examples of this policy was the extensive levels of ODA provided to Tanzania under the leadership of former president Julius Nyerere, the so-called dean of African socialism and prominent leader of the anti-apartheid struggle against South Africa.

As with French ODA policies toward francophone Africa, a country's colonial past seemingly played an important role in Japanese ODA calculations. However, in contrast to France, Japan targeted a vast portion of its ODA toward former British colonies during the 1980s, whereas only 23 percent was directed toward former French colonies. Although many reasons for this relationship can be offered (e.g., greater facility of doing business in English-speaking, former British colonies), Japanese business leaders often noted that the francophone economies were more difficult to penetrate because of powerful French monopolies and a conscious governmental policy that supported them. By the end of the 1980s, France remained the premiere, if not unchallenged, ODA actor within francophone Africa.

AID PATTERNS AFTER THE COLD WAR

The most notable political development that accompanied the end of the Cold War across Africa was the rise of democratic reform movements seeking an end to single-party rule (e.g., see Schraeder, 1994a; Martin, 1993; Hyden and Bratton, 1992). Out of fifty-four African countries for which data were provided to international organizations, fifteen (roughly 28 percent) were described as either maintaining or having ensured a successful transition to democratic forms of governance. This number stood in sharp contrast to the five democracies (roughly 9 percent of the total) that existed as late as 1990. Another twenty-six countries were described as being "in transition" as of 1994 from various types of authoritarian rule to more democratic forms of governance.

France's initial behavior suggested that the democratization process would become the guiding principle of French ODA in francophone Africa in the post–Cold War era. At the sixteenth Franco-African summit, held in June 1990, Mitterrand announced that French ODA commitments henceforth would favor those countries that either were democratic or undergoing democratic change. Individuals from all major elite groups were invited to take part in a political summit to debate the outlines of a new democratic political order (Boulaga, 1993). In the case of Benin, the summit declared its sovereignty over the political process, stripped dictator Mathieu Kerekou of his official powers (but granted him political amnesty), and drafted an electoral calendar that led to the country's first free multiparty elections (Nzouankeu, 1993).

In addition to assuming that other authoritarian leaders could be forced out by pressure from a summit conference, proponents also believed that France would punish recalcitrant leaders by applying economic and political sanctions. As demonstrated by the distribution of French ODA in the years immediately following the La Baule summit, however, it became clear that the idealistic goals associated with African "Paristroïka" were never intended to replace the more traditional goals of preserving and strengthening *la francophonie* (see Bayart, 1991). In the case of Côte d'Ivoire, despite President Félix Houphouët-Boigny's co-optation of the democratization process, the Mitterand administration sent its favored client more than $1.5 billion in official development assistance from 1990 to 1992—a dramatic increase from the already high level of $549 million in ODA provided during the preceding three-year period.

France's unwillingness to embrace democratization movements when accompanied by instability was underscored at the seventeenth Franco-African summit, held in October 1992. At this meeting, Prime Minister Pierre Bérégovoy stated that when confronted with the simultaneous and potentially conflicting goals of promoting democracy, ensuring development, and maintaining security, francophone African leaders should adhere to the following order of priorities: first and foremost, security, followed by development and then democratization (Glaser and Smith, 1994: 102). This shift in priorities also reflected growing support for a "cohabitation" model of governance that became the hallmark of French politics during the 1980s. Under the Africanized version, often referred to as a *gouvernement de l'unité nationale* (government of national unity), incumbent regimes that had no intention of relinquishing power were expected to compensate for the lack of democracy by asking opposition leaders and parties to join a government of national unity (Glaser and Smith, 1994: 103).

A second trend that significantly affected French ODA policy in the post–Cold War era was the intensification of a continentwide economic crisis that strongly affected francophone Africa. An important dimension of this crisis was the often severe economic dislocation that accompanied the implementation of structural-adjustment programs imposed by the IMF and the World Bank. Equally important, internal economic decline, often resulting from bad policy choices, was hastened by bloated, corrupt, and inefficient bureaucracies—the so-called "crisis of the state"—that increasingly were incapable of responding to the day-to-day needs of their populations (e.g., see Widner, 1994; Callaghy and Ravenhill, 1993; Sandbrook, 1993). In response to this economic crisis, France devalued the previously sacred CFA franc for the first time since the franc zone's creation in 1948. The extraordinary decision clearly suggested the rising importance of economic factors in French foreign-policy calculations in the post–Cold War era.

The seriousness French officials accorded to the growing necessity of bailing out financially threatened francophone regimes rather than devaluing was clearly demonstrated by a dramatic increase in ODA commitments at the beginning of the 1990s. From 1990 to 1992, total French ODA to francophone Africa exceeded $8.2 billion—a more than $2 billion increase over the amount of ODA provided during the previous three-year period. Franc-zone members constituted a privileged subgroup of an already privileged group (francophone Africa) in that they received the largest share (79 percent) of French ODA in 1992 despite constituting only 56 percent of francophone African countries.

Nonetheless, the end of the Cold War was accompanied by a concomitant increase in global economic competition that forced France seriously to reconsider its relationship with francophone Africa. "Ultimately," concluded Martin (1995: 175), "the deepening economic and financial crisis in francophone Africa, coupled with a severe recession in the former metropole, led to the sobering realization that France could no longer afford to foot the bill." Interestingly enough, but clearly not by accident, the French decision to devalue the CFA franc was only announced and implemented after the death on December 7, 1992, of the dean of francophone Africa, President Houphouët-Boigny of Côte d'Ivoire (see Whiteman, 1994; French, 1994). Before his death, Houphouët-Boigny could be counted on by other francophone leaders to utilize his diplomatic clout to squelch any French attempts at devaluation.

A third security-related trend of the post–Cold War era that has captured the attention of French policymakers is the rise of Islamic revivalist movements, particularly in the Maghreb region of North Africa, which includes Algeria, Egypt, Morocco, Libya, Mauritania, and Tunisia. Algeria offers an especially poignant example of this evolving French security concern. Having fought a bloody war to gain independence from France in 1962, Algeria in the early 1990s was engulfed in an intensifying civil war. Tensions began to mount in 1991 after the Algerian army annulled the country's first round of multiparty elections since independence, then assumed governmental control in a military coup d'état. Tensions peaked when the military government canceled parliamentary elections scheduled for 1992. The military intervened because an Islamic revivalist party, the Islamic Salvation Front (FIS), was on the verge of winning democratic elections.

France's concerns over Islamic fundamentalism were evident beginning in the 1980s. Fearing that an Algeria governed by fundamentalists would pose a direct threat to French interests in the Maghreb region and radicalize the substantial Islamic community in France itself, French policymakers increased ODA commitments from the $192 million provided between 1986 and 1988 to $574 million over the following three years. The Mitterrand administration supported Algeria's decision in 1992 to cancel parliamentary elections by providing an additional $103 million in ODA. France's preoccupation with Islamic revivalism in Algeria was not unique; it simply was the latest manifestation of a long-term security interest in francophone Maghreb states.[10]

The French response to genocide in Rwanda in 1994 is also illustrative of how French security interests evolved in the post–Cold War era. Due to a conscious effort to integrate the former Belgian colonies of Central Africa into the French sphere of influence, the Mitterrand administration during the 1980s provided significant amounts of ODA to Burundi ($243 million), Zaire ($461 million), and Rwanda ($199 million). The ODA provided to Rwanda was especially noteworthy in that the annual amount provided during the 1980s was doubled, to an average of $40 million, during the initial three years of the 1990s.

Specifically, the Mitterrand administration sought to stem the invasion and steady advance beginning in October 1990 of the Rwandan Patriotic Front (RPF), a guerrilla army supported by Uganda and perceived by French policymakers as hostile to France and "under Anglo-Saxon influence" (Smith, 1995: 452). The RPF's military victory constituted the first time that a francophone country had "fallen" to Anglo-Saxon influence, and some French officials perceived Rwanda as the first in a series of regional dominos that eventually could bring Burundi and an independent Shaba (the southeastern province of Zaire) under Anglo-Saxon domination, to the detriment of France and *la francophonie* (Glaser and Smith, 1994: 182–185). Despite the fact that the new RPF regime neither initiated nor participated in the genocide by ethnic Hutus (which ultimately ended when the RPF achieved military victory), the Mitterrand administration refused to invite Rwanda to the Franco-African summit of November 1994.

As for U.S. aid, the end of the Cold War reinforced the historical tendency among U.S. policymakers to place Africa on the back burner. Adopting a play on words of the Reagan administration's much-debated policy of "constructive engagement," Clough (1992: 1) pointedly argued that the Bush administration engaged in "cynical disengagement," in which policymakers were guided by three principles:

1. Do not spend much money [on Africa] unless Congress makes you.
2. Do not let African issues complicate policy toward other, more important parts of the world. And, above all else,
3. Do not take stands that might create domestic political controversies in the United States.

Although one can argue that the Clinton administration's neglect of sub-Saharan Africa is not cynically motivated (see Schraeder, 1995), these three guiding principles still appear to characterize Washington's approach to francophone Africa in the post–Cold War era.

The Clinton administration's avoidance of policies that might create domestic controversies was clearly demonstrated by its tentative response to the genocide in Rwanda in 1994. Fearful of reviving the domestic uproar that accompanied the killing in October 1993 of eighteen U.S. soldiers taking part in Operation Restore Hope in Somalia, the Clinton White House not only initially blocked the dispatch to Rwanda of 5,500 peacekeeping troops requested by UN Secretary-General Boutros Boutros-Ghali but actually instructed U.S. spokespersons to avoid labeling the unfolding ethnic conflict "genocide"—lest such a label inflame U.S. public opinion and cause demands for U.S. intervention (see Des Forges, 1995). A variety of Africanist groups, such as Human Rights Watch/Africa, claimed that the administration's foot-dragging contributed to the deaths of thousands of civilians (see Human Rights Watch/Africa, 1994: 2), but Clinton's decision nonetheless matched the growing popular sentiment against U.S. involvement in UN-sponsored peacemaking operations.

The second guiding principle for U.S. policymakers in the post–Cold War era—avoiding issues that will complicate policies toward other, more important regions of the world—was demonstrated by U.S. policy toward Zaire. During the 1992 presidential election campaign, candidate Clinton attacked the Bush administration for failing to distance itself from "corrupt and dictatorial leaders" in Africa, specifically in terms of being "tepid, when it should have been decisive" with respect to terminating aid to the Mobutu regime (quoted in Cason and Martin, 1993: 2). Contrary to his espoused intentions, however, Clinton ultimately adopted a more status quo policy before finally being persuaded to suspend aid to Zaire by congressional critics.[11]

The avoidance of financial commitments to Africa—the third guiding principle for U.S. policymakers in the post–Cold War era—constituted the consensus viewpoint within both the White House and Congress in the mid-1990s. Regardless of whether the White House has been occupied by a Democrat or a Republican, since the mid-1980s U.S. foreign assistance to Africa has been steadily cut because of popular pressures to trim the budget deficit. From 1985 to 1995, U.S. bilateral assistance to Africa declined both in aggregate terms (from $1.9 to $1.1 billion) and as a percentage of the U.S. foreign-aid budget (from 10.3 to 6 percent). Although military and other security-related forms of assistance (such as economic support funds) have been almost totally abolished and account for the majority of these cuts, the Republican Party—which as of January 1995 controlled both the Senate and the House of Representatives—vowed to slash even these lower ODA levels because of the lack of U.S. strategic interests in Africa in the post–Cold War era.

The growing centrality of promoting democracy, in terms of both rhetoric and viable policies, is the most notable change in U.S. policies toward Africa during the post–Cold War era (e.g., see Diamond, 1995). In numerous countries throughout francophone Africa, relatively small but effective amounts of ODA have been provided to facilitate the transition to democracy (e.g., sending representatives to monitor elections) as well as to consolidate successful transitions that already have taken place. In the case of Benin, the U.S. provided $41 million in ODA during the election year of 1991 and $14 million in ODA in 1992 after the installation of a democratically elected administration.

The gradual decline of ideologically based policies in favor of ones based on economic self-interest is a second important element of changing U.S. involvement in Africa in the post–Cold War era. U.S. policymakers increasingly are in agreement that foreign policy should facilitate U.S. private enterprise in all regions of the world, including francophone Africa. The net result of this growing economic component of U.S. foreign policy is to strengthen further the small but growing expansion into francophone Africa of certain key U.S. industries, most notably oil and telecommunications, that has accompanied the end of the Cold War.

In the eyes of many French policymakers, however, the growing penetration of U.S. companies into francophone Africa constitutes "at best an intrusion" and "at worst an aggression" into their *chasse gardée* (Glaser and Smith, 1994: 186). The seriousness with which this issue was treated at the highest levels of the French government was demonstrated by the public admission of Minister of Cooperation Michel Roussin that a series of meetings was held on the theme of how best to "defend" French interests— including those within the economic realm—against those of the United States (Glaser and Smith, 1994: 187).

A growing cultural interest in African affairs, which led to greater economic interaction, has served as another dimension of U.S. foreign policy toward francophone Africa in the post–Cold War era. The first U.S.-African summit was held in Côte d'Ivoire in April 1991, an expanded second summit was held in Gabon two years later, and a third summit, which took place in May 1995 in Senegal, earned the distinction of the largest U.S.-African gathering ever held. Originally designed to strengthen African/African-American cultural ties, the summit evolved into a major forum for promoting trade and investment between the United States and Africa and threatened to overshadow the only other comparable francophone equivalent—the Franco-African summit (see Triay, 1993).

As in the case of France, a final element of U.S. policies toward Africa in the post–Cold War era is a growing fear that the spread of Islamic fundamentalism on the African continent threatens U.S. interests (Esposito, 1992). Many officials observed that the demise of the Soviet Union and communism created a power vacuum on the African continent that was partially being filled by what they perceived as radical forms of Islamic revivalism sponsored by Iran, Libya, and the Sudan (e.g., see Lesser, 1993). This perception of Islamic fundamentalism as a threat to U.S. interests is not new, dating back to the Iranian revolution. But it has been heightened in the 1990s in the wake of political turmoil in Egypt and its potential impact on the Middle East peace process.

Unlike their French and U.S. counterparts, who had to realign ODA policies in light of changing national interests after the end of the Cold War, Japanese policymakers simply reinforced their ongoing pursuit of economic self-interest in francophone Africa. In order to enhance Japanese trade and investment opportunities, the Japanese government hosted a major conference on African development in October 1993. A substantial rise in Japanese ODA in the post–Cold War era underscores the seriousness with which Japanese policymakers have sought to penetrate francophone Africa. Whereas an average of $101 million in Japanese ODA was provided between 1980 and 1982, this average increased significantly, to $460 million, between 1990 and 1992. Not surprisingly, major Japanese trading partners—most notably Morocco, Senegal, and Côte d'Ivoire—received large increases in Japanese ODA.

It is interesting to note that despite the fact that Japan's ODA average for the 1990–1992 period was not much lower than the U.S. ODA average for the same period ($560 million), Japanese efforts in francophone Africa have not attracted the same level of criticism leveled by France at the United States. Japan, like Germany, is not perceived as encroaching upon French cultural institutions and leadership, as the United States was in the case of the African/African-American summit or Canada is within the francophone summit. Moreover, Japan does not compete within the extremely lucrative and jealously protected oil industry. However, significant Japanese inroads within the telecommunications and automobile industries of francophone Africa clearly underscore Japan's movement away from its past role as purchaser of primary products and toward greater penetration of traditional French export realms.

Whatever the reason for its success relative to U.S. aid, the expanding Japanese ODA program in francophone Africa nonetheless has generated both criticisms and concerns. Japan has nothing to lose and everything to gain by pressing for the political and economic liberalization of francophone African states (witness its provision of $14 million in ODA to Benin in 1992) and is criticized as a strong supporter of Anglo-Saxon culture, most notably in terms of its adoption of English as the language of international diplomacy and business (see Mazrui, 1995: 81–84).

The greatest potential impact on French interests lies in what is often referred to as the Japanese model of development. As highlighted by Prime Minister Habib Thiam of Senegal, the virtues of this model are its openness to modernity, its utilization of the state as a motor for rapid economic development, and its allowing the country to "preserve its own identity" (see Samb, 1995: 4). The implication of the latter portion of this statement is that francophone Africa can and perhaps should develop in association with foreign partners who do not seek to impose their ideological and cultural biases and preconceptions on LDCs.

CONCLUSION

The end of the Cold War has had a dramatic effect on the flows of foreign aid from all donors to francophone Africa, particularly the three primary donors of France, the United States, and Japan. Although Japan simply reinforced and expanded its focus on trade and private investment, French policymakers were prompted to reassess a culturally based ODA policy of promoting *la francophonie,* and U.S. policymakers had to restructure its containment-based policy once the threat of communism no longer existed. The common element of each of these three cases was a growing recognition (or reaffirmation, in the case of Japan) of the importance of economics in the emerging post–Cold War era.

Despite their continued strong attachment to promoting the cultural ideal of *la francophonie,* French policymakers have emerged as the protectors of the status quo in an increasingly competitive international economic environment. If one perceives economics as a zero-sum game, as French policymakers appear to do, the process of economic and political liberalization throughout francophone Africa poses strong risks to the high levels of influence previously enjoyed by France. According to this perspective, both the United States and Japan have much to gain from the creation in francophone Africa of multiparty democracies that are more fully integrated into the international economic system. In this regard, French policymakers have perceived a growing U.S. threat and, to a lesser degree, have begun to voice concern over rising Japanese influence.

Whereas Japan in the early 1980s committed only 6 percent of the total ODA provided by the three major donors, its share rose to 9 percent in the mid-1980s and to 12 percent at the beginning of the 1990s.[12] In March 1995 it signed a major foreign-assistance agreement with the Senegalese government, and other major packages were under consideration. In this regard, the observation of a Cameroonian businessman (quoted in Maunick, 1993: 25) concerning the U.S. economic threat to French interests in francophone Africa is revealing: "If one looks closely, it is not the Americans that are threatening the French, but rather the Japanese."

NOTES

1. The U.S. attended the proceedings as an observer nation, and its representative, John A. Kasson, signed the Berlin Convention (see M'Bokolo, 1992: 278–282).

2. According to Martin (1995: 63), among the other factors that make francophone Africa distinctive are 1) "a common (French or Belgian) colonial experience"; 2) "a broad cultural unity" resulting from a fusion of African and French cul-

tures"; 3) "a tradition of moderation and compromise arising out of a peaceful transfer of power at independence"; and 4) "the perpetuation of Franco-African relations characterized by a pattern of continuing French political, economic, and cultural power and influence."

3. For the purposes of this chapter, francophone Africa includes twenty-five independent states from the following regions: Central Africa (Burundi, Cameroon, Central African Republic, Chad, Congo, Gabon, Rwanda, and Zaire); East Africa (Djibouti); Indian Ocean (Comoros, Madagascar, Mauritius, and Seychelles); North Africa or the Maghreb (Algeria, Morocco, and Tunisia); and West Africa (Benin, Burkina Faso, Côte d'Ivoire, Guinea, Mali, Mauritania, Niger, Senegal, and Togo).

4. Neither Germany nor Canada will be treated in this chapter.

5. All statistical references, unless otherwise cited, are derived from a data set of thirty-six African countries that served as the basis of Schraeder, Hook, and Taylor (1996).

6. These countries include Benin, Burkina Faso, Cameroon, Central African Republic, Chad, Comoros, Congo, Côte d'Ivoire, Gabon, Mali, Niger, Senegal, Togo.

7. U.S. aid to Africa, of course, has been overshadowed by its massive annual transfers to Egypt, but these are listed by USAID as aid for the Near East, not Africa.

8. The largest ODA package in 1992 was $55 million for Morocco, but this represented a deep cut from the $127 million allocation of the previous year (OECD, 1994a).

9. The importance of ideology in U.S. calculations was further illustrated by the fact that capitalist countries received, on average, 88 percent of all U.S. ODA to Africa during the 1980s, whereas Marxist and socialist countries received only 6 percent each.

10. Other outlets of French concern included Morocco and Tunisia, which together received approximately $1 billion in French ODA from 1990 to 1992.

11. At the heart of the Clinton administration's revised approach to Zaire in 1993 and 1994 was an apparent acceptance of the "Mobutu or chaos" argument advanced by Zairian specialists in the State Department, the Pentagon, and the Central Intelligence Agency since Mobutu took power in the mid-1960s (Schatzberg, 1991). "Regardless of the fact that we are no longer faced with a communist threat," explained a foreign service officer of the State Department (quoted in Schraeder, 1994b: 107), "the destabilization of Zaire—which borders nine other African countries—could have a tremendously negative impact on regional stability."

12. The rising economic importance of Japan suggested by these figures is perhaps best symbolized by the ongoing construction of a massive Japanese cultural center overlooking the Atlantic Ocean in Dakar, Senegal.

12

Aid and Developmentalism in Southern Africa

Goran Hyden

As in the case of francophone Africa, foreign aid has increasingly become a lifeline for less developed countries elsewhere on the African continent. Foreign aid, largely in the form of cash grants designed to meet humanitarian needs, is virtually the only kind of foreign capital inflow that takes place now that private investment has gone elsewhere. Even if living conditions improve dramatically in the coming years, which itself is unlikely, foreign aid will be a dominant factor in development policy among the anglophone (English-speaking) and lusophone (Portuguese-speaking) states well into the next millennium.[1]

This central reality is due to the growing gap between socioeconomic conditions in much of Africa and those in other parts of the developing world. In 1961 the per capita income of Ghana and South Korea was the same. Thirty years later, Ghana's remained at virtually the same level (about $100), but South Korea's had risen many times over. Conditions in southern Africa improved marginally during the first decade after the peak of decolonization in 1960. But progress slowed in the 1970s and actually reversed course in the 1980s, widely viewed as the "lost decade" of development in the world's poorest countries. When Tanzania became independent, its per-capita income was approximately $100. In 1981 it had reached a peak of $310 per year, but by the early 1990s it had sunk to the same level as in 1961. For this and other reasons, LDCs in southern Africa have emerged as the leading per capita aid recipients in the world.

These and similar figures from other countries clearly demonstrate that many African populations have suffered a drastic decline in living standard in the last two decades of this century. While much of the developing world has moved ahead, both on absolute and relative terms, states in what was once termed the Fourth World have treaded water or even sunk lower than before. Not only must their fledgling governments struggle to retain internal control, the specter of intrusion by industrialized states (many of which serve as their primary foreign-aid donors) continues to loom very heavily. And wherever living conditions continue to worsen, the prospect of direct intervention in the affairs of these politically sovereign nations on the continent increases. Countries such as Liberia and Somalia are examples in which the collapse of political authority has led to the imposition by external forces of law and order.

Against this gloomy background, it is distressing how little public debate there is about the future of foreign aid in southern Africa. Equally disturbing is how little self-examination is being displayed by the donors themselves, who continue to claim that the burden of reform lies squarely with the recipients. That they may be as much part of the problem as the solution does not seem to enter donors' minds.

This chapter examines the role of foreign aid in southern Africa's development by looking more specifically at what has happened in a select number of recipient countries. My main argument is that donors must share responsibility for what has gone wrong across Africa, including the francophone and Maghreb regions, and that foreign aid is unlikely to bring about positive results in the future unless both donors and recipients rethink the ways aid is dispensed. The chapter is organized into three sections. In the first I review the most basic aid data and consider the extent of aid dependency in various southern African states. In the second I discuss how southern Africa arrived at the predicament in which it finds itself between the Cold War and the new millennium. In the third I suggest a new way of organizing relations between donors and recipients—not only within this region but across the continent—which may overcome many of the structural impediments to economic growth.

AID DEPENDENCY IN SOUTHERN AFRICA

As noted above, standards of living in southern Africa are among the most desperate of any developing region, and in many cases conditions are deteriorating. Five of the poorest ten states in the world were in southern Africa in the immediate post–Cold War period, including the two poorest states, Mozambique and Tanzania, whose inhabitants earned an average 1993 income of just $90 (World Bank, 1995a: 162). Other grossly impoverished states included Sierra Leone ($150), Uganda ($180), and Malawi ($200). Seven additional southern Africa states reported per capita incomes of less than $700 in 1993, placing them in the World Bank's poorest category, low-income countries.[2]

These economic figures only tell part of the story. Between 1980 and 1993 life expectancy, which reflects more basic social-welfare conditions, decreased in five of these states, including Mozambique (47 to 46 years), Sierra Leone (47 to 39), Uganda (54 to 45), Zambia (49 to 48), and Zimbabwe (55 to 53). Most other African states reported life expectancies well below the 1993 world average of 66 years, including 51 years in Nigeria, the continent's most populous state, and 63 years in South Africa, its most productive state in terms of economic output (World Bank, 1995a, 1982a).

The international aid community recognized the distress in southern Africa. Yet after rising steadily from the early 1960s to a 1989 peak of $18.3 billion, overall aid flows to sub-Saharan Africa fell in the early 1990s in real terms (OECD, 1996a). This decrease reflected widespread cutbacks in aid flows and a diversion of some aid to the former Soviet Union.

Primary anglophone recipients during the first three years of the post–Cold War period (1992–1994) included Tanzania ($3.3 billion), Ethiopia ($2.9 billion), Uganda ($2.0 billion), Kenya ($1.7 billion), and Somalia ($1.7 million). Among lusophone states, Mozambique has consistently received the largest volumes of development assistance, including $3.7 billion between 1992 and 1994. Angola, in the midst of fragile peace negotiations, received $914 million during this period (OECD, 1995c). Scandinavian donors, Great Britain, the United States, and Japan provided the most aid to this seriously impoverished and indebted region.

More so than LDCs in other parts of the world, many countries in southern Africa have become chronically dependent on continued aid to sustain many basic programs. One way to illustrate this pattern is to examine the share of the recipient's GDP represented by net ODA. This figure indicates how much capital is being generated externally as opposed to domestically. The higher the ratio of net ODA to GDP, the lower the degree of national self-reliance.

According to the United Nations Development Programme (UNDP, 1992), foreign aid accounted for 43.7 percent of the GDPs of the five developing states in lusophone Africa. By comparison, aid made up just 14 percent of the GDPs of the sixteen anglophone recipients and 13 percent of the GDPs of the twenty-two francophone recipients in Africa. The most striking thing about these patterns is the significance of ODA's role in the economies of lusophone countries. The foreign aid component of GDP was very small in Angola (1.9 percent), moderate in Cape Verde (26.4 percent) and it approached 60 percent in Guinea-Bissau and Mozambique during the early 1990s. Even if questions can be raised about how adequately national accounts record economic transactions—a good number take place informally and may not be counted—it is evident that approximately half of GDP, possibly more, was generated by foreign aid in these two countries. Among anglophone states, the most aid-dependent countries were Gambia (42.1 percent), Tanzania (32.6 percent), and Lesotho (28.3 percent).[3] Francophone states on average depended less heavily on foreign aid to fund their government budgets, but they received other support from Paris through the integrated franc zone and through military cooperation (see Chapter 11).[4]

Even if the francophone countries are in statistical terms the least aid dependent, it is important to note that they tend to be more dependent on the flow from one major donor, France, partly because of French ambitions to dominate economic relations with its former colonies and partly because of language (many donor nations do not feel comfortable working in countries that speak French). By contrast, a wide range of donors—including the United States, Japan, Scandinavian states, and Great Britain—maintain parallel aid projects in southern Africa. In some cases the donors jockey to gain the most influence with these LDCs; in others the multiple aid programs produce confusion, duplication, and inefficient management of development assistance.

Non-French donors have been selective in giving aid to francophone recipients. For instance, the United States has at different points been active in the Côte d'Ivoire and Zaire (originally the Belgian Congo, now considered part of francophone Africa). France used to concentrate its aid almost exclusively on its former colonies, but in the 1980s, after President François Mitterrand took office, it has pursued a conscious strategy to provide aid to select anglophone countries. For example, in 1989 France was Kenya's third-largest donor (Government of Kenya, 1990: 5, 65). But France's basic emphasis on francophone African recipients, as well as its remaining overseas possessions remained intact.

There is no evidence that aid inherently fosters dependency, but it is quite obvious that dependency is real in sub-Saharan Africa. In the 1990s, many countries are so heavily reliant on foreign aid that without it new investment would be virtually nonexistent (the latter is often predicated upon the former). Moreover, without aid these countries would not be able to pay salaries and meet other expenses needed to maintain ongoing activities. Compared to those in other regions of the world, the ratios of ODA to GDP for African countries are considerably higher: 8.6 percent for developing countries in sub-Saharan Africa, 1.7 percent in South Asia, 0.7 percent in East Asia, and 0.4 percent in Latin America (Serageldin, 1990: 11).

Africa's dependence on aid has generally increased rather than decreased in the 1990s. One major reason for this trend is that, contrary to the experience of many Latin American states, Africa's debt burden has not been reduced during the decade. For example, Nigeria's external debt burden amounted to 95 percent of its GDP in 1992, and its debt-service obligations constituted 37 percent of its national budget. The situation in southern Africa is no different. Though some progress has been made over the years to relieve the debt burden in the anglophone states, mainly by softening repayment terms, the presence of an external debt burden remains a major obstacle to economic progress across the region in the late 1990s.

This situation does not excuse Africans from responsibility for turning the situation around. Corruption, poor governance, and bureaucratic regulations in African nations continue to keep away private investors, who have noted that the rate of return in sub-Saharan Africa is only 2.5 percent, compared to 23 percent in South Asia (Chege, 1992: 158). It is not surprising that private investments in southern Africa fell from $2.3 billion in 1982 to $900 million in 1989. Without the ability to attract private investors, including from within the continent, LDCs across southern Africa are likely to remain highly dependent on foreign aid into the next millennium.

PHASES OF AFRICAN DEVELOPMENTALISM

It is difficult to appreciate fully the causes of the ongoing socioeconomic problems in southern Africa and the role played by foreign aid if we do not critically examine "developmentalism," the ideology that donors and recipient governments have followed much to their detriment since decolonization. Although this ideology is not the sole cause of Africa's malaise, it is certainly a factor that is often wholly overlooked. If we accept, however, that development is a deliberate course of action—an effort to control the process of social change—it is not difficult to see that hegemonic influences are important. This is particularly so in southern Africa, where, at independence, the perceived need to "catch up" with wealthier countries was particularly strong. A vague but widespread feeling among Western liberals that industrialized countries needed to compensate Africa for the opportunities lost under colonialism (a feeling reinforced by the strategic considerations engendered by Africa's incorporation into the Cold War) combined with African aspirations to lay the ideological foundation on which development policies have been pursued on the continent since the 1960s.

It is possible to discern four separate phases, roughly coinciding with the first four decades of the postcolonization era, through which developmentalism has passed. This process has been observable throughout Africa but particularly within the anglophone states, where I have conducted extensive field research and interviewed hundreds of government officials and private actors working in the area of foreign assistance.

Phase I: Trickle-down Development

The first of these phases, lasting into the latter part of the 1960s, may be best labeled the "trickle-down period" because of the widespread belief that development comes from above. This notion was the natural outgrowth of the orientations prevailing among donors and recipients alike. Responding to Keynesian ideas about economic-demand management and drawing on the successful rebuilding of Western Europe through the Marshall Plan, donors endorsed the idea that government was the principal development actor. This view also suited leaders of the new nation-states in Africa, who were eager to create strong governments to promote development.

As a result, emphasis was laid squarely on economic growth, which development policy analysts thought could be best achieved by selectively funneling inputs to well-endowed and entrepreneurial individuals. Progressive farmers, for example, were expected to modernize their agricultural practices and thus encourage others to follow suit. Rural cooperatives were viewed as key institutional instruments to ensure the trickle-down effect. Kept under close supervision by government, these institutions would provide credit and necessary inputs to interested and willing members. Backup services were provided by government extension agencies. Agricultural research stations were expected to provide valuable support for this drive to modernize. Even community development was a government affair in those days.

The Indian and Pakistani governments were the first to launch ambitious community-development programs to foster local development in the 1950s, but leaders in southern Africa adopted the same approach in the 1960s. The general assumption in those days was that social and economic modernization was a sine qua non for the emergence of more democratic forms of governance. In other words, politics was reduced to the status of a dependent variable.

This initial phase left behind a legacy that has continued to affect policy in southern Africa ever since. One aspect of this legacy was the idea of development as a top-down exercise, with donors playing a vital backup role for recipients. A second aspect was the rejection of things African. Development, as viewed from the perspective of catching up, meant imitation rather than innovation, a rejection rather than adoption of indigenous customs and values. A third element of this legacy was that development was a nonpolitical affair, the prerogative of experts. This depoliticization of development suited donors and recipients alike. The former endorsed it because it legitimized development as an exercise in social engineering. The latter approved it because it implied that donors would not question the political sovereignty of the new nation-state.

Phase II: Integrated Development

The second phase in the evolution of developmentalism on the African continent may best be labeled "integrated development," a phase that spanned the 1970s. In many respects it was an attempt to refine the ideas born in the first phase. The emphasis still lay on the political will of strong governments. The centralized nature of policymaking that had characterized the first years, however, was now seen as a limitation. To realize development objectives it was considered necessary to decentralize, more specifically to fragment administrative authority to field levels at which policy implementation was taking place. When governments proved weak, special integrated development structures were set up. For example, following the success of the Chilalo Agricultural Development Unit (CADU), an integrated development program in southern Ethiopia, bilateral and multilateral donors alike began using it as a model for rural development purposes.

A major reason for this turn was disillusionment with the trickle-down approach, which diffused information and innovations too slowly to suit the more radical mood of the late 1960s and early 1970s. Development had to include not just the better-off but also the poorer segments of the population. The peasant farmer replaced the progressive farmer as the prime target of rural development. Furthermore, development was viewed as promoting not merely economic but also social objectives. Programs and projects had to respond in an integrated fashion to the full range of human needs. To deal with this more complex version of development, it became necessary to pay even more attention to design. Development without a plan or a blueprint was viewed as inconceivable.

This phase had the effect of reinforcing the trends that had been set in motion during the early years of developmentalism in Africa. Development continued to be seen as a top-down exercise, with management emphasized even more strongly than before. The solution to Africa's problems was to come from administrators and experts involved in coordinating and delivering particular programs. People were still treated as recipients of ideas formulated and handed down by an elite. For donors, this approach extended the scope of intervention and constituted a step forward from the overly optimistic and simplistic notions of development that had prevailed in the 1960s. For recipient governments, the new approach provided the outside legitimation of the monopolistic party-state. Without donor objections, organizations such as cooperatives and trade unions that hitherto had been independent were subordinated to the idiosyncracies of a small political elite. The call for unity had now been turned into one demanding uniformity. In many countries, the death knell was sounded for civil society.

The case of Tanzania, a major aid recipient in anglophone Africa and the largest aid recipient on a per capita basis, is illustrative here. Because its first president, Julius Nyerere, was able to invent an indigenous twist to the basic arguments of modernization through his socialist *ujamaa* policies, Tanzania became in many respects a model in the eyes of the donor community. Bilateral donors and the World Bank subsequently heaped money on

Tanzania, although countless World Bank reports, some dating as far back as the early 1960s, had warned of the country's limited implementation capacity (Msemakweli, 1994). Given the donor community's endorsement of a statist strategy of development, however, African leaders like Nyerere may be excused for believing that what they were doing was right.

Phase III: Structural Adjustment

It came as a shock to African leaders, therefore, when the donors, without much warning, initiated the third development phase by demanding structural adjustment in the early 1980s. The catalyst for action was the so-called Berg Report (World Bank, 1981), named for its principal author, U.S. economist Elliott Berg. Its main thrust was the gradual dismantling of the monopolistic state sector that had been created—with donors' blessings—in the previous two decades and the return to a market-based approach to development. The latter implied a host of policy measures, such as deregulation, privatization, currency devaluation, and related measures of financial stabilization (see Chapter 2).

In an attempt to mitigate the impact of the Berg Report, African leaders, with the help of the UN Economic Commission for Africa, launched their own strategy. They produced a document—the Lagos Plan of Action—that called for far less adjustment and in essence a continuation of policies of national self-reliance centered in governments. This move by the African leaders gave them some bargaining space in their negotiations with the donors. In some countries it was used as an excuse for rejecting World Bank and IMF demands for new financial and economic policies.

For example, it is not surprising that Tanzania's Nyerere, who had been the principal benefactor of donor Keynesianism in the 1970s, proved to be the most politically resilient leader in the battle against emerging IMF/World Bank hegemony. Complaining about what he termed the IMF's role as a "global finance police," he refused to accept the structural adjustments required by the two international finance institutions. As the Tanzanian economy continued to spin out of control, however, it became increasingly clear that he was losing the battle. Rather than accepting the bitter medicine of the IMF, he decided to retire as head of state in 1985.

Events in other anglophone countries were less dramatic. Ghana, the first to accept the new strategy, was used by the World Bank and IMF as a model of what could and should be done. Nigeria objected to the approach of the international finance institutions and decided to invent its own adjustment strategy, borrowing its principal elements from the Berg Report. For other countries, such as Kenya, the required adjustments were not so extensive and politically easier to swallow. Regardless of what approach they adopted, however, it was clear by the late 1980s that African countries had no choice but to comply with the demands of the international finance institutions.

At least two factors contributed to this situation. First, the export-oriented policies fostered by the structural-adjustment strategy led to a glut in the global commodity market. Without a significant rise in demand in the industrial world for coffee, tea, cocoa, cotton, groundnuts, and other primary commodities produced by African countries, the latter found themselves increasingly competing with each other and thus keeping prices down. Instead of reaping increased export incomes, African countries in the 1980s began to suffer a decline in revenues. Structural adjustment, though economically necessary, proved to be a double-edged sword.

The second reason southern African LDCs had no choice but to accept structural adjustment was that all the principal donors in Africa supported the conditions for further aid established by the IMF and the World Bank. African governments could no longer play one donor against the other, as they had in earlier years. Furthermore, after Mikhail Gorbachev took over leadership of the Soviet Union in the mid-1980s, its role as a supporter of African countries began to dwindle. The overall effect was to reduce African governments' political opportunities to negotiate favorable deals with donors. Faced with this no-win situation, these governments gradually adopted the adjustment packages recommended by the donors.[5]

Phase IV: Democratization

The most recent phase in the history of foreign aid to African development is that of democratization. With the demise of communism and the end of the Cold War, Western donors became increasingly insistent that African governments reform their political systems in a democratic direction. Political intervention was now justified on the grounds that structural adjustment alone had not improved the utilization of foreign aid. African governments remained secretive and arbitrary in their actions. Political reforms were necessary to make them more open and accountable to the public.

Since the beginning of the 1990s, therefore, donors have been preoccupied with supporting political reforms aimed at promoting good governance and introducing elements of political democracy that had never before been present or had been swept aside by the authoritarian regimes installed during the 1970s. A minimum condition imposed upon African recipients has been that they allow multiple political parties and free elections. Much donor energy has gone into facilitating such elections through provision of international election monitors, sponsorship of local organizations with the same objective, printing of ballot papers, and management of related technical and logistical issues.

Parallel to these efforts has been sponsorship of activities aimed at enhancing respect for human rights and the growth of associational life in southern Africa's fledgling civil societies. The assumption here is that organizations outside of government need to be strengthened in Africa to counterbalance the power of incumbent political leaders, who only reluctantly seem willing to accommodate more democratic forms of governance. Unfortunately, the democratic wave that has swept across Latin America, Eastern Europe, and parts of the Far East has been slower in coming to southern Africa. According to Freedom House (1994), only Botswana, Gambia, Namibia, São Tomé, and Príncipe had become "free" states by 1993, whereas nine states (Angola, Ghana, Kenya, Liberia, Malawi, Mozambique, Nigeria, Sierra Leone, and Uganda) remained "not free." The remaining states in this region, many of which were in the midst of democratic transitions, were listed as "partly free."[6]

This latter group included South Africa, where the dismantling of apartheid in 1993 was the most visible example of democratic reform in the region. Industrialized states committed more than $600 million in 1993 and 1994 to President Nelson Mandela's government. Of these commitments, $150 million originated in the United States, and other large aid flows were approved by Nordic and Western European donors (OECD, 1995c). Donors hoped the political transformation would stimulate regional economic growth and propel democratization throughout southern Africa; skeptics noted that South Africa possessed far greater economic resources and strategic assets than its neighbors.

The new donor approach contrasts sharply with the approach of the 1960s, when the assumption was that social and economic modernization were prerequisites for successful democratization. In the 1990s this thesis has been turned upside down. The argument is now that democratization is a condition for social and economic development. However, this proposition remains largely inconclusive. There is some evidence that public criticism of governments has increased. Particularly encouraging has been the role played by independent newspapers in exposing corruption and other malpractice in public institutions. Civic consciousness is also growing as donors put their support behind organizations that demand greater professionalism and accountability in public transactions.

Nonetheless, there persists a fundamental question about what contribution these measures make to national development. Donors seem overwhelmed by their own belief in the righteousness of liberal democracy, confident that it will magically change anglophone Africa's predicament for the better. Democratization across sub-Saharan Africa, however, is likely to require a very long time. The question is whether the donors will show the necessary patience and sensitivity to local conditions that this process demands.

OBSTACLES TO REFORM IN SOUTHERN AFRICA

Four obstacles to development continue to dominate the political scene in the anglophone and lusophone countries of Africa in the mid-1990s.

First, the prevailing form of governance is still the patronage system. African governments are not policy-oriented, as donors have assumed throughout three decades of support. African leaders take pride in two things: their ability to oppose outside pressures and their ability to distribute benefits and rewards to potential supporters. Pleasing people is what matters—regardless of the macroeconomic consequences. Professional considerations are overshadowed by political concerns; long-term perspectives are overwhelmed by the prospect of short-term gains.

Second, corruption continues to be pervasive in spite of efforts to strengthen accountability. Much of this corruption can be attributed to wages and salaries that have not risen to reflect higher costs of living as a result of structural adjustment. Improvement is expected if the public sector can be cut to a size that allows government to pay livable salaries to those who perform essential functions. But corruption will not necessarily cease with such reforms. Public records continue to be in such an abominable state that the chance of getting away with illegal behavior is very great. In many countries corruption has become a way of life, an integral part of the political culture. Beating the system has become a sport in which large numbers of people, both rich and poor, excel. In one respect multiparty democracy may even have intensified corruption: With the risk of losing the next election, many leaders are eager to seize personal advantages before they are voted out of power. In short, respect for things public remains very weak across southern Africa.

The third problem is that relations between African governments and civil society remain strained and characterized by mutual suspicion. Both view politics largely as a zero-sum game, in which one must win, the other lose. Competitive politics, therefore, tends to have a polarizing effect, because there is no shared normative foundation on which democracy can be built. This situation has been exacerbated by donors' clear stand in support of NGOs and of measures that give the emerging political opposition an equal chance to compete for power. African governments continue to view democratization as a threat, not an opportunity, and avoid taking any goodwill measures of their own to promote the process of democratization. Were it not for the pressures exercised by the donors, the process might have stalled long ago.

All of these factors lead ODA donors to become enmeshed within the internal affairs of African recipients, the fourth major obstacle to development. As they continue to pump money into these countries without seeing the expected results, donors find it hard to define where their responsibility begins and ends. At a time when their financial presence is already so vital to these countries, donors ask themselves whether they should assume executive responsibility, even if doing so amounts to an effective recolonization of Africa. Or should they withdraw and allow the African countries to assume the consequences on their own, even if it may mean greater sufferings for people, especially the poor?

As the millennium approaches, the choices for donors in southern Africa have become that stark. Against this background, it is not surprising that critics want to terminate foreign aid, arguing that it does more harm than good (e.g., Hancock, 1989). The important question is whether there is an alternative route forward between total withdrawal and recolonization, whether foreign aid can be salvaged and reinvigorated in ways that restore some of the public confidence that has been lost over the years.

A NEW MODEL FOR AFRICAN AID

It ought to be clear from the discussion above that continuing to give foreign aid in the same forms as in the past would only be a further waste of donor money. Moreover, it would do no good for the recipients in southern Africa or in the francophone states; it would only reinforce aid dependency. A new approach is needed that addresses the principal shortcomings listed above. Such an approach would entail the creation of a credible intermediary between donors and recipients, one that is independent of both government and civil society. Such an initiative would utilize foreign aid to strengthen institutions in the public, private, and voluntary sectors in Africa. The model for this approach is the politically and legally independent development fund.

Development funds are not new in Africa; many donors have experimented with them for years. In the 1970s, for instance, regional or rural development funds were often supported in the hope that they would benefit small-scale community-development activities that were impossible to include in conventional aid packages. However, because their institutional home was usually the office of the president or some key ministry, these funds became part of the political patronage available to the leadership. Feasibility and other professional considerations were ignored. No independent boards or accountability mechanisms were established. Because the funds had so little to show for themselves after several years of operation, donor support for this type of fund gradually ceased in the 1980s.

The idea has since been resuscitated in two different ways. The first version finances village or community development activities through support to NGOs. A number of bilateral and multilateral donors have experimented with this approach as a way of getting their money to the people who need it. These funds tend to be controlled by one donor; they cater to only one type of client (NGOs); and they are often confined to one particular region of the recipient country. Because they are controlled by one donor, they enjoy a measure of autonomy from government. On the other hand, their dependence on the financier is almost total.

Social-action funds constitute the second type. These have been established with the help of World Bank resources to support social development under the overall structural-adjustment umbrella. They have helped spread responsibility for activities that hitherto had been carried out by government departments but had been eliminated because of enforced contractions of the national budget. These funds have been commonplace in both Africa and Latin America in the last ten years, the Emergency Social Fund of Bolivia being perhaps the best known. Their scope has usually been national. Because the World Bank is an intergovernmental organization, however, it has been impossible for these funds to enjoy autonomy from the recipient governments.

The model proposed here draws on the lessons learned from these earlier efforts at using funds to dispense aid money in recipient countries. In addressing the peculiar challenges facing donors in African countries, the new funds must have the following five qualities: They must be national in scope, sectoral in orientation, autonomous in status, nondiscriminatory in practice, and versatile in operation.

The importance of a national scope stems foremost from the experience of regional funds. The latter have often had the effect of generating opinions that certain parts of the country are being favored over others. At a time when multiparty politics already seem to encourage centrifugal tendencies, it is important that donors preserve the notion of national mandates for the institutions they support. Donor funds should in principle be available to people from any region of the recipient country, regardless of whether or not that region is dominated by the party in power.

A sectoral orientation is important in order to ensure a feasible mandate. Thus, there would typically be more than one development fund in each country, one for each sector identified as a national priority. A given fund would support projects and programs relating to food security, public health, education, or any other set of socioeconomic issues identified as national priorities by the country's representative organs.

Legal and political independence is the most critical feature of this model. Although the notion of institutional autonomy was abandoned in most African countries after independence, most have laws enabling the delegation of authority to public national institutions such as the funds suggested here. Where they do not exist, it would be necessary to introduce legislation that insulates the funds from political and economic pressures. There are different ways of ensuring this autonomy. The appointed trustees of these funds can be made contractually responsible for adhering to the principles of fairness and professionalism. The board can be constituted as a self-appointing body to prevent its being controlled by an outside actor, including the head of state, and/or it can include a minority of representatives from outside the recipient country.[7]

The fourth feature of the development fund is nondiscrimination among clients. In African countries, neither government nor civil society tends to be strong; both need strengthening. One way of achieving this is to encourage them to compete with each other on equal terms for public money channeled through these development funds. Thus, contrary to current donor practice, whereby one set of government departments or NGOs is identified in advance as the preferred institutional channel, judgment on who deserves the money would be suspended until a comparative assessment could be made of the potential institutional beneficiaries. In societies where government institutions lack the legal and rational qualities that donors prefer, foreign aid flows must create a climate and an environment in which these qualities can be fostered. The development funds proposed here are an ideal mechanism precisely because they encourage recipients to demonstrate that they are capable of doing work in a professional manner.

Versatility in operation is the fifth feature associated with this model. These funds must be more than regular credit institutions in order to serve the broadest segment of the potential actors in development. The development funds, therefore, should operate through three separate windows. The first would support activities that have no immediate return on capital. The mechanism for dispensing money would be grants. The second window would cater to those actors who are locked out of access to regular commercial credits but whose projects have such potential for development that they are worth funding. The mechanism used in this window would be the soft loan. The third window would be similar to a regular credit institution in that it would make available loans on regular commercial terms. It would thus be possible for the fund to cater to a broad range of actors involved in social and economic development.

The funds proposed above would not cover all foreign aid. For example, large infrastructure projects and humanitarian assistance would not fall into the categories covered by the fund model. The latter addresses the challenges associated with foreign aid currently channeled to governments, NGOs, cooperatives, or private companies for purposes of social and economic development. Because it touches so many actors and is expected to have long-term benefits, it is particularly important. This kind of development is more difficult to achieve, however. It is no coincidence that most failures of foreign aid have occurred in the social and economic sectors (Cassen, 1986).

CONCLUSION

As we have argued in this chapter, the failures of past foreign-aid efforts in southern Africa are not inevitable. They largely have been determined by the shortcomings in previous approaches to using foreign aid in development. Obviously, the poor performance of foreign aid throughout Africa, as compared to that of South Asia or other regions of the world, cannot be allowed to continue. Many countries on the continent are already on the brink of becoming so weak that only recolonization can save them.

Donor governments, for their part, cannot afford to let their money be squandered without undercutting the credibility of the whole exercise, a point vividly illustrated by current debates within the United States, which has already approved widespread cutbacks to sub-Saharan Africa yet retained aid programs to the Middle East and expanded those to Eastern Europe and the former Soviet Union (see Chapter 4). Foreign aid is in a similar political crisis in many other donor countries. Increasing numbers of people ask why their governments should continue giving aid to countries that seem unable to make good use of it.

Foreign aid, therefore, must be given a new lease on life in southern Africa and in other parts of this impoverished, imperiled continent. African recipients must begin to show that they can use aid as effectively as can recipients in other parts of the world. This means, however, that both donors and recipients must address the challenges now facing the African continent. They must demonstrate courage and vision to transcend the limitations inherent in the ways foreign aid has been allocated and dispensed across Africa during the decolonization process. The model suggested here is not beyond reach and provides one route to reinvigorating the aid industry and increasing the benefits to donors and recipients. It may be the only way out if foreign aid to Africa in the next millennium is not going to be reduced merely to global charity.

The final question is whether these reforms are politically feasible. Will African governments give up control of external funding? The answer is that with the rise of multiparty politics, the understanding of the need for independent institutions that, like the courts, are accessible to all on equal terms has increased. Recipient governments also realize that they may need this approach to get continued financing from increasingly critical and reluctant donors.

Reluctance to adopt this model may be greater among the donors, who have been used to treating foreign aid as an integral part of their foreign policies, allowing it to be guided more by domestic policy concerns than by the real needs and opportunities of recipient countries. To facilitate the approach proposed here, donors must overcome this perspective. If they do not, Africa is in the long run going to prove a much more serious foreign-policy problem. The continent will not disappear. That is why constructive action at this juncture will benefit the donors and why it should be in their political interest to act accordingly.

Ironically, because Africa in the post–Cold War era has lost its strategic significance to the West, it ought to be possible for the world's wealthiest states to make foreign-aid considerations that go beyond their own narrow security and economic interests. The willingness of industrialized countries to transcend these interests during a period of profound flux in world politics remains the key factor that will determine the course of African development in the coming years.

NOTES

1. The anglophone states of Africa include Botswana, Gambia, Ghana, Kenya, Lesotho, Liberia, Malawi, Namibia, Nigeria, Sierra Leone, Swaziland, South Africa, Tanzania, Uganda, Zambia, and Zimbabwe. Lusophone countries include Angola, Guinea-Bissau, Mozambique, and the island of São Tomé and Príncipe. It is acknowledged, of course, that national and regional languages and dialects are also spoken in these countries. In the interest of brevity, and to differentiate these states from those in francophone Africa reviewed in the previous chapter, these countries will be collectively referred to as southern Africa.

2. These included Gambia, Ghana, Guinea-Bissau, Kenya, Lesotho, Nigeria, and São Tomé and Príncipe.

3. Nigeria was lowest, with an ODA/GNP level of 1.2 percent, followed by Namibia (3.1 percent) and Zimbabwe (4.5 percent).

4. At the top end of the ODA/GNP scale among francophone LDCs in 1989 were Mauritania (24.3 percent), Chad (23.9 percent), Mali (22.9 percent), and Comoros (22.4 percent). In contrast, Mauritius (2.8 percent), Congo (3.6 percent), and Côte d'Ivoire (4.5 percent) were the least aid dependent among the French-speaking countries.

5. Some did so with greater vigor than others. A report on the performance of structural-adjustment policies in twenty-nine African countries identified six as having done especially well; nine had shown a small improvement; and the remainder suffered a deterioration (World Bank, 1994b). Among the more successful countries were Nigeria and Tanzania, the two countries that ten years earlier had been the most vocal against the approach.

6. It should be noted, however, that in some cases (e.g., Nigeria, Sierra Leone, and Uganda) the transitions were in the opposite direction, from partly free to not free (Freedom House, 1994).

7. A formula that is used in the regional development banks is two-thirds from domestic sources and one-third from outside. This way, the minority is big enough to blow the whistle, if necessary, and small enough not to erode the principle of local accountability.

13

Progressive Aid
to Latin America?

David Louis Cingranelli & SimonPeter Gomez

As with other developing regions reviewed in this volume, foreign assistance to Latin America has been overshadowed by the Cold War and its pernicious effects on North-South relations. But this region—extending from the Mexico to Cape Horn and including the Caribbean—has had a peculiar experience given its relatively long history since decolonization, its paucity of armed interstate conflicts, and, perhaps most significant, the geopolitical interests and hegemonic control of the United States.

But the era of U.S. preeminence in this region is quickly passing, as is its long-standing domination of the foreign-aid network. Now that the perceived communist threat has ended, democratic governments have taken control in most states, and integrated free-market economies have been established, many in the U.S. government believe the major justification for providing concessional funding to this part of the developing world has disappeared. If the aid program is not eliminated outright, as some in the Republican-led U.S. Congress have proposed, it is nonetheless certain that resources designated for Latin America will continue to be reduced greatly.

Even without the need to send aid to new recipients in Eastern Europe and the former Soviet Union, Congress and the Clinton administration would likely have reduced Latin American aid intended to slow the flow of drugs to the United States because of a growing consensus that the "cut the supply" policy failed to produce the desired effect (Jehl, 1993). As a result of these and other factors, some estimate that U.S. military and economic aid to the region will drop by as much as 50 percent by the year 2005 (Scott, 1994).

Though some reductions in overall U.S. assistance to Latin America will undoubtedly continue—and already most military aid packages have been eliminated—we believe these estimates in the area of development assistance are exaggerated. As its March 1995 effort to help Mexico avoid a financial crisis demonstrates, the United States still has compelling long-

term stakes in the economic development of the region. The uncertain future
of the Amazon rain forest, narcotics production and distribution, illegal
immigration, and long-standing economic linkages will assure sustained
attention from Washington and other industrialized states.

Aid flows from the twenty-one OECD donors to Latin America in 1994
amounted to $5.1 billion, more than double the 1984 level of $2.3 billion
and consistently about 12 percent of global development aid flows (OECD,
1996a: A67–A68). Bolivia received the largest commitments of official
development assistance in the first three years of the post–Cold War period,
followed by El Salvador, Nicaragua, Brazil, and Mexico (see Table 13.1).
Aid revenues represented 10 percent of Bolivia's GNP in 1993–1994, but in
general Latin American governments have become less dependent than
those in sub-Saharan Africa and southern Asia on aid flows.

Table 13.1   Major Recipients of Development Aid in Latin America, 1992–1994

	1993 Population (millions)	1992–1994 Development Aid Commitments[a]	1993 GDP (per capita)	1993 External Debt
Bolivia	7.1	$2,116	$5,382 ($760)	$4,213
El Salvador	5.5	1,809	7,625 (1,320)	2,012
Nicaragua	4.1	1,743	1,800 (340)	8,773
Brazil	156.5	1,349	444,205 (2,930)	132,749
Mexico	90.0	1,141	343,472 (3,610)	118,028

Sources: OECD (1995c), World Bank (1995a)
Note:
a. Economic figures in millions of current U.S. dollars.

Even in the face of continued cutbacks by the United States, there is an
emerging progressive trend in the policies of other donor states toward Latin
America. This trend has to a large degree compensated for the reductions in
U.S. assistance and is likely to accelerate in the near future. In the following
pages we will refer to this as the "progressive-trend hypothesis." A progressive foreign-aid regime is one that is designed not only to advance the self-
interests of the donor states but also to realize more universally accepted

values and principles. Some elements of this outlook are described in the UN Charter and the Universal Declaration of Human Rights and illustrated in recent efforts to encourage sustainable development in the Southern Hemisphere. Within Latin America, such principles are routinely articulated by the Organization of American States (OAS).

We believe evidence for this hypothesis can be drawn from eight categories of appropriate state behavior identified by Jones (1991): sovereign equality of states; territorial integrity and political independence of states; equal rights and self-determination of peoples; nonintervention in the internal affairs of states; peaceful settlement of interstate disputes; abstention from the threat or use of force; fulfillment of international obligations; and respect for human rights and fundamental freedoms. Three other principles have achieved near-universal acceptance and are relevant to this analysis: the promotion of self-sustaining economic growth; protection of the global environment; and the use of multilateral rather than unilateral means to solve international problems.

To be consistent with these values and principles, a progressive foreign-aid regime would disburse substantial aggregate volumes of ODA to developing countries, commit more aid to states whose governments respect human rights, offer more aid to least developed countries, reduce the proportion of aid that is tied to purchases of goods and services produced by the donor country, provide a higher proportion of economic versus military aid, enlist a diverse set of bilateral donors as development partners for each developing country, emphasize multilateral instead of bilateral aid, and give a higher proportion of aid in the form of grants as opposed to loans (Cingranelli, 1993: 221).[1]

Our argument is not that the foreign-aid regime as it operates in Latin America is progressive in an absolute sense but that it has become more progressive over time and is likely to continue in this direction. Recent developments in world politics, particularly the cessation of the superpower rivalry that undermined regional stability throughout the developing world, and an emergent consensus regarding the advantages of democratic governance and economic integration provide cause for optimism.

In the pages to come we will first describe the origins and evolution of the U.S. aid program, given the centrality of the United States in Latin American development. We will then discuss the other major donors in the region, especially Japan, along with multilateral aid sources such as the IMF, the World Bank, and the OECD. Finally, we will consider the effects of the ongoing debt crisis, which has been particularly acute in Latin America, and we will demonstrate how the distribution of aid between the Cold War and millennium is being affected by emerging considerations, interests, and realities.

THE CENTRALITY OF U.S. AID FLOWS

At least since the Monroe Doctrine of 1823 and the Mexican-American War of the 1840s, the United States has profoundly affected the politics and policies of all Latin American states. This region was central to U.S. geopolitical considerations before and during the Cold War, and it remains so in the late 1990s. Latin America is not a major supplier of strategic raw materials, nor is it a particularly important market for U.S. goods and services. Instead, its importance derives from its location within the Western Hemisphere, a location that gives Latin America a geostrategic significance in U.S. foreign policy that it would not have otherwise. Because the United States has traditionally sought to keep Latin America firmly within its sphere of influence, and because it had the only industrialized economy still intact at the end of World War II, it quickly assumed the role of major foreign-aid donor to the region.

Latin America received more U.S. bilateral economic and military aid in the mid-1960s than at any other time, enjoying a steep rise in U.S. foreign aid under the Kennedy administration's Alliance for Progress. As the decolonization process reached its peak in sub-Saharan Africa, the United States focused on Latin America in devising state-building programs. Between 1962 and 1993, the U.S. government transferred a total of $33 billion to Latin American recipients (USAID, 1994a: 83). Of this total, $29 billion was in the form of economic aid, $4 billion in the form of military aid. Primary recipients included strategically important states in the Caribbean such as the Dominican Republic and Central American states such as El Salvador and Honduras.

Although the United States traditionally has played a predominant role in the flow of foreign aid to Latin America, its aggregate commitments to the region have lagged behind those to other regions. Since the signing of the Camp David peace accords in 1978, the largest share of U.S. foreign aid has been devoted to the Middle East—especially Egypt and Israel. The Middle East now receives about three times as much foreign aid as Asia and Latin America and about five times as much as Africa (Bandow, 1992: 79), a stark reality that vividly illustrates the geopolitical orientation of U.S. aid.[2]

Within Latin America, the primary recipients of U.S. assistance during the period have included El Salvador, Brazil, Honduras, Peru, Bolivia, and Colombia. As these and other patterns suggest, U.S. assistance was widely disbursed within the region rather than being concentrated among a few recipients, as in the Middle East. The patterns do reflect, however, the importance of Central America vis-à-vis South America in U.S. aid calculations and—since the Cold War's demise—of the narcotics problem in propelling large bilateral aid flows to Bolivia, Colombia, and Peru.

One important reason to seek a dominant bilateral foreign-aid policy in a region is that dependency on a single donor gives that donor disproportionate influence over the politics and policies of the recipient. That pattern clearly was evident during the early period of the Cold War and extended beyond foreign aid to other aspects of U.S. economic relations with Latin America. Since the mid-1970s the U.S. aid program has become less intertwined with geostrategic interests and more oriented toward advancing universal values such as respect for human rights; self-determination and autonomy; social, political, and economic justice; and multilateral rather than unilateral solutions to international problems (Cingranelli, 1993, 7–8). These patterns were contrary to widespread perceptions of the U.S. aid program, which continued to anticipate the dominance of Cold War motivations.

There were, of course, notable exceptions to this general trend. U.S. policy toward Nicaragua and El Salvador during the 1980s serves as a prominent example, but it is a mistake to judge the U.S. foreign-aid effort in Latin America on the basis of a few well-publicized cases in which geostrategic interests trumped more progressive foreign-policy goals. Even when we shift our focus to more routine foreign-aid decisions by U.S. policymakers, the evidence is not monolithic in support of the progressive trend hypothesis. Some evidence clearly contradicts it; some evidence is unclear; and some definitely supports it.

Given the continuing needs of strategically important recipients in the Middle East, South and East Asia, and Eastern Europe, we expect the percentage of U.S. GNP devoted to foreign aid to increase gradually by the year 2000 and remain stable. The increased size of the foreign-aid program will accommodate new recipients and respond to worsening transnational problems. But the share of the U.S. foreign-aid program devoted to Latin America, and the total volume of aid provided to the region, is likely to decline from its levels in the mid-1990s.

During the Cold War, Latin American states received more aid when the former Soviet Union's influence in the region was perceived to be expanding. Seventy percent of all U.S. aid to Latin America over the period 1946–1992 was delivered between the 1960s and the 1980s (Pastor, 1992: 179). In the 1960s the perceived Soviet proxy was Cuba; in the 1980s the proxies for the Soviet Union were the Sandinistas in Nicaragua and Marxist rebels in El Salvador. Superpower competition stimulated U.S. foreign-aid spending in the past but is unlikely to do so again unless renewed rivalry of some kind develops in the region.

In this sense the reductions in U.S. aid to Latin America in the post–Cold War period should not be surprising. But the shrinking role of the United States as a foreign-aid provider in Latin America reflects other factors, including the relative decline of the United States in the world economy. As will be discussed, however, other donors are filling the gaps in the global flow of foreign aid to Latin America.

The United States has been less willing in the 1980s and 1990s to use its tax dollars to help developing countries but more willing to use the private sector to stimulate economic development in the Latin American region. The Reagan administration in 1982 proposed a package of trade concessions and investment incentives under the Caribbean Basin Initiative (CBI). The trade-concessions portion of the CBI proposal was passed in a weakened form by Congress, however, because opponents complained that the bill would take jobs away from U.S. citizens. In 1993 the Clinton administration led the successful fight for passage of the North American Free Trade Agreement (NAFTA), establishing a regional trading bloc among the United States, Canada, and Mexico. If NAFTA works as the United States hopes, other Latin American states gradually will be incorporated, and the entire region may attract the vast sums of private investment that are now flowing primarily to East Asia.

This process of inclusion will likely begin with the stronger Latin American economies, such as Argentina and Brazil, and eventually will incorporate the whole region; the Chilean government already has been provisionally accepted into NAFTA. Critics of this policy believe it is regressive because it will enable U.S.-based corporations to exploit the poorest people in Latin America. Defenders predict free trade will lead to higher wages in developing countries. In any event, the passage of NAFTA and other forms of economic integration presages a continuing role by the United States in promoting Latin American economic development.

As a foreign-policy goal, advancing human rights has received greater recognition in U.S. foreign-policy rhetoric since the mid-1970s. This change in U.S. policy has stimulated extensive research on the relationship between the human-rights practices of Latin American governments and the amount of U.S. bilateral assistance each has received (e.g., Poe and Tate, 1994). Although analyses of this relationship have led to mixed conclusions, it is clear that U.S. foreign aid to several Latin American countries has been suspended because their governments were believed systematically to violate the human rights of their citizens. The most recent cases were the suspensions of aid to Haiti in 1991 for not allowing President-elect Jean-Bertrand Aristide to take power after he had won a fair election in 1990 and to Peru in 1991 after its president suspended democratic practices to combat the insurgent group Shining Path. Indeed, U.S. human-rights laws governing the disbursement of foreign aid have been invoked more often in Latin America than in any other region of the world.

U.S. human-rights legislation in the 1970s also marked the beginning of a widespread practice by which donors conditioned developmental assistance on the human-rights record of recipient governments. All major donors with lending programs in Latin America have declared acceptable human-rights performance a major precondition of concessional funding. Although other performance criteria vary from donor to donor, most bilateral and multilateral aid programs use development aid as an incentive to promote good governance in developing countries (see Chapter 1).

This practice has not escaped criticism, however. Some consider such conditions an intrusion into the domestic affairs of recipient states. But clearly the use of foreign aid to promote better human-rights practices is morally justified and in many cases long overdue. Because it is no longer necessary to prop up unsavory regimes in Latin America for Cold War reasons, there will be fewer constraints on tying foreign aid to good governance.

The danger is that performance criteria for receiving development aid will rapidly proliferate and become more complex and contradictory. Respect for human rights now represents one of many goals, alongside fiscal restraint, environmental protection, and social equality. The rise of such conditions has caused confusion and resentment within recipient states in other regions, particularly the Central and Eastern European countries and the newly independent states of the former Soviet Union (CEEC/NIS).[3] As an example of this diffusion of aid conditionalities, the Clinton administration's foreign-aid proposal submitted to Congress in September 1993 established five goals: protecting the environment, managing population growth, dealing with the plight of refugees, promoting economic development, and promoting democracy. Converting these principles into practice has become a formidable task for an administration whose aid program is under constant assault, both from the U.S. Congress and a wary public.

More than thirty years earlier, John F. Kennedy's short-lived Alliance for Progress was launched to help the neediest countries and poorest people in Latin America. Acknowledging the extraordinary responsibility of the United States for economic and social conditions in Latin America, Kennedy proclaimed: "To our sister republics south of our border, we offer a special pledge to convert our good words into good deeds, in a new alliance for progress, to assist free men and free governments in casting off the chains of poverty."

These words were clear, but the actions of the Kennedy administration and its successors were more ambiguous. Lumsdaine (1993: 91–93), for example, found no statistical relationship between the level of U.S. economic assistance provided and the poverty of the recipient. When he disaggregated U.S. economic assistance into "security-supporting assistance" (given only to military allies) and development aid based on human needs, however, he found that the latter was highly correlated with recipient poverty, a finding clearly applicable to Latin America.

In these respects there is substantial reason to question the progressive-trend hypothesis. There is less foreign aid being provided on an aggregate basis. Improving human rights may be a symbolic but not a real goal of U.S. policy in many cases. Conditioning aid on good governance by recipients may constitute an intrusive practice, and, depending on what data are examined, foreign aid may or may not be targeted to the neediest recipients.

But there also are clear signs of increasing progressiveness in other aspects of the U.S. aid program. There is greater willingness to give economic aid instead of military aid. In the early years of the Cold War (1946–1952) the United States transferred about 20 percent of its bilateral aid to Latin America in the form of military support. In the aftermath of the Korean War the military proportion rose gradually—especially under the Reagan administration—but since the Cold War's conclusion it has fallen to less than 5 percent. In absolute terms, U.S. military-aid flows to the region, which amounted to $237 million in 1991, fell to $124 million in 1992, to $74 million in 1993, and to just $17 million in 1994, a reflection of more widespread reductions in U.S. military assistance during the post–Cold War period (USAID, 1996a: 83).

Most of the remaining flows ($50 million in 1993) were directed to two recipients—Bolivia and Colombia—to support their campaign against drug traffickers, a far cry from the days when U.S. arms were shipped in massive volumes to military dictators on dubious Cold War grounds. But, as noted above, support even for this policy has waned in the mid-1990s. Congress now requires that for a country with a large drug trade to receive military assistance, the president must certify that the country is making progress in fighting drug trafficking.[4]

In still other qualitative respects the U.S. record has been encouraging in the wake of the Cold War. There is decreasing insistence that the giving of U.S. foreign aid dollars be tied to the purchase of goods and services from the United States. The percentage of U.S. foreign aid that is fully tied has declined since the mid-1960s from around 90 percent to about 37 percent. For all members of the OECD's Development Assistance Committee, the percentage has declined from 67 percent to 31 percent (Lumsdaine, 1993, 263). Thus, recipients have greater autonomy and can spend limited ODA more efficiently.

The United States also has been willing to make way for other donors (particularly Japan) to provide bilateral grants rather than loans and to channel more economic aid through multilateral channels. A key shift in the U.S. program welcomed by Latin American leaders is the gradual shift away from loans to grants. Because funds given as grants do not require repayment, they do not add to the debt problems many Latin American states already face. After climbing steadily for thirty years after the signing of the Foreign Assistance Act of 1961, bilateral loans as a percentage of total U.S. ODA to Latin America fell to less than 10 percent in the early 1990s. The grant element has increased in most aid packages offered to Latin American LDCs; this pattern held in fourteen of the eighteen cases over the fifteen-year period from 1976 to 1991. Grant aid increased from 27 percent to 100 percent in the case of Colombia; from 40 percent to 96 percent in the case of Brazil; and from 16 to 72 percent in that of Nicaragua. Of the four exceptions, three are among the richest Latin American nations (Argentina, Mexico, and Uruguay), and the fourth, Ecuador, is one of the region's largest oil producers. Thus, more grants have appropriately flowed to states that needed help the most.

We will describe the gradual shift from bilateral to multilateral aid and toward stronger aid roles for other donors in the next section of this chapter. Both these developments are progressive in the sense that they allow greater autonomy on the part of recipients. It is unlikely that the U.S. foreign aid program will ever become entirely multilateral, however, because the United States has many distinctive interests in Latin America that are best served through a bilateral relationship. But the trend in this category of aid quality is unmistakable.

In the face of widespread opposition to U.S. foreign aid to all regions, the Clinton administration has countered that the United States in the post–Cold War period has interests abroad that can best be served by the continued provision of foreign aid. The United States has an ongoing stake in the economic prosperity of other nations, especially in the geographically proximate region of Latin America. Economic problems in Mexico have a direct effect on the United States, as exemplified by the continued wave of illegal immigration from Mexico, caused mainly by a lack of economic opportunity in that country. Thus, eliminating foreign aid, or even restricting it, would limit the power of the president in this increasingly vital area of foreign economic policy.

As we have seen, qualitative improvements in U.S. aid to Latin America are evident and they should play a meaningful role in extending economic and political reforms. The overall U.S. aid program will likely increase to accommodate the former Soviet bloc, the Middle East peace process, and other ongoing priorities, but the net volumes allocated to Latin America will likely continue their decline. This trend will inevitably raise the profile of other major donors to the region, a subject to which we now turn.

OTHER MAJOR AID DONORS TO LATIN AMERICA

In 1976 the United States was among the top two bilateral donors to fifteen of the seventeen Latin American recipients. By the mid-1990s it has lost this distinction in many cases. Japan, France, Germany, the Netherlands, and

Spain, among other donors, have become primary donors to at least one Latin American LDC, complicating the aid picture considerably. Major increases in contributions to Latin America as a percentage of total ODA flows were reported in 1994 by the governments of Belgium, Denmark, Italy, the Netherlands, Norway, and Sweden (OECD, 1996a: A68).

The Japanese government has played a key role in this diversification of ODA sources, increasing its disbursements to Latin America to more than $1 billion in 1994. Of all Japanese ODA, the share designated for Latin America grew from 7.8 percent in 1983–1984 to 9.3 percent a decade later (OECD, 1996a: A68). In 1994 Tokyo approved large-scale bilateral ODA packages to Brazil ($389 million), Peru ($177 million), Paraguay ($176 million), El Salvador ($124 million), the Dominican Republic ($120 million), Honduras ($90 million), and Nicaragua ($83 million).

As during the heyday of U.S. aid to Latin America, however, the rise of Japanese aid remains laced with a heavy element of donor self-interest. Japan has a continuing need for lumber, so it is no coincidence that many of these countries contain large areas of rain forest. This evidence of economic self-interest is supported by recent statistical analyses showing that the Japanese aid program has long been motivated by economic factors (Hook, 1995). The disproportionate share of this aid committed to Central America, however, may indicate an additional objective—filling the vacuum created by U.S. ODA cutbacks to a region once considered critical to its Cold War strategy.

The French government has long maintained active aid relationships with its overseas possessions in the Caribbean. On the continent, France emerged in the early 1990s as the primary aid donor to Colombia, Ecuador, and Mexico and the secondary donor to Haiti. In 1994 its aid to Latin America was more limited and lower as a proportion of total aid than in 1984, but major bilateral aid packages were approved for Chile ($88 million) and Mexico ($76 million).

The decline of Germany as a major donor to Latin America in the 1980s and 1990s is more surprising. In 1976 Germany was among the top two donors to twelve Latin American LDCs, but in 1991 that number fell to six. This decline in Germany's role as a development partner in Latin America is due to strategic readjustments stemming from the Federal Republic's reunification with the former East Germany. Given Germany's proximity to and attendant responsibilities in Eastern Europe and Russia, to which it has become the preeminent donor of economic assistance, its reduced ODA role in Latin America may be long-lasting.

Another major change in the matrix of aid to Latin America in the 1980s and 1990s is the increased role of international financial institutions as conduits of concessional financing.[5] Multilateral aid has increased as a percentage of total aid to most recipients in the region, and it has entailed an ever-expanding list of conditionalities, which have drawn fire from development analysts.[6] Structural-adjustment requirements of the IMF and the World Bank are illustrative of the interests of multilateral lenders. Unless the creditworthiness of the recipient is clearly established, the World Bank insists upon reduced trade barriers, greater reliance on market forces (requiring an end to price controls and subsidies to economic sectors), reduced public expenditures and public-sector employment, increased accountability, a framework of law to guide public and private action, and information and transparency in policymaking (Moore and Robinson, 1994).

These standards have been resented within many LDCs because, in the short run, decreases in public-sector expenditures and employment may cause hardships for the poorest people in the debtor state. However, when aid is channeled through multilateral agencies, direct self-interests are much harder to advance by individual states. In order for donor interest to play a part, the donor must have control over where and for what the aid is being given; by funneling aid through multilateral sources, individual donors relinquish some control over the destination of and the strings attached to foreign aid (see Chapter 2). So the channeling of a relatively large amount of aid through multilateral financial institutions is evidence of a decline in direct donor self-interest as a determinant of aid flows.

FOREIGN AID AND LATIN AMERICAN DEBT

Among the world's developing countries, those in Latin America were among the primary victims of the debt crisis that occurred in the 1980s. The effects of this crisis were still being felt in the mid-1990s, when the total external debts of Brazil ($133 billion) and Mexico ($118 billion) remained the largest in the developing world (World Bank, 1995a: 200).[7] A thorough examination of the Latin American debt crisis is beyond the scope of this chapter, but a brief overview of how the states of the region came to their present position is necessary before we assess their future prospects.

The decade following the initiation of President Kennedy's Alliance for Progress in 1961 was one of unprecedented economic growth across Latin America (Todaro, 1989). However, large amounts of goods, including oil, were imported to fuel this growth. The first oil shock (1973–1974) and the concomitant world recession abruptly stunted the region's economic growth. In the face of declining revenues and increasing expenses, many Latin America states tried to maintain their high growth rates through borrowing. Official sources such as the IMF and World Bank were shunned in favor of private loans on commercial terms. These loans were considered more attractive, although the interest rates were much higher, because they lacked the many strings attached to concessional loans and bilateral grants. Further, the coffers of private lending institutions, mainly U.S.-based transnational banks, were glutted with OPEC petrodollars, so they were more than eager to lend money to the region.

The second oil shock, in 1979, coupled with stagnant commodity prices and the demise of import-substitution strategies, further stifled Latin American growth and left the region with huge debts on which the interest often could not even be paid. The result was a massive debt crisis—most acutely felt in Argentina, Brazil, and Mexico—that persists into the 1990s. Since the mid-1980s the United States, the World Bank and the IMF have worked with commercial lenders to help these indebted states meet their obligations without imperiling their prospects for economic growth. These strategies, manifested in the Baker and Brady plans, combined outright forgiveness of much of this outstanding debt with structural-adjustment demands for future support.

The pattern of Latin American aid flows in the mid-1990s suggests that foreign indebtedness remains a major determinant. However, this pattern calls into question the sincerity of the motives behind the aid programs to these highly indebted countries. With debt so high, the aid received has been barely sufficient to meet interest-payment obligations. Thus, rather than promoting economic growth and social reforms, foreign aid merely prevents the aid recipients from falling into economic chaos. Meanwhile, other LDCs in the region, many of which suffer from poor living standards but have not accumulated massive debts, have been neglected.

The modest ODA disbursements to Mexico and Brazil (relative to their large populations) illustrate the process of graduation from concessional aid to commercial funding outlined in Chapter 2 of this volume. Although both countries have high national debts, both also have relatively prosperous economies that have attracted large-scale infusions of private capital. The amount of ODA each receives equals less than 1 percent of GNP. As the Mexican and Brazilian economies have become stronger, more industrialized, and more integrated into the international economic system, both have been weaned from a reliance on U.S. aid. As the economies of other Latin American countries develop in similar fashion, we expect a similar reduction in the relative amount of ODA, a greater reliance on loans instead of grants, and a lowered reliance on U.S. aid.

Of course, integration in the international economic system makes any state more vulnerable to economic shocks such as inflation, high interest rates, or sharp fluctuations in commodity prices. For those Latin American states with large continuing debts, a worldwide recession in the late 1990s would be catastrophic, because they still must pay the large interest payments on their debts. Thus, no amount of ODA will result in economic development if the debt problem is not seriously addressed. Unfortunately, cutbacks in many bilateral aid programs and new demands from Eastern Europe and the Middle East will likely drain development resources that could be used to sustain Latin America's economic recovery.

CONCLUSION

As the cross-national patterns suggest, foreign aid to Latin America has been at one level guided by recipient needs, including their level of indebtedness, and at another level driven by donor interests. Both forces are at work, as they are in aid flows to other regions, as reviewed in previous chapters. The uneasy coexistence of recipient need and donor interests has always been a central aspect of the foreign-aid regime, and Latin America has been no exception to this rule.

Nonetheless, our examination of the foreign aid regime in Latin America has revealed evidence of a progressive trend, one that stresses the achievement of universal values and principles over the national self-interests of donors. This trend is by no means unidimensional, as donor interests continue to coincide with more progressive aid policies. From the patterns we described, however, we are able to advance some predictions about the distribution of development assistance to Latin American countries in the future.

We expect that the net volumes of development aid provided to Latin America from all sources will decline moderately as donors respond to new demands from the CEEC/NIS region and to growing domestic priorities and as many Latin American LDCs graduate to less concessional sources of capital. For those aid programs that continue at comparable levels, there likely will be increased emphasis on market-friendly means to economic growth rather than the nationalistic practices of the 1970s and 1980s, when Latin America served as the centerpiece of the new international economic order. Demands by donors for structural adjustment and good governance on the part of recipients will become even more insistent, and prospective recipients who ignore those demands will see their aid levels further reduced.

Amid these quantitative shifts, the quality of aid to Latin American will likely continue to improve as the millennium approaches. There will be increased emphasis on recipient need as a determinant of the level of ODA provided, although need may be narrowly defined on the basis of recipient indebtedness. Less aid will be explicitly tied to donor goods and services, and military aid as a proportion of total aid, already declining, will fall further. (It is hoped that lowered military aid will mean lower arms sales to the region, an issue raised in Chapter 3 of this volume.) Of the volumes of bilateral aid transferred to LDCs in the region, a higher proportion will be provided in the form of grants rather than loans, and a higher proportion will flow through multilateral channels.

As some states in Latin America achieve sustained economic growth and reach the status of newly industrialized countries, they may actually be transformed into net *donors* of ODA, as have many countries in East Asia. South Korea, for example, was scheduled to join the OECD in 1996. Finally, as the process of regional economic integration expands, aid flows will be increasingly supplemented by private investment and domestic and intraregional commerce. As we have seen in other developing regions, however, the linkage of aid flows with investments, multinational corporate expansions, and commercial lending to firms has been concentrated among the relatively prosperous Latin American LDCs, widening the already gaping intraregional cleavages between rich and poor.

The 1994 U.S. intervention in Haiti, designed to return a democratically elected regime to power, contrasted fundamentally with those that occurred all too frequently during the Cold War, and the subsequent UN-supervised peacekeeping mission on the island has served as a second departure from the historic pattern. Democratic elections in early 1996 were supervised and accredited by international observers, raising expectations that foreign powers and international organizations may play a more generalized, constructive role in Latin America in the future. The rapid democratization of this region in the post–Cold War is surely a most progressive trend, one conducive to an emerging period of pacific relations in the next millennium if the theories of "democratic peace" hold true (see Russett, 1994).

Profound systemic changes in world politics since the Cold War's conclusion have obscured many extraordinary developments in foreign aid. In Nicaragua, for example, for much of the 1980s the U.S. government overtly and covertly supported the anti-Sandinista contras, many of whom were based in U.S. military installations in Honduras. In the 1990s the United States has committed nearly $1 billion to the democratic government of Violeta Chamorro, which defeated the Sandinista regime in free elections. Large volumes of U.S. ODA are intended to rebuild the war-torn country and lead to economic progress, presumably reducing the potential appeal of the Sandinista Party, which continues to have widespread support. In El Salvador, the persistence of radical opposition groups has driven U.S. aid well past the Cold War. Elections held in March 1994 and reconciliation between the government and the opposition were thus critical to its future prospects as a foreign-aid recipient.

Taken together, these trends demonstrate that the foreign-aid regime in Latin America has become more progressive over time. What is startling, in our view, is that this trend began during the latter stages of the Cold War, an era when realpolitik took precedence in the foreign policies of donor states.

In the post–Cold War era, when more LDCs in Latin America have become democratic than ever before and when donor states have begun to address the mounting environmental challenges in the region, there is every reason to believe this trend will continue.

NOTES

1. Many of these provisions have already been accepted and are annually documented by the OECD (1979–1996a).

2. Recipients in the Near East accepted $112 billion in U.S. assistance during the thirty-one-year period, including $56 billion for Israel and $37 billion for Egypt, both of which received more bilateral U.S. aid than all of Latin America. Asian states received an additional $79 billion in U.S. aid during the period, also greater than Latin America's share (USAID, 1994a: 7, 117).

3. See Chapter 9 for a discussion of this problem in Eastern Europe and Chapter 10 for a similar review of the problem in South Asia.

4. Because a large proportion of military aid is used to purchase military hardware, the reduction in military assistance from the United States may lead to reduced arms sales in the region. See Chapter 3 for an elaboration of this point and others relating to the worldwide flow of U.S. weaponry both on concessional and market terms.

5. In those cases where multilateral aid did not increase, there were serious domestic problems, such as civil war in Nicaragua and El Salvador, domestic unrest in Bolivia, and military intervention by the United States in Panama.

6. Hayter (1985), for example, argued that the conditions imposed by many multilateral donor institutions are designed to serve the interests of the advanced capitalist states that donate to and manage these institutions. Thus, in her view, the switch from bilateral to multilateral aid is not evidence of progressivity in the foreign-aid regime.

7. Other major debtors included India ($92 billion), Indonesia ($90 billion), China ($84 billion), and Russia ($83 billion).

Part 4

Conclusion

14

Foreign Aid and the
Illogic of Collective Action

Steven W. Hook

According to a well-known African aphorism, "When elephants fight, the grass suffers." These words were often used to describe the Cold War's pernicious effects on LDCs in Africa, Latin America, and South Asia, many of which served as surrogate battlegrounds during the nearly half century of superpower competition.

In the late 1990s, a corollary has gained widespread currency: "When elephants make love, the grass suffers equally."

Such is the ironic fate of many impoverished states that escaped from the shadow of the United States and Soviet Union only to find themselves as financially distressed as ever in the mid-1990s. Ambitious plans to implement the UN's program for sustainable development have been scaled back in the face of cutbacks in many aid budgets. The bulk of remaining aid flows has been concentrated among strategic allies of the United States, trading partners of Japan, former colonies of France and Great Britain, heavily indebted middle-income countries, and transition states in the former Soviet bloc. For the inhabitants of the world's poorest areas, still suffering from acute malnutrition, overcrowding, and political repression, hegemonic meddling by the major powers has been replaced in many instances by indifference and neglect.

The crest in worldwide aid flows took many by surprise, as the euphoria surrounding the Cold War's demise gave way to a new era of fiscal austerity and economic competition in the industrialized world. Without influential domestic constituencies to promote aid on a humanitarian basis, and in the absence of the geopolitical rationales that had driven U.S. and Soviet aid flows for decades, many long-standing aid programs were reduced or eliminated outright. Those that survived were often those that most benefited the donor countries—either directly, through the tying of aid funds to domestic purchases, or indirectly, through the securing of export markets, sources of raw materials, or destinations for overseas investments. As they became more selective in their aid relationships, donors imposed increasingly stringent conditions upon recipients regarding their use of the aid funds.

The contributors to this volume have examined the many pieces of the foreign-aid puzzle and have shed new light on the trends in aid flows between the Cold War and the new millennium. They have described these trends in the context of the volatile and rapidly changing international climate of the 1990s, which has witnessed tenuous political and economic transitions in Eastern Europe, the resurgence of many regional conflicts, tightening economic integration, and a wave of democratization that has swept across much of the developing world. Military assistance has given way to development aid in the post–Cold War era, although arms transfers on market terms have accelerated in many conflict-prone regions. Thus, the emphasis of this anthology has been on the shifting logic of development-aid programs and their application to the broader policy goals of both rich and poor states.

Along the way, these contributors have illuminated the many ways in which developmental problems and solutions are unique to each areas of study. This was the intended purpose of their collective effort—to move beyond a generalized treatment of international development and to examine its complexities in a wide variety of discrete functional and regional contexts.

Yet readers of this volume may have noticed commonalities across the chapters, both in terms of the problems facing aid donors and recipients and in the solutions embraced to resolve them. Thus, without minimizing the distinctive aspects of the individual contributions, we may profitably explore some consistent themes and lessons.

TWO-LEVEL GAMES IN DONOR STATES

Among the recurring themes found in Part 2 of this volume is the coexistence of both domestic and systemic pressures that pulled policymakers and aid administrators in often contradictory directions during the post–Cold War period. To Putnam (1988), such "two-level games" often constrain the ability of policymakers to pursue optimal solutions based upon objective evaluations of existing problems and goals.

In the case of foreign aid, our contributors observed a pattern by which both donor and recipient governments, having enunciated clear policy goals, were constrained by multiple and frequently competing domestic actors. These included heads of state, legislative bodies, aid bureaucracies, foreign ministries, nongovernmental organizations, and elites from the business sector, who exerted greater leverage in an era of geoeconomics. The foreign-aid regime became more diffused, involving the OECD, IMF, World Bank, United Nations, European Union, and a network of regional development banks, each of which brought discrete institutional biases to the table. As a result, the proclaimed ends and the executed means of foreign aid were increasingly disconnected, resulting in compromises that undercut the efficacy of aid strategies.

Like other aspects of U.S. foreign relations, U.S. policy toward the Third World has lacked a common orienting principle in the post–Cold War era, shifting spasmodically across regions and issue areas in an ad hoc manner (see Spanier and Hook, 1995). President Clinton's initial embrace of UN-sponsored sustainable-development efforts was almost entirely suspended after the 1994 congressional elections, and U.S. support for multilateral development efforts decreased considerably in their aftermath. The new Republican majority in Congress opted instead for unilateral solutions, symbolized in 1995 by a $262 billion defense budget for fiscal year 1996 that was $12 billion *more* than the Pentagon requested. And a presidential campaign that dominated national attention was largely silent on foreign policy.

More generally, the executive-legislative impasse within the U.S. government, which forced the repeated closing of the federal government in 1995, prevented a redefinition of U.S. "grand strategy" in the post–Cold War era. Given his domestic preoccupations, Clinton largely abandoned his earlier attempt to redefine U.S. policy based upon the enlargement of democratic rule. As a result, many aspects of U.S. foreign policy—including foreign aid—were placed on automatic pilot, with little innovation or central coordination. The United States, though the world's wealthiest and most powerful state by virtually any measure, was unable to exploit its advantages and to lead the effort to address global problems in the wake of the Cold War. Secretary of State Warren Christopher's April 1996 proclamation that the global environment had become a vital ingredient of U.S. national security consequently fell on deaf ears, overshadowed by presidential politics.

During the early 1990s the Japanese government faced its own protracted internal crisis, which overshadowed its expanding involvement in international development efforts. This political and economic crisis left Japan's inefficient system of disbursing economic aid largely intact. As a result, Japan continued to lag behind other major donors in closely watched qualitative aspects of foreign aid, as proclaimed reforms were undercut by domestic infighting. More broadly, Japan's domestic difficulties hindered its ability to exploit its stature as an economic superpower and to play a stronger role in the United Nations and other multilateral fora.

As described in Chapter 6, Western European donors fell victim to the cross-pressures of national and transnational concerns. As the Cold War receded into history, a wide range of domestic priorities emerged, and these in turn elicited a revival of ethnic and nationalist tensions. The European Union expanded its membership and pursued a Common Foreign and Security Policy as part of the 1992 Maastricht Treaty but persistent strains at the state level limited the prospects for collaboration in important policy areas. And the EU's failure to take concerted or coherent action in response to the spreading Balkan crisis revealed fundamental shortcomings in its plan for foreign-policy integration. Nordic donors, meanwhile, abandoned their recipient-oriented approach to international development in the name of both domestic austerity and regional coalescence with the EU.

Meanwhile, OPEC was never able to reconcile the clashing interests of its member states with the proclaimed collective objectives of the cartel. Within these states a small number of political elites embarked upon lavish domestic projects in the name of modernization, but by the mid-1990s the living conditions in most OPEC nations had improved only marginally from their levels of the early 1970s, when OPEC exploded onto the international scene. The tangible contributions of OPEC donors to international development fell below expectations from the outset, and the prolonged slump in oil prices eliminated their prospects to play a meaningful role in North-South relations.

Domestic politics also plays a critical role within recipient governments, of course, as many chapters of this volume have illustrated. Converting aid into effective development relies on credible administration within LDCs along with adequate means to implement aid-funded programs. Frequently during the Cold War, however, neither condition pertained; the mere presence of bilateral aid from either of the great powers was seen as sufficient to serve its geopolitical, ideological, or neocolonial interests within recipient states. Thus aid was often transferred to autocratic LDCs whose leaders exploited the funds for personal gain or used them for cosmetic projects that did little to alleviate poverty or stimulate long-term development. By contrast, in the less ideologically charged climate of the post–Cold War period, with democratic governments established in a growing number of LDCs, conditions are more favorable for the effective implementation of development projects funded through foreign aid.

Taken together, these essays illustrate the precarious role of foreign aid as an instrument of statecraft, which to some degree is understandable given the relative youth of the global aid regime. Most bilateral aid programs will be less than forty years old at the turn of the century, and the organized and well-documented aid behavior of OECD states is a product of the 1970s. The cross-national malaise may also be understandable given the habitually slow adaptation of national governments to fundamental systemic changes. Foreign-aid donors initiated most aid programs in the context of the superpower rivalry and in the midst of a decolonization process that tripled the number of nation-states and introduced the pernicious term "Third World." Many recipients, meanwhile, became accustomed to annual infusions of concessional funding from several sources and were not prepared when the rationales for them came under scrutiny after the Cold War.

Industrialized states outside of Japan, so long accustomed to utilizing foreign aid to pursue narrow Cold War goals or to sustain postcolonial ties, have only in the 1990s turned to transnational concerns of sustainable development. Although their leaders were loath to admit it, these donor governments faced a continuing uphill battle to claim legitimacy for large-scale aid efforts only indirectly and ephemerally connected to their perceived national interests. The problems outlined in the Earth Summit's concluding manifesto, *Agenda 21*, were unarguably salient at the global level but difficult to prioritize domestically in the context of more tangible and short-term concerns. Given that all twenty-one members of the OECD's Development Assistance Committee were representative democracies with multiple channels of access, the subordination of abstract transnational initiatives to diffused subnational priorities was a logical outcome. In this respect the level of support for sustainable development that remained after strategic allies, trading partners, domestic interest groups, and debt-ridden NICs were accommodated is somewhat surprising.

Members of the OECD (1995a: 73) remained optimistic that the leveling off of aid flows recorded in the early and mid-1990s was "a bout of weakness, rather than an incipient collapse." Most donors and international development agencies were encouraged by the proliferation of private financial flows to LDCs, even though such flows were largely restricted to states already liberated from the most desperate living conditions. Future prospects for aid depended upon the performance of the remaining recipients in utilizing the more limited funds they received. But, as always, their performance was dependent upon wealthy states' political and economic conditions and their willingness to expend their public resources in the form of foreign aid.

The development-aid regime appears to have attained a sufficiently broad base within the international political economy to withstand this period of uncertainty. Leaders of industrialized countries have found common cause with the OECD, IMF, and other multilateral conduits of aid and have clearly recognized the growing dangers of rapid population growth in LDCs, mounting foreign debt, the exhaustion of finite natural resources, and the unrest and regional conflict that so often springs from socioeconomic distress. Of greater relevance for the longevity of the aid regime, developed nations have apprehended the benefits they can realize when LDCs become viable actors in the global economy. All of these motivations have assured the extension of foreign aid well into the new millennium, although coherent collective action to preserve the global commons is still a long way off.

PROSPECTS FOR AID RECIPIENTS

The contributors to Part 3 of this volume considered the experience of aid recipients, and their essays demonstrated the variability of foreign aid processes and outcomes across regional boundaries. Recipients of foreign aid must frequently align their political, economic, and security interests with those of wealthy aid donors, a practice that preceded the Cold War and will remain a mainstay of the aid regime far into the future. Thus, aid-recipient behavior must be viewed, in part, as refracting the policy preferences of donor governments and multilateral development agencies.

For many LDCs struggling in the wake of the Cold War, the conditionalities of development aid effectively structure their government and business sectors. Standards of good governance must be met through tangible expenditures on police, court, and electoral systems; recipient transparency requires the presence of a sizable and professionally trained civil service; and liberal macroeconomic policies reward and encourage private investors, often from overseas, along with a commercial class that transforms indigenous cultures and mores. In the past, these same LDCs had to pass ideological litmus tests to receive foreign aid. The substantive contours of aid conditionalities have changed in the post–Cold War period. But the aid relationship's basic asymmetry, which transcends temporal and spatial boundaries and reflects more basic material inequalities, is the central reality for the developing states reviewed in this volume.

Recipients in Eastern Europe have utilized massive infusions of Western aid largely for purposes of reindustrialization—to rebuild factories, electrical utilities, communication networks, and other infrastructure that had become decrepit under Soviet control. Private investments were not far behind in Poland, Hungary, and the Czech Republic, and these nations' progress toward integrating with the world economy has been considerable. By contrast, leaders in Bulgaria, Romania, Slovakia, and other transition states have had a difficult time attracting both public and private capital, and across the former Soviet Union the obstacles to economic and political reform remain daunting. A massive $10 billion IMF loan to Boris Yeltsin's tottering regime in Moscow was seen as giving him a chance to stay in power and save his reform efforts from collapse.

In South Asia, home to the largest segment of the world's population and its largest networks of foreign aid, LDCs have fragmented along numerous regional, ethnic, religious, and economic fault lines. The Middle East remains a primary recipient of U.S. military and economic assistance; the Indian subcontinent attracts development aid from most major donors; and LDCs along the Pacific Rim have become accustomed to complementary aid and trade ties to Japan. Private investment, however, has been largely limited to East Asia, where Japan and the Asian Tigers have become role models of state-driven, export-led industrialization. Given the continuing strategic interests of major donors—quite apart from the degree of human need in South Asia—the concentration of global aid flows to this region is likely to continue.

The peoples of sub-Saharan Africa, the most distressed region of the developing world, face a much more uncertain future. Both the Cold War and decolonization rationales that once guided many bilateral aid programs have dissolved, and private investors have been conspicuously absent. Leaders in sub-Saharan Africa have watched as the United States has closed several missions, reduced funding levels, and redirected aid resources to Eastern Europe and the former Soviet Union. The Japanese government has failed to play a significant role in the region, further limiting the availability of development assistance. As we found, however, the traditional involvement of France and Great Britain—former colonial rulers in sub-Saharan Africa—and of Scandinavian donors has provided some relief. But in an era when public aid is increasingly predicated upon private investment with tangible short-term returns, sub-Saharan Africa will likely be further isolated within the international system in general and the developing world in particular.

In Latin America, living conditions have improved in many areas, and democratically elected governments have assumed power in virtually every state. But high levels of foreign debt continue to soak up foreign aid, removing capital from more productive uses that might improve living conditions in these largely impoverished states. As always, the foreign-policy priorities of the United States have dominated the process; most recently, the drug war rendered Bolivia its primary Latin American recipient in the early 1990s. The Japanese government has in some cases compensated for U.S. aid cutbacks across South America, where Tokyo has discovered fertile territory for corporate expansion and commercial lending. In general, the terms of aid transfers to Latin America have improved in the post–Cold War era, now that the era of the anticommunist dictator is behind us.

In general, we have witnessed a paradoxical pattern among recipients of foreign assistance in the post–Cold War period. Foreign aid has increasingly been directed toward more affluent LDCs and middle-income countries that already have established a record of economic growth, internal political stability, and pacific relations with their neighbors. On the one hand, this is an encouraging trend that promises to hasten the economic ascension of these middle-income states. On the other hand, in a stagnant or contracting global aid network, less support is available to those in greatest need. For these and other reasons, the economic polarization of the developing world is likely to widen, as is the gap between rich and poor, abetted both by the growing role of private capital transfers and by the tightening linkages between private capital and foreign aid. In the short and medium term this pattern likely will sustain the aid regime, which since its inception has been based upon the convergence of donor and recipient interests. In the long run, however, the worsening plight of marginalized societies will demand international attention. As their needs continue to be neglected because of the domestic constraints of donors and the new paradigm of development thought reviewed throughout this volume, the human costs of this neglect will escalate. This problem will only be resolved after the incentives for collaboration have improved or the costs of ignoring transnational problems have become prohibitive.

THE DEVELOPMENT PARADOX

Most foreign-aid programs today encourage recipients to build the foundations for market-driven, export-led industrial expansion. It is axiomatic that rapid industrialization and urbanization provide the best hope for curbing global population growth, which has emerged as the most urgent problem facing humankind. But what are the costs of this strategy?

The world's population, which reached 1 billion in 1800, doubled to 2 billion in just 125 years and to 4 billion by 1976. It is generally assumed that today's world population of 5.7 billion will reach 11 billion by 2100 before stabilizing at this level or turning downward (United Nations, 1990). Nearly all of this growth will occur in the developing world, more specifically in the most impoverished societies, where fertility rates are the highest. The population of Africa, for example, is expected to more than double from its current 650 million, reaching 1.6 billion by 2025, whereas the populations of the United States and Western Europe are expected to grow at a much smaller rate. As Kennedy (1993: 46) correctly observed, "The issue of global demographic imbalances between richer and poorer societies forms the backdrop to all the other important forces for change that are taking place."

The linkage between industrialization and improved living standards— higher life expectancies, personal incomes, and literacy rates—is also axiomatic. The causal chain then extends from economic structure to regime type, following Kantian and Schumpeterian assumptions about the democratic correlates of advanced industrial economies and their reliance upon stable, representative governments. Finally, the model holds that these societies will be necessarily pacific toward one another, induced to cooperation by mutual self-interest and pluralistic governments.

This is the basic logic of contemporary development thought, which has assumed widespread currency in the absence of the Cold War's geopolitical pressures and ideological polarization. Although fundamental differences

remain over the scope of state action in furthering economic growth and distributing resources to its citizens, this model pervades the development man-
ifestos of the United Nations, World Bank, IMF, and OECD, providing a
blueprint for developing countries hoping to attract concessional funding as
well as private investment.

This model, an outgrowth of demographic-transition theories that project a stabilizing world population in the mid-twenty-first century, is unarguably supported by empirical evidence, although birth and death rates have
varied widely even among states at similar levels of development (Kegley
and Wittkopf, 1995: 301–305). More fundamentally, it raises vexing environmental issues which have yet to be resolved. I shall refer to this as the
"development paradox."

The development paradox centers upon the ecological consequences of
rapid industrialization: accelerating habitat destruction, air and water pollution, and skyrocketing rates of consumption. It is inevitable that in the short
run greater ecological decay will be the correlate of accelerated industrialization. If megacities such as Mexico City, São Paulo, and Jakarta are repro-
duced throughout the developing world, their inhabitants will find the benefits of population control to be overshadowed by the costs of ecological
contamination. Further, the environmental damage they face will be felt far
beyond their borders.

The environmental maladies noted above, of course, all characterized
U.S. industrial expansion in the early decades of the twentieth century. With
just 4 percent of the world's population in the mid-1990s, the United States
accounted for approximately 25 percent of annual world oil consumption
(Wald, 1990). As other states experience their own industrial revolutions in
the next millennium, they likely will replicate the U.S. penchant for national consumption on a global scale.

The Chinese government announced in 1994 that among its major economic priorities in the second half of the decade would be the expansion of
the PRC's automotive industry. Not only would the PRC produce more vehicles for export, in keeping with the Japanese mold, but government plans
also called for developing the vast interior of China and extending a network
of modern highways across the country. As a result the PRC, whose densely crowded population of 1.2 billion has largely retained traditional modes
of transportation and agriculture to the benefit of the country's ecological
balance, will likely witness an ominous explosion of oil consumption and
emissions, accentuated by the planned expansion of coal-fired power plants.
Other heavily populated LDCs have announced similar plans for modernization and likely will repeat China's reliance on coal-burning electrical utilities.

One need not proclaim that the sky is falling to recognize the precarious
nature of the environment and to demonstrate how disruptive these key

demographic and ecological trends are for its ongoing stability. The human race has shown an impressive ability both to overwhelm its natural environment and to adapt to the fundamental changes in economic conditions, societal customs, and modes of governance that ensue.

The central question is not so much when the world's population will peak but how the corresponding increases of fuel consumption, habitat and wildlife destruction, and air and water pollution can be held in check. For development to be truly sustainable, it must not only utilize privatization and good governance—both of which are essential components—but also make provision for limiting toxic industrial emissions, preserving sufficient natural habitat, building adequate water-treatment facilities, and requiring the use of fuel-efficient vehicles.

A related development paradox, unfortunately, calls this effort into question. Simply put, environmental restraint violates the logic of collective action (Olson, 1971). Political and economic leaders today face neither incentives nor the penalties sufficient to prevent them from ignoring those aspects of sustainable development whose short-term costs outweigh their potential long-term benefits. Immediate concerns (such as preventing the demise of reform in Russia) do indeed warrant the attention they have received, but as a result less pressing but equally vital concerns go unaddressed.

The demise of most military-aid programs is one of the most welcome developments of the post–Cold War era, although continued large-scale transfers of weaponry on market terms are just as problematic as concessional military aid. It will be a colossal folly if the demise of the Soviet arms industry and the post–Cold War relaxation of global tensions does not lead to demilitarization in many poor regions and a tragedy if LDCs are compelled to follow the U.S. lead and consider military exports a viable source of national income. But that is the probable outcome of current trends, and a natural consequence of free riding by the world's most affluent states.

The growing amalgamation of foreign aid and private investment has lessened the influence of the UN and, to a lesser extent, the OECD in many development debates and expanded that of the World Bank, IMF, and regional development banks. Though they rhetorically embrace the UN's call for sustainable development, the latter agents of foreign aid have been more preoccupied with global economic emergencies such as the Mexican peso crisis and the precarious reform effort in Russia. Such cases have demonstrated both the fragility of the global economy and the potential for isolated economic crises to overwhelm concessional funding sources. In an era of belt-tightening within many governments and of backlash against foreign aid, they have magnified the diversion of aid from long-term ecological priorities to short-term economic ones. This may ultimately represent the least "sustainable" aspect of the contemporary foreign-aid regime.

Despite these obstacles and the growing deficiencies of many aid policies, development assistance will continue to play a crucial role in the international political economy, as demonstrated by the numerous and diverse
ways in which it has been applied to global relations since World War II. It
has served as a most malleable policy instrument—in the sheer quantity of
aid, the selection of aid recipients, the functions of aid-funded projects, and
the terms upon which grants and concessional loans are disbursed. As noted
throughout this volume, foreign aid has contributed greatly to the improvement of living conditions in many distressed parts of the world; there are
many success stories of international development. In the 1980s and 1990s
aid programs have paid for many of the crucial costs of democratization—
supervising and certifying elections, creating effective and just police
forces, and establishing court systems that consistently enforce constitutional protections. The failure of UN-sponsored peacekeeping missions in
Somalia and Bosnia, furthermore, must not obscure successful efforts in
Southeast Asia, Central America, and southwest Africa.

For all of these reasons, foreign aid remains a vital issue in world politics at the end of the second millennium. It has proven itself to be a force for
constructive change, even while serving as an agent for the perceived self-
interests of wealthy states. As the contributors to this volume have argued,
the central and intractable tension between these two opposing forces will
likely shape international development long into the future.

Acronyms

ADB	Asian Development Bank
ALAMED	Asia, Latin America, and Mediterranean agreements
BITS	Swedish Agency for International Technical and Economic Cooperation
CADU	Chilalo Agricultural Development Unit
CATT	Conventional Arms Transfer Talks
CBI	Caribbean Basin Initiative
CDB	Caribbean Development Bank
CEEC	Central and Eastern European countries
CFA	Communauté Financière Africaine
CFE	Conventional Forces in Europe
CFF	Compensatory Financing Facility
CFSP	Common Foreign and Security Policy
CIS	Commonwealth of Independent States
CSCE	Conference on Security Cooperation in Europe
DAC	Development Assistance Committee
DANIDA	Danish International Development Agency
EBRD	European Bank for Reconstruction and Development
EC	European Community
EDF	European Development Fund
EEC	European Economic Community
ESF	economic support funds
EU	European Union
FINNIDA	Finnish International Development Agency
G-24	Group of 24
G-77	Group of 77
GATT	General Agreement on Tariffs and Trade
GDR	German Democratic Republic
GSP	General System of Preferences
IBRD	International Bank for Reconstruction and Development
IDA	International Development Association
IDB	Inter-American Development Bank
IFC	International Finance Corporation

IMET	International Military Education and Training
IMF	International Monetary Fund
JICA	Japan International Cooperation Agency
LDC	less developed country
LIC	low-income country
LIEO	liberal international economic order
LLDC	least developed country
MIDC	middle-income developing country
MITI	Ministry of International Trade and Industry
MNC	multinational corporation
MTCR	Missile Technology Control Regime
NAFTA	North American Free Trade Agreement
NATO	North Atlantic Treaty Organization
NDF	Nordic Development Fund
NGO	nongovernmental organization
NIC	newly industrialized country
NIEO	new international economic order
NIS	new independent states
NMFA	Norwegian Ministry of Foreign Affairs
NORAD	Norwegian Development Agency
NPT	Nuclear Non-Proliferation Treaty
OAS	Organization of American States
OAU	Organization for African Unity
ODA	Official Development Assistance
OECD	Organization for Economic Cooperation and Development
OECF	Overseas Economic Cooperation Fund
OPEC	Organization of Petroleum Exporting Countries
OSCE	Organization of Security Cooperation in Europe
PLO	Palestine Liberation Organization
PRC	People's Republic of China
PHARE	Poland-Hungary: Assistance for Restructuring of the Economy
RDB	regional development bank
SADEC	Southern African Development Cooperation
SEA	Single European Act
SIDA	Swedish International Development Agency
STABEX	System for the Stabilization of Export Earnings
SWEDFUND	Swedish Fund for Industrial Cooperation with Developing Countries
UN	United Nations
UNCED	United Nations Conference on Environment and Development

UNCTAD	United Nations Conference on Trade and Development
UNDP	United Nations Development Programme
UNICEF	United Nations Children's Fund
USACDA	United States Arms Control and Disarmament Agency
USIA	United States Information Agency
USAID	U.S. Agency for International Development
WTO	World Trade Organization

References

Adas, Michael (1989). *Machines as the Measure of Men: Science, Technology, and Ideologies of Western Dominance.* Ithaca: Cornell University.

Agrawal, Nisha, Zafar Ahmed, Michael Mered, and Roger Nord (1993). *Structural Adjustment, Economic Performance, and Aid Dependency in Tanzania.* Policy Research Working Paper No. 1204. Washington, D.C.: World Bank.

Amsden, Alice H. (1989). *Asia's Next Giant: South Korea and Late Industrialization.* New York: Oxford University Press.

Andreen, Rolf (1986). "The International Commitment: Swedish Participation in Multilateral Development Cooperation," pp. 129–146 in Pierre Frühling, ed., *Swedish Development Aid in Perspective: Policies, Problems and Results Since 1952.* Stockholm: Almqvist & Wiksell.

Andrén, Nils (1981). "The Nordic Countries and North-South Relations," pp. 690–706 in Erik Allardt, ed., *Nordic Democracy.* Copenhagen: Det Danske Selskab.

Antola, Esko (1978). "The Evolution of Official Finnish Development Policy," *Cooperation and Conflict* 13 (No. 3): 231–241.

Arase, David (1993). "Japanese Policy Toward Democracy and Human Rights in Asia," *Asian Survey* 33 (October): 935–952.

Arnold, Steven H. (1982). *Implementing Development Assistance: European Approaches to Basic Needs.* Boulder, CO: Westview Press.

Baldwin, David A. (1985). *Economic Statecraft.* Princeton, NJ: Princeton University Press.

——— (1969). "Foreign Aid, Intervention and Influence," *World Politics* 21 (April): 425–447.

——— (1966). *Economic Development and American Foreign Policy, 1943–1962.* Chicago: University of Chicago Press.

——— (1965). "The International Bank in Political Perspective," *World Politics* 18 (October): 68–81.

Ball, George (1968). *The Disciples of Power.* Boston: Little, Brown, and Company.

Ball, Nicole (1988). *Security and Economy in the Third World.* Princeton, NJ: Princeton University Press.

Bandow, Doug (1992). "Economic and Military Aid," pp. 75–96 in Peter J. Schraeder, ed., *Intervention Into the 1990s: U.S. Foreign Policy in the Third World.* Boulder, CO: Lynne Rienner Publishers.

Bauer, Peter T. (1981). *Equality, the Third World, and Economic Delusion.* London: Methuen.

——— (1972). *Dissent on Development.* London: Weidenfeld and Nicolson.

Bayart, Jean-François (1991). "La problématique de la démocratie en Afrique noire: la Baule et puis après," *Politique Africaine* 43 (October): 5–20.

——— (1984) *La politique Africaine de François Mitterrand.* Paris: Karthala.

Beckman, Björn (1979). "Aid and Foreign Investments: The Swedish Case," *Cooperation and Conflict* 14 (No. 1): 133–148.

Bellah, Robert Neelly, et al. (1991). *The Good Society.* New York: Knopf.

Berthelot, Yves (1973). "French Aid Performance and Development Policy," pp. 36–49 in Bruce Dinwiddy, ed., *European Development Policies: The UK, Sweden, France, the EEC, and Multilateral Organizations.* New York: Praeger.

Biarnès, Pierre (1987). *Les français en Afrique noire de Richelieu à Mitterrand.* Paris: Armond Colin.

Bissell, Richard (1992). "Foreign Aid and the American Interest," *The World and I* 7 (No. 5): 32–35.

Blair, John M. (1976). *The Control of Oil.* New York: Pantheon.

Blake, David H., and Robert S. Walters (1987). *The Politics of Global Economic Relations.* Englewood Cliffs, NJ: Prentice-Hall.

Block, Fred L. (1977). *The Origins of International Economic Disorder.* Berkeley: University of California Press.

Booth, David (1993). "Development Research: From Impasse to New Agenda," pp. 49–76 in Frans J. Schurman, ed., *Beyond the Impasse: New Directions in Development Theory.* London: Zed Books.

Bose, Anuradha, and Peter Burnell, eds. (1991). *Britain's Overseas Aid Since 1979: Between Idealism and Self-Interest.* New York: St. Martin's Press.

Boulaga, F. Eboussi (1993). *Les conférences nationales en Afrique noire: une affaire à suivre.* Paris: Karthala.

Bourguignon, Francois, and Christian Morrison (1992). *Adjustment and Equity in Developing Countries: A New Approach.* Paris: OECD.

Boustany, Nora (1994). "At Saudi's Rich Table, the Alien Taste of Austerity," *The Washington Post* (August 13): 1–14.

Brandt Commission (1983). *Common Crisis: North-South Cooperation for World Recovery.* London: Pan Books.

——— (1980). *North-South: A Program for Survival. Report of the Independent Commission on International Development Issues.* Cambridge, MA: MIT Press.

Brooks, William L., and Robert M. Orr, Jr. (1985). "Japan's Foreign Economic Assistance," *Asian Survey* 25 (March): 322–340.

Brzoska, Michael (1983). "Third World Arms Control: The Problems of Verification," *Bulletin of Peace Proposals* 14 (No. 2): 165–173.

Burnell, Peter (1991). "Introduction to Britain's Overseas Aid: Between Idealism and Self-Interest," pp. 1–31 in Anuradha Bose and Peter Burnell, eds. *Britain's Overseas Aid Since 1979: Between Idealism and Self-Interest.* New York: St. Martin's Press.

Callaghy, Thomas M. (1989). "Toward State Capability and Embedded Liberalism in the Third World: Lessons for Adjustment," pp. 115–138 in Joan M. Nelson, et al., *Fragile Coalitions: The Politics of Economic Adjustment.* New Brunswick, NJ: Transaction Books.

Callaghy, Thomas M., and John Ravenhill, eds. (1993). *Hemmed In: Responses to Africa's Economic Decline.* New York: Columbia University Press.

Cardoso, Fernando Henrique (1972). "Dependency and Development in Latin America," *New Left Review* 74 (July–August): 83–95.

Cason, Jim, and Bill Martin (1993). "Clinton and Africa: Searching for a Post–Cold War Order," *ACAS Bulletin* 38–39 (Winter): 2–8.

Cassen, Robert, and Associates (1986). *Does Aid Work? Report to an Intergovernmental Task Force.* Oxford: Clarendon Press.

Cerny, Philip G. (1980). *The Politics of Grandeur: Ideological Aspects of de Gaulle's Foreign Policy.* New York: Cambridge University Press.

Chege, Michael (1992). "Remembering Africa," *Foreign Affairs* 71 (January–February): 146–163.

Chilcote, Ronald H. (1985). *Theories of Development and Underdevelopment.* Boulder, CO: Westview Press.

——— (1981). *Theories of Comparative Politics.* Boulder, CO: Westview Press.

Chipman, John (1989). *French Power in Africa.* Cambridge, MA: Basil Blackwell.

Cingranelli, David Louis (1993). *Ethics, American Foreign Policy, and the Third World.* New York: St. Martin's Press.

Clark, John (1990) *Democratizing Development: The Role of Voluntary Organizations.* West Hartford, CT: Kumarian Press.

Clough, Michael (1994). *Free at Last? U.S. Foreign Policy Toward Africa and the End of the Cold War.* New York: Council on Foreign Relations Press.

——— (1992). "The United States and Africa: The Policy of Cynical Disengagement," *Current History* 91 (May): 193–198.

Cohen, Benjamin J. (1982). "Balance of Payments Financing: Evolution of a Regime," *International Organization* 35 (Spring): 457–478.

Commission of the European Communities (1990). *Official Development Assistance from the European Community and Its Member States.* Brussels: Information of the European Communities.

Cornia, Giovanni Andrea, Richard Jolly, and Frances Stewart, eds. (1987). *Adjustment with a Human Face: Protecting the Vulnerable and Promoting Growth.* Oxford: Clarendon Press.

Danish International Development Agency [DANIDA] (1993a). *DANIDA Information: Denmark's Development Assistance 1992.* Copenhagen: DANIDA.

——— (1993b). *Women in Development: DANIDA's WID Policy Towards the Year 2000.* Copenhagen: DANIDA.

——— (1992). *Denmark's Development Assistance 1990/91.* Copenhagen: DANIDA.

Des Forges, Alison (1995). "Face au génocide, une réponse désastreuse des États-Unis et des Nations Unies," in André Guichaoua, ed., *Les crises politiques au Burundi et Rwanda (1993–1994): analyses, faits et documents.* Paris: Karthala.

Deutsche Bundesbank (1990). "Recent Trends in the Development Policy Cooperation of the FRG," *Deutsche Bundesbank Monthly Report* 42 (October): 32–39.

Diamond, Larry (1995). "Promoting Democracy in Africa: U.S. and International Policies in Transition," pp. 250–277 in John W. Harbeson and Donald Rothchild, eds., *Africa in World Politics*, 2d rev. ed. Boulder, CO: Westview Press.

Dinan, Desmond (1994). *Ever Closer Union? An Introduction to the European Community.* Boulder, CO: Lynne Rienner Publishers.

Dinwiddy, Bruce, ed. (1973). *European Development Policies: The UK, Sweden, France, the EEC, and Multilateral Organizations.* New York: Praeger.

Diop, Momar Coumba, and Mamadou Diouf (1990). *Le Sénégal sous Abdou Diouf: état et société.* Paris: Editions Karthala.

Dupont, Stéphane (1995). "Francophonie: une stérile rivalité Franco-Canadienne," *Jeune Afrique Economie* 187 (January 2): 24–25.

Eberstadt, Nicholas (1988). *Foreign Aid and American Purpose.* Washington, DC: American Enterprise Institute.

Edgren, Gösta (1986). "Changing Terms: Procedures and Relationships in Swedish Development Assistance," pp. 47–64 in Pierre Frühling, ed., *Swedish Development Aid in Perspective: Policies, Problems, and Results Since 1952*. Stockholm: Almqvist & Wiksell.

Eikenberry, Karl W. (1995). *Explaining and Influencing Chinese Arms Transfers*. Washington, DC: National Defense University.

Ensign, Margee (1992). *Doing Good or Doing Well? Japan's Foreign Aid Program*. New York: Columbia University Press.

Esposito, John L. (1992). *The Islamic Threat: Myth or Reality?* New York: Oxford University Press.

Faquih, Osama J. (1993). "Arab Aid Agencies and Their Contribution to Arab Economic Development," *OPEC Bulletin* 24 (October): 12–14.

Finnish International Development Agency [FINNIDA] (1993a). *Finland's Development Assistance 1992: Annual Report*. Helsinki: Ministry of Foreign Affairs.

——— (1993b). *Finland's Development Cooperation in the 1990s: Strategic Goals and Means*. Helsinki: Ministry of Foreign Affairs.

Foccart, Jacques, with Philippe Gaillard (1995). *Foccart parle: entretiens avec Philippe Gaillard*, Vol. 1. Paris: Fayard/Jeune Afrique.

Freedom House (1994). *Freedom in the World: The Annual Survey of Political Rights and Civil Liberties, 1993–1994*. Lanham, MD: University Press of America.

French, Howard (1995). "France's Master Puppeteer in Africa Drops the Veil," *International Herald Tribune* (March 12): 1, 8.

——— (1994). "Closing a Chapter," *Africa Report* 39 (March–April): 13–18.

Frey-Wouters, Ellen (1980). *The European Community and the Third World*. New York: Praeger.

Friedman, Alan (1995). "France and the IMF Press Aid for Algeria," *International Herald Tribune* (January 10): 1, 4.

Frühling, Pierre (1986). *Swedish Development Aid in Perspective: Policies, Problems, and Results Since 1952*. Stockholm: Almqvist and Wiksell.

Gaimusho, Keizai Kyoryokukyoku (1993). *Wagakuni no seifu kaihatsu enjo*, 2 vols. Tokyo: Kokusai kyôryoku suishin kyôkai.

——— (1988). *Wagakuni no seifu kaihatsu enjo*. Tokyo: Kokusai kyôryoku suishin kyôkai.

Gause, F. Gregory (1994). *Oil Monarchies: Domestic and Security Challenges in the Arab Gulf States*. New York: Council on Foreign Relations Press.

Gibbs, David N. (1991). *The Political Economy of Third World Intervention: Mines, Money, and U.S. Policy in the Congo Crisis*. Chicago: University of Chicago Press.

Gilpin, Robert (1987). *The Political Economy of International Relations*. Princeton, NJ: Princeton University Press.

Glaser, Antoine, and Stephen Smith (1994). *L'Afrique sans Africaines: le rêve blanc du continent noir*. Paris: Stock.

Gordon, Michael R. (1996). "Russia and IMF Agree on a Loan for $10.2 Billion," *New York Times* (February 23): 1A–2A.

Greenhouse, Steven (1995). "Administration Resists Pressures to Cut Foreign Aid for 1996," *New York Times* (February 7): 1A.

Griffin, Keith (1991). "Foreign Aid After the Cold War," *Development and Change* 22 (October): 645–685.

Grilli, Enzo R. (1993). *The European Community and the Developing Countries*. New York: Cambridge University Press.

Grimmett, Richard F. (1994). *Conventional Arms Transfers to the Third World, 1986–1993.* Washington, DC: Congressional Research Service.

———— (1991) *Conventional Arms Transfers to the Third World, 1983–1990.* Washington, DC: Congressional Research Service.

Grosser, Alfred (1965). *French Foreign Policy Under de Gaulle.* Boston: Little, Brown, and Company.

Guillaumont, Patrick, and Sylvianne Guillaumont (1984). *Zone franc et développement Africain.* Paris: Economica.

Gunder Frank, Andre (1967). "Sociology of Development and Underdevelopment of Sociology," *Catalyst* 3 (Summer): 20–73.

Haas, Peter M. (1992). "Introduction: Epistemic Communities and International Policy Coordination," *International Organization* 46 (Winter): 1–35.

Haggard, Stephen (1990). *Pathways from the Periphery: The Politics of Growth in the Newly Industrializing Countries.* Ithaca, NY: Cornell University Press.

Haggard, Stephen, and Robert R. Kaufman, eds. (1992). *The Politics of Economic Adjustment: International Constraints, Distributive Conflicts, and the State.* Princeton, NJ: Princeton University Press.

Halliday, Jon, and Gavan McCormack (1973). *Japanese Imperialism Today.* Harmondsworth: Penguin Books.

Hammarskjöld, Dag (1964). *Markings.* New York: Knopf.

Hammond, Paul Y. (1983). *The Reluctant Supplier.* Cambridge, MA: Oelgeschlager, Gunn, and Hain.

Hanabusa, Masamichi (1991). "A Japanese Perspective on Aid and Development," pp. 88–104 in Shafiqul Islam, ed., *Yen for Development: Japanese Foreign Aid and the Politics of Burden-Sharing.* New York: Council on Foreign Relations Press.

Hancock, Graham (1989). *Lords of Poverty: The Power, Prestige, and Corruption of the International Aid Business.* New York: Atlantic Monthly Press.

Hartung, William (1994). *And Weapons for All.* New York: HarperCollins.

Hasegawa, Sukehiro (1975). *Japanese Foreign Aid: Policy and Practice.* New York: Praeger.

Hayter, Theresa (1985). *Aid: Rhetoric and Reality.* London: Pluto Press.

———— (1971). *Aid as Imperialism.* Harmondsworth: Penguin Books.

———— (1966). *French Aid.* London: Overseas Development Institute.

Heppling, Sixten (1986). "The Very First Years: Memories of an Insider," pp. 13–26 in Pierre Frühling, ed., *Swedish Development Aid in Perspective: Policies, Problems, and Results Since 1952.* Stockholm: Almqvist and Wiksell.

Hewitt, Adrian (1989). "ACP and the Developing World," pp. 258–300 in Juliet Lodge, ed., *The European Community and the Challenge of the Future.* New York: St. Martin's Press.

Hirabayashi Hiroshi (1993). "ODA taikô o zahyôjiku ni," *Kokusai kaihatsu jânaru* (December): 27–29.

Hofmeier, Rolf, and Siegfried Schultz (1984). "German Aid: Policy and Performance," pp. 206–238 in Olav Stokke, ed., *European Development Assistance: Policies and Performance.* Oslo: European Association of Development Research and Training Institutes Working Group.

Holm, Hans-Henrik (1979). "Danish Third World Policy: The Feedback Problem," *Cooperation and Conflict* 14 (No. 1): 87–103.

Holmberg, Susan (1989). "Welfare Abroad: Swedish Development Assistance," pp. 123–166 in Bengt Sundelius, ed., *The Committed Neutral.* Boulder, CO: Westview Press.

Holtsberg, Christer (1986). "The Development of Rural Development," pp. 157–164 in Pierre Frühling, ed., *Swedish Development Aid in Perspective: Policies, Problems, and Results since 1952.* Stockholm: Almqvist & Wiksell.

Hook, Steven W. (1995) *National Interest and Foreign Aid.* Boulder, CO: Lynne Rienner Publishers.

Hopkins, Raymond F. (1992). "Reform in the International Food Aid Regime: The Role of Consensual Knowledge," *International Organization* 46 (Winter): 225–264.

——— (1987). "The Evolution of Food Aid: Toward a Development-First Regime," pp. 246–259 in J. Price Gittinger, et al., eds., *Food Policy: Integrating Supply, Distribution, and Consumption.* Baltimore: Johns Hopkins University Press.

Horesh, Edward (1984). "British Aid: Policy and Performance," pp. 110–128 in Olav Stokke, ed., *European Development Assistance, Policies and Performance,* Vol. 1. Tilburg, Netherlands: European Association of Development Research and Training Institute.

Huband, Mark (1993). "Cameroon: A Flawed Victory," *Africa Report* 38 (January–February): 41–44.

Hugon, Philippe (1984). "French Development Cooperation: Policy and Performance," pp. 178–205 in Olav Stokke, ed., *European Development Assistance: Policies and Performance.* Tilburg, Netherlands: European Association of Development Research and Training Institute.

Human Rights Watch/Africa (1994). *Human Rights in Africa and U.S. Policy.* Special Report by Human Rights Watch/Africa for the White House Conference on Africa, June 26–27, 1994.

Huntington, Samuel (1968). *Political Order in Changing Societies.* New Haven, CT: Yale University Press.

Hyden, Goran, and Michael Bratton, eds. (1992). *Governance and Politics in Africa.* Boulder, CO: Lynne Rienner Publishers.

Hyden, Goran, and Bø Karlstrom (1993). "Structural Adjustment as a Policy Process: The Case of Tanzania," *World Development* 21 (September): 1395–1404.

International Finance Corporation (IFC) (1992). *Contributing to Development.* Washington, DC: International Finance Corporation.

——— (1981). *Annual Report.* Washington, DC: International Finance Corporation.

Isaak, Robert A. (1995). *Managing World Economic Change,* 2d ed. Englewood Cliffs, NJ: Prentice-Hall.

Islam, Shafiqul, ed. (1991). *Yen for Development: Japanese Foreign Aid and the Politics of Burden-Sharing.* New York: Council on Foreign Relations Press.

Jacoby, Ruth (1986). "Idealism versus Economics: Swedish Aid and Commercial Interests," pp. 85–100 in Pierre Frühling, ed., *Swedish Development Aid in Perspective: Policies, Problems and Results Since 1952.* Stockholm: Almqvist and Wiksell.

Jaidah, Ali M. (1983). *An Appraisal of OPEC Oil Policies.* London: Longman.

Japanese Government (1993). *Japan's ODA 1992.* Tokyo: Ministry of Foreign Affairs.

Jehl, Douglas (1993). "U.S. Is Cutting Aid to Latin Drug War," *New York Times* (March 25): 8:1.

Jepma, Catrinus J. (1991). *The Tying of Aid.* Paris: OECD.

Jinadu, L. Adele (1984). "The Political Economy of Sweden's Development Policy in Africa," *Cooperation and Conflict* 19 (No. 3): 177–196.

Johansen, Robert (1994). "Building World Security," pp. 372–397 in Michael T.

Klare and Daniel C. Thomas, eds., *World Security: Challenges for a New Century.* New York: St. Martin's Press.

Johnson, Chalmers (1982). *MITI and the Japanese Miracle.* Palo Alto, CA: Stanford University Press.

Jones, Dorothy V. (1991). *Code of Peace.* Chicago: University of Chicago Press.

Kadar, Bela (1993). "Where Have All the Dollars Gone?" *Transition: The Newsletter about Reforming Economies.* Washington, DC: World Bank.

Kalb, Madeleine G. (1982) *The Congo Cables: The Cold War in Africa From Eisenhower to Kennedy.* New York: Macmillan.

Kaminski, Antoni A., and Roanna Kurczewska (1994). "Main Actors of Transformation: The Nomadic Elites." In Eric Allardt and W. Wesolowski, eds., *The General Outlines of Transformation.* Warsaw: IFIS PAN Publishing.

Kanté, Babacar (1994). "Senegal's Empty Elections," *Journal of Democracy* 5 (No. 1): 96–108.

Kaplan, Jacob J. (1967). *The Challenge of Foreign Aid: Policies, Problems, and Possibilities.* New York: Praeger Publishers.

Kardam, Nuket (1993). "Development Approaches and the Role of Policy Advocacy: The Case of the World Bank," *World Development* 21 (November): 1773–1786.

Kawakami, Takao (1993). "Aid in the Post–Cold War Era," *Japan Views Quarterly* (Spring): 14–17.

Kegley, Charles W., Jr., and Steven W. Hook (1991). "U.S. Foreign Aid and U.N. Voting: Did Reagan's Linkage Strategy Buy Deference or Defiance?" *International Studies Quarterly* 35 (September): 295–312.

Kegley, Charles W., Jr., and Eugene R. Wittkopf (1995). *World Politics: Trend and Transformation,* 5th ed. New York: St. Martin's Press.

Kelly, John Barnett (1980). *Arabia, the Gulf, and the West.* New York: Basic Books.

Kelly, Sean (1993). *America's Tyrant: The CIA and Mobutu of Zaire.* Washington, DC: American University Press.

Kemp, Geoffrey (1992). *The Control of the Middle East Arms Race.* Washington, DC: Carnegie Endowment for International Peace.

Kemp, Peter (1993). "Oil Tide Turns in OPEC's Favor," *Middle East Economic Digest* 37 (February): 2–3.

Kennedy, John F. (1961). "The Peace Corps," *Vital Speeches* 27 (March 15): 325–326.

Kennedy, Paul (1993). *Preparing for the Twenty-First Century.* New York: Random House.

Kenya, Government of (1990). *Development Estimates 1990/91: Details of Projects with External Resources and Programme Finance.* Nairobi: Office of the Vice President and Minister of Finance.

Khadiagala, Gilbert M. (1993). "Uganda's Domestic and Regional Security Since the 1970s." *The Journal of Modern African Studies* 31 (June): 231–255.

Kielmas, Maria (1993). "Saudi Arabia: Cash Crisis Looms," *Petroleum Economist* 60 (September): 20.

Kiljunen, Kimmo (1983). *Finnish Aid in Progress: Premises and Practice of ODA.* Institute of Development Studies: University of Helsinki.

Killick, Tony, and Christopher Stevens (1991). "Eastern Europe: Lessons on Economic Adjustment from the Third World," *International Affairs* 67 (No. 4): 679–696.

Kitajima, Shinichi (1994). "Atarashii jidai no niizu ni taiô shi naigai ni rikai sareru ODA o," *Kokusai kaihatsu jânaru* (January): 117–119.

250 REFERENCES

Klare, Michael T. (1993). "The Next Great Arms Race," *Foreign Affairs* 72 (Summer): 136–152.

―――― (1992). "Controlling the Trade in Conventional Weapons," *Transnational Law and Contemporary Problems* (Fall): 493–536.

―――― (1991). "Gaining Control: Building a Comprehensive Arms Restraint System," *Arms Control Today* (June): 9–13.

―――― (1984). *American Arms Supermarket.* Austin, TX: University of Texas Press.

Kolko, Gabriel, and Joyce Kolko (1972). *The Limits of Power: The World and United States Foreign Policy.* New York: Harper and Row.

Kolodziej, Edward A. (1974). *French Foreign Policy Under De Gaulle and Pompidou: The Politics of Grandeur.* Ithaca, NY: Cornell University Press.

Koppel, Bruce M., and Robert M. Orr, Jr. (1993). *Japan's Foreign Aid: Power and Policy in a New Era.* Boulder, CO: Westview Press.

Krasner, Stephen D. (1982). "Structural Causes and Regime Consequences: Regimes as Intervening Variables," *International Organization* 36 (Spring): 185–205.

Laatikainen, Katie V. (1995). "Nordic EU Membership: The Swan Song of Nordic Development Assistance" *Scandinavian Review* 83 (Spring–Summer): 30–36.

Labrie, Roger P. (1982). *U.S. Arms Sales Policy: Background and Issues.* Washington, DC: American Enterprise Institute.

Lappé, Frances Moore, Joseph Collins, and David Kinley (1980). *Aid as Obstacle: Twenty Questions About Our Foreign Aid and the Hungry.* San Francisco: Institute for Food and Development Policy.

Lele, Uma, and Ijaz Nabi, eds. (1991). *Transitions in Development: The Role of Aid and Commercial Flows.* San Francisco: Institute for Contemporary Studies Press.

Lesser, Ian O. (1993). *Security in North Africa: Internal and External Challenges.* Santa Monica, CA: Rand.

Le Vine, Victor T., and Timothy W. Luke (1979). *The Arab-African Connection: Political and Economic Realities.* Boulder, CO: Westview Press.

Libby, Ronald T. (1975). "International Development Association: A Legal Fiction Designed to Secure an LDC Constituency," *International Organization* 29 (Autumn): 1065–1072.

Liebenow, J. Gus (1986). *African Politics: Crises and Challenges.* Bloomington: Indiana University Press.

Ling, Hou (1992). "Foreign Aid Policy in the USA, Japan, and Germany," *Beijing Review* 35 (November): 31–33.

Lipson, Charles (1981). "The International Organization of Third World Debt," *International Organization* 35 (Autumn): 603–631.

Lipton, Michael, and John Toye (1990). *Does Aid Work in India? A Country Study of the Impact of Official Development Assistance.* London: Routledge.

Luke, Timothy W. (1985). "Dependent Development and the OPEC States: State Formation in Saudi Arabia and Iran Under the International Energy Regime," *Studies in Comparative International Development* 20 (Spring): 31–54.

―――― (1983). "Dependent Development and the Arab OPEC States," *Journal of Politics* 45 (November): 588–601.

Lumsdaine, David Halloran (1993). *Moral Vision in International Politics: The Foreign Aid Regime, 1949–1989.* Princeton, NJ: Princeton University Press.

Luttwak, Edward N. (1990). "From Geo-Politics to Geoeconomics," *The National Interest* 20 (Summer): 17–23.

McNamara, Francis T. (1989) *France in Black Africa.* Washington, DC: National Defense University Press.

Magnard, F., and N. Tenzer (1988). *La Crise Africaine: Quelle Politique de Cooperation pour la France.* Paris: Presses Universitaires de France.

Malik, Mohammed H., ed. (1991). *Contemporary Issues in European Development Aid.* Aldershot, UK: Avebury.

Martin, Guy (1995). "Francophone Africa in the Context of Franco-African Relations," pp. 163–188 in John W. Harbeson and Donald Rothchild, eds., *Africa in World Politics,* 2d rev. ed. Boulder, CO: Westview Press.

——— (1993). "Democratic Transition in Africa," *Issue: A Journal of Opinion* 21 (Nos. 1–2): 6–7.

Maunick, Edouard J. (1993). "Ce qui restera de Libvreville," *Jeune Afrique* 1692 (June 10–16): 23–24.

Mazrui, Ali A. (1995). "Africa and Other Civilizations: Conquest and Counter-conquest," pp. 69–94 in John W. Harbeson and Donald Rothchild, eds., *Africa in World Politics,* 2d rev. ed. Boulder, CO: Westview Press.

M'Bokolo, Elikia (1992). "Conquêtes européenes et résistances africaines, ca. 1880-ca. 1910." In Elikia M'Bokolo, ed. *Afrique noire: histoire et civilisations,* Vol. 2. Paris: Hatier.

Montgomery, John D. (1967). *The Politics of Foreign Aid.* New York: Praeger.

Moore, Mick, and Mark Robinson (1994). "Can Foreign Aid Be Used to Promote Good Government in Developing Countries?" *Ethics and International Affairs* 8: 141–158.

Moose, George E. (1985). "French Military Policy in Africa," pp. 59–97 in William J. Foltz and Henry S. Bienen, eds., *Arms and the African: Military Influences on Africa's International Relations.* New Haven, CT: Yale University Press.

Moravcsik, Andrew M. (1989). "Disciplining Trade Finance: The OECD Export Credit Arrangement," *International Organization* 43 (Winter): 173–205.

Morrison, Elizabeth, and Randall B. Purcell (1988) *Players and Issues in U.S. Foreign Aid.* West Hartford, CT: Kumarian Press.

Morse, Edward L. (1973). *Foreign Policy and Interdependence in Gaullist France.* Princeton, NJ: Princeton University Press.

Mosley, Paul (1987). *Overseas Aid: Its Defence and Reform.* Brighton, UK: Wheatsheaf Books, Ltd.

Mosley, Paul, Jane Harrigan, and John Toye (1991a). *Aid and Power: The World Bank and Policy-based Lending,* Vol. 1. London: Routledge.

——— (1991b). *Aid and Power: The World Bank and Policy-based Lending,* Vol. 2. London: Routledge.

Moss, Joanna, and John Ravenhill (1989). "Trade Diversification in Black Africa," *The Journal of Modern African Studies* 27 (September): 521–545.

Msemakweli, John (1994). "Tanzania–World Bank Relations: Development Aid at Its Worst?" *The Express* (Dar es Salaam) 150 (May 15–18).

Myrdal, Gunnar (1971). *Economic Theory and Underdeveloped Regions.* New York: Harper and Row.

Nathan, James A., and James K. Oliver (1987). *Foreign Policy Making and the American Political System,* 2d ed. Boston: Little, Brown, and Company.

Nelson, Joan M. (1993). "The Politics of Economic Transformation: Is Third World Experience Relevant in Eastern Europe?" *World Politics* 45 (April): 433–463.

——— (1992). "Beyond Conditionality: Foreign Aid and the Changing Global Agenda," *Harvard International Review* 15 (Fall): 4–7, 61.

Nelson, Joan M., et al. (1989). *Fragile Coalitions: The Politics of Economic Adjustment.* New Brunswick, NJ: Transaction Books.

Nisbet, Robert A. (1969) *Social Change and History.* New York: Oxford University Press.

Nolan, Janne E. (1991a). "The Global Arms Market after the Gulf War: Prospects for Control," *The Washington Quarterly* 14 (Summer): 125–138.

———— (1991b). *Trappings of Power: Ballistic Missiles in the Third World.* Washington, DC: Brookings Institution.

Nordic Council of Ministers (1990). *Yearbook of Nordic Statistics 1989–90.* Stockholm: Norstedts Tryckeri.

Nordic Development Fund (1992). *Annual Report.* Helsinki.

Nordic UN Project (1991). *The United Nations in Development: Reform Issues in the Economic and Social Fields: A Nordic Perspective.* Stockholm: Almqvist and Wiksell.

———— (1990). *Perspectives on Multilateral Assistance: A Review by the Nordic UN Project.* Stockholm: Almqvist and Wiksell.

Norwegian Development Agency [NORAD] (1993). *NORAD and Norwegian Development Cooperation in the 1990s.* Oslo: NORAD.

Norwegian Ministry of Foreign Affairs [NMFA] (1993). *Norwegian Development Cooperation in a Nutshell.* Oslo: NMFA.

Nzongola-Ntalaja, Georges (1994). "Zaire I: Moving Beyond Mobutu," *Current History* 93 (May): 222.

Nzouankeu, Jacques Mariel (1993). "The Role of the National Conference in the Transition to Democracy in Africa: The Cases of Benin and Mali," *Issue* 21 (No. 1–2): 44–50.

Ohlin, Göran (1973). "Swedish Aid Performance and Policy," pp. 50–62 in Bruce Dinwiddy, ed., *European Development Policies: The United Kingdom, Sweden, France, the EEC, and Multilateral Organizations.* New York: Praeger.

Olson, Lawrence (1970). *Japan in Postwar Asia.* London: Pall Mall Press.

Olson, Mancur (1971). *The Logic of Collective Action.* Cambridge, MA: Harvard University Press.

OPEC Fund for International Development (1990). *OPEC Aid and OPEC Aid Institutions: A Profile.* Vienna: OPEC Fund for International Development.

Organization for Economic Cooperation and Development (OECD) (1979–1996a). *Development Cooperation: Efforts and Policies of the Members of the Development Assistance Committee.* Paris: OECD.

———— (1994–1996b). *Geographical Distribution of Financial Flows to Developing Countries.* Paris: OECD.

———— (1995c). *Financial Flows to Developing Countries in 1994: Smaller Decline in Aid, Sustained High Private Flows.* Paris: OECD.

———— (1993c). *Development Assistance Manual: DAC Principles for Effective Aid.* Paris: OECD.

Organization of Petroleum Exporting Countries (OPEC) (1990, 1984). *Official Resolutions and Press Releases.* Vienna: OPEC.

Organski, A.F.K. (1965). *Stages of Political Development.* New York: Knopf.

Orr, Robert M., Jr. (1990). *The Emergence of Japan's Foreign Aid Power.* New York: Columbia University Press.

Osgood, Robert E. (1953). *Ideals and Self-Interest in America's Foreign Relations.* Chicago: University of Chicago Press.

Overseas Economic Cooperation Fund (OECF) (1993). *Annual Report 1993.* Tokyo: OECF.

Pastor, Robert A. (1992). *Whirlpool: U.S. Foreign Policy Toward Latin America and the Caribbean.* Princeton, NJ: Princeton University Press.

Payer, Cheryl (1989). "Causes of the Debt Crisis," pp. 7–16 in Bade Onimode, ed., *The IMF, the World Bank, and the African Debt: The Social and Political Impact.* London: Zed Books.

———— (1982). *The World Bank: A Critical Analysis.* New York: Monthly Review Press.

Phillips, Leslie (1995). "'Senator No' Puts U.S. Foreign Policy on Hold," *USA Today* (December 5): 7A.

Pierre, Andrew J. (1982). *The Global Politics of Arms Sales.* Princeton, NJ: Princeton University Press.

Poe, Steven C., and C. Neal Tate (1994). "Repression of Human Rights to Personal Integrity in the 1980s: A Global Analysis," *American Political Science Review* 88 (December): 853–872.

Pool, John Charles, and Stephen C. Stamos (1989). *International Economic Policy.* Lexington, MA: Lexington Books.

Putnam, Robert (1988). "Diplomacy and Domestic Politics: The Logic of Two-Level Games," *International Organization* 42 (Summer): 427–460.

Ravenhill, John (1995). "Dependent By Default: Africa's Relations with the European Union," pp. 95–126 in John W. Harbeson and Donald Rothchild, eds., *Africa in World Politics,* 2d rev. ed. Boulder, CO: Westview Press.

Riddell, Roger C. (1987). *Foreign Aid Reconsidered.* Baltimore: Johns Hopkins University Press.

Rix, Alan (1993). *Japan's Foreign Aid Challenge: Policy Reform and Aid Leadership.* London: Routledge.

——— (1990). *Japan's Aid Program: A New Global Agenda.* Canberra: Australian Government Publishing Service.

——— (1980). *Japan's Economic Aid: Policy-making and Politics.* London: Croom Helm.

Rondinelli, Dennis (1989). "Reforming U.S. Foreign Aid Policy: Constraints on Development Assistance," *Policy Studies Journal* 18 (Fall): 67–85.

Rostow, W. W. (1971) *Politics and the Stages of Growth.* New York: Cambridge University Press.

Rudebeck, Lars (1982). "Nordic Policies Toward the Third World," pp. 143–175 in Bengt Sundelius, ed., *The Foreign Policies of Northern Europe.* Boulder, CO: Westview Press.

Ruggie, John Gerard (1983). "Political Structure and Change in the International Economic Order: The North-South Dimension," pp. 423–487 in John Gerard Ruggie, ed., *The Antinomies of Interdependence.* New York: Columbia University Press.

Ruttan, Vernon W. (1989). "Why Foreign Economic Assistance?" *Economic Development and Cultural Change* 37 (January): 411–424.

Samb, Pape Boubacar (1995). "Sénégal-Japon: nouvel élan à la coopération," *Le Soleil* (March 9): 4.

Sandbrook, Richard (1993). *The Politics of Africa's Economic Recovery.* New York: Cambridge University Press.

Scalapino, Robert A. (1992). "The Foreign Policy of Modern Japan," pp. 186–221 in Roy A. Macridis, ed., *Foreign Policy in World Politics,* 8th ed. Englewood Cliffs, NJ: Prentice-Hall.

Schatzberg, Michael G. (1991). *Mobutu or Chaos? The United States and Zaire, 1960–1990.* Lanham, MD: University Press of America.

Schneider, Steven A. (1983). *The Oil Price Revolution.* Baltimore: Johns Hopkins University Press.

Schraeder, Peter J. (1995). "The Clinton Administration's Africa Policies: Some Comments on Continuity and Change at Mid-Term." *L'Afrique Politique:* 47–72.

——— (1994a). "Elites as Facilitators or Impediments to Political Development? Some Lessons from the 'Third Wave' of Democratization in Africa," *The Journal of Developing Areas* 29 (October): 69–90.

——— (1994b). *United States Foreign Policy Toward Africa: Incrementalism, Crisis, and Change.* New York: Cambridge University Press.

———, ed. (1992). *Intervention into the 1990s: U.S. Foreign Policy in the Third World.* Boulder, CO: Lynne Rienner Publishers.

Schraeder, Peter J., Steven W. Hook, and Bruce Taylor (1996). "Determinants of Foreign Aid to Africa: A Cross-National Assessment." Paper delivered at the annual meetings of the International Studies Association, April 17.

Scott, David Clark (1994). "U.S. to Cut Foreign Aid to Latin America," *The Christian Science Monitor* (January 26): 4:1.

Serageldin, Ismael (1990). *Development Partners: Aid and Cooperation in the 1990s.* Stockholm: Swedish International Development Authority.

Shihata, Ibrahim F. (1983). *The OPEC Fund for International Development.* London: Croom Helm.

——— (1982). *The Other Face of OPEC Financial Assistance to the Third World.* New York: Longman.

Silberman, James B., and Charles Weiss, Jr. (1992). *A History of the Technical Assistance Programs of the Marshall Plan and Successor Agencies, 1948–1961.* Washington, DC: World Bank Industrial Policy Group.

Smith, Stephen (1995). "France-Rwanda: lévirat colonial et abandon dans la region des grands lacs." In André Guichaoua, ed., *Les crises politiques au Burundi et Rwanda (1993–1994): analyses, faits et documents.* Paris: Karthala.

——— (1994). "Afrique noire: le duel Washington-Paris," *Politique Internationale* 63 (Spring): 355–367.

Soroos, Marvin S. (1988). "Global Interdependence and the Responsibilities of States: Learning from the Japanese Experience," *Journal of Peace Research* 25 (March): 17–29.

Spanier, John, and Steven W. Hook (1995). *American Foreign Policy Since World War II,* 13th ed. Washington, DC: CQ Press.

Stallings, Barbara (1992). "International Influence on Economic Policy: Debt, Stabilization, and Structural Reform," pp. 41–88 in Stephen Haggard and Robert R. Kaufman, eds., *The Politics of Economic Adjustment: International Constraints, Distributive Conflicts, and the State.* Princeton, NJ: Princeton University Press.

Stockholm International Peace Research Institute (SIPRI) (1992). *SIPRI Yearbook 1992: World Armament and Disarmament.* New York: Oxford University Press.

Stokke, Olav (1985). "Norwegian Development Cooperation Policy: Altruism and International Solidarity," pp. 120–143 in Johan J. Holst, ed., *Norwegian Foreign Policy in the 1980s.* Oslo: Norwegian University Press.

——— (1984). *European Development Assistance.* Oslo: European Association of Development Research and Training Institutes Working Group.

Streeten, Paul (1993). "Markets and States: Against Minimalism," *World Development* 21 (August): 1281–1298.

Swedish Ministry of Foreign Affairs (MFA) (1993). *Sweden's Development Assistance 1992/93.* Stockholm: MFA.

Takahashi, Akira (1993). "From Reparations to *Katagawari:* Japan's ODA to the Philippines," pp. 63–90 in Bruce M. Koppel and Robert M. Orr, Jr., eds., *Japan's Foreign Aid: Power and Policy in a New Era.* Boulder, CO: Westview Press.

Tansky, Leo (1967). *U.S. and USSR Aid to Developing Countries.* New York: Praeger.

Taylor, Lance (1988). *Varieties of Stabilization Experience: Toward Sensible Macroeconomics in the Third World.* Oxford: Clarendon Press.

Todaro, Michael P. (1989). *Economic Development in the Third World,* 4th ed. New York: Longman.

Toye, John (1987). *Dilemmas of Development: Reflections on the Counter-Revolution in Development Theory and Policy.* Oxford: Basil Blackwell.

Triay, Philippe (1993). "Deuxième sommet Africain/Africain-Américain: la consécration d'une idée," *Jeune Afrique Economie* 169 (July): 17–33.

United Nations (1991). *Study on Ways and Means of Promoting Transparency in International Transfers of Conventional Arms.* U.N. Report A/46/301. New York: United Nations.

———— (1990). *World Resources 1990–1991.* New York: Oxford University Press.

United Nations Development Program (1980–1994a). *Human Development Report.* New York: Oxford University Press.

———— (1994b). *Development Cooperation Ukraine.* New York: UNDP.

United Nations Development Program and the World Bank (1992). *African Development Indicators.* Washington, DC: The World Bank.

U.S. Agency for International Development (USAID) (1982–1996a). *U.S. Overseas Loans and Grants and Assistance from International Organizations.* Washington, DC: U.S. Government Printing Office.

———— (1990b). *Development and the National Interest.* Washington, DC: U.S. Government Printing Office.

U.S. Arms Control and Disarmament Agency (1990–1995). *World Military Expenditures and Arms Transfers.* Washington, D.C.: U.S. Government Printing Office.

U.S. Department of State (1995). *Security Assistance for Foreign Operations.* Washington, DC: U.S. Government Printing Office.

———— (1994a). *United States Assistance and Economic Cooperation Strategy for the Newly Independent States.* Washington, DC: U.S. Government Printing Office.

———— (1994b). *SEED Act Implementation Report: Fiscal Year 1993.* Washington, DC: U.S. Government Printing Office.

U.S. Department of the Treasury (1982). *United States Participation in Multilateral Development Banks in the 1980s.* Washington, DC: Department of the Treasury.

U.S. General Accounting Office (USGAO) (1995). *Former Soviet Union: U.S. Bilateral Program Lacks Effective Coordination.* Washington, DC: U.S. Government Printing Office.

———— (1994). *Eastern Europe: AID's Indefinite Contracts Assist Privatization Efforts but Lack Adequate Oversight.* Washington, DC: U.S. Government Printing Office.

———— (1992). *Poland and Hungary: Economic Transition and U.S. Assistance.* Washington, DC: U.S. Government Printing Office.

———— (1991). *Eastern Europe: Status of U.S. Assistance.* Washington, DC: U.S. Government Printing Office.

Uri, Pierre (1976). *Development Without Dependence.* New York: Praeger.

Uvin, Peter (1992). "Regime, Surplus, and Self-Interest: The International Politics of Food Aid," *International Studies Quarterly* 36 (September): 293–312.

Vesa, Unto (1979). "Finland and the New International Economic Order," *Cooperation and Conflict* 12 (No. 2): 105–120.

Wade, Robert (1993). "Managing Trade: Taiwan and South Korea as Challenges to Economics and Political Science," *Comparative Politics* 25 (January): 147–167.

———— (1990). *Governing the Market: Economic Theory and the Role of Government in East Asian Industrialization.* Princeton, NJ: Princeton University Press.

Wald, M. L. (1990). "America Is Still Demanding a Full Tank," *The New York Times* (August 12): E3.

Waxman, Sharon (1995). "Congress Could Set Off Foreign Aid Dominoes," *Chicago Tribune* (June 18): 4C.

Webber, Mark (1993). "The Third World and the Dissolution of the USSR," *Third World Quarterly* 13 (No. 4): 692–712.

Wedel, Janine R. (1995). "In Russia, Don't Tie US Aid to Privatization," *The Christian Science Monitor* 87 (March 1): 18.

——— (1994). "U.S. Aid to Central and Eastern Europe, 1990–1994: An Analysis of Aid Models and Responses," *Joint Economic Committee Publications, U.S. Congress.* Washington, DC: U.S. Government Printing Office.

——— (1992a). *The Unplanned Society: Poland During and After Communism.* New York: Columbia University Press.

——— (1992b). "The Unintended Consequences of Western Aid to Post-Communist Europe," *Telos* 92 (Summer): 131–138.

——— (1992c). U.S. Congressional Testimony: U.S. Assistance to Eastern Europe and the Former Soviet Union, U.S. House of Representatives Committee on Foreign Relations, Subcommittee on Europe and the Middle East, April. 7. Washington, DC: U.S. Government Printing Office.

——— (1992d). "Beware Western Governments Sending Gifts," *The Wall Street Journal Europe* (January 14).

Weissman, Steve (1974). *The Trojan Horse: A Radical Look at Foreign Aid.* Palo Alto, CA: Ramparts Press.

Wharton, Clifton (1993). "USAID and Foreign Aid Reform," *U.S. Department of State Dispatch* 14 (July 26): 526–531.

Whiteman, Kaye (1994). "The Party's Over," *Africa Report* 39 (No. 2): 13–18.

Widner, Jennifer A., ed. (1994). *Economic Change and Political Liberalization in Sub-Saharan Africa.* Baltimore: Johns Hopkins University Press.

Willis, F. Roy (1982). *The French Paradox.* Stanford, CA: Hoover Institution Press.

Woo, Jung-en (1991). *Race to the Swift: State and Finance in Korean Industrialization.* New York: Columbia University Press.

Woo, Wing Thye (1990). "The Art of Economic Development: Markets, Politics, and Externalities," *International Organization* 44 (Summer): 401–429.

Wood, Robert E. (1986). *From Marshall Plan to Debt Crisis: Foreign Aid and Development Choices in the World Economy.* Berkeley: University of California Press.

——— (1980). "Foreign Aid and the Capitalist State in Underdeveloped Countries," *Politics and Society* 10 (No. 1): 1–34.

World Bank (1980–1995a). *World Development Report.* New York: Oxford University Press.

——— (1994b). *Adjustment in Africa: Reforms, Results and the Road Ahead.* New York: Oxford University Press.

——— (1993b). *Annual Report.* Washington, DC: World Bank.

——— (1993c). *The East Asian Miracle: Economic Growth and Public Policy.* Washington, DC: World Bank.

——— (1993d). *Getting Results: The World Bank's Agenda for Improving Development Effectiveness.* Washington, DC: World Bank.

——— (1993e). *World Debt Tables 1993–94,* Vol. 1. Washington, DC: World Bank.

——— (1981). *Accelerating Development in Sub-Saharan Africa.* Washington, DC: World Bank.

Yanagihara, Toru, and Anne Emig (1991). "An Overview of Japan's Foreign Aid," pp. 37–69 in Shafiqul Islam, ed., *Yen for Development: Japanese Foreign Aid and the Politics of Burden-Sharing.* New York: Council on Foreign Relations Press.

Yasutomo, Dennis (1986). *The Manner of Giving: Strategic Aid and Japanese Foreign Policy.* Lexington: Lexington Books.

Yergin, Daniel (1991). *The Prize: The Epic Quest for Oil, Money, and Power.* New York: Simon and Schuster.

Young, Crawford and Thomas Turner (1985). *The Rise and Decline of the Zairian State.* Madison, WI: University of Wisconsin Press.

Zimmerman, Robert F. (1993). *Dollars, Diplomacy, and Dependency: Dilemmas of U.S. Economic Aid.* Boulder, CO: Lynne Rienner Publishers.

About the Authors

M. LEANN BROWN is an associate professor of political science at The University of Florida. A specialist on international political economy and Western European integration, she is the author most recently of *Developing Countries and Regional Economic Cooperation* (1994).

DAVID LOUIS CINGRANELLI is professor of political science at Binghamton University, where he serves as department chairman and conducts research on American politics, foreign policy, and political economy. He is the author of several books and articles, including *Ethics, American Foreign Policy, and the Third World* (1993).

SIMONPETER GOMEZ is the Clifford Geertz Fellow of Political Science at Binghamton University. His research focuses on the quantitative study of human rights and politics of Latin America.

STEVEN W. HOOK, the editor of this volume, is an assistant professor of political science at Kent State University, where he teaches a variety of courses in world politics and foreign policy. He is the author of *National Interest and Foreign Aid* (1995) and is coauthor, with John Spanier, of *American Foreign Policy Since World War II* (13th edition, 1995).

GORAN HYDEN is professor of political science at the University of Florida and the 1994–1996 director of its Center for African Studies. The author of several books on North-South relations and international development, including *No Shortcuts to Progress* (1983) and *Governance and Politics in Africa* (1992, coedited with Michael Bratton), he is currently studying the impact of Chinese, Swedish, and U.S. foreign aid in Tanzania.

MICHAEL T. KLARE is the Five College Professor of Peace and World Security Studies, based at Hampshire College. He is the author of *Rogue States and Nuclear Outlaws* (1995) and *American Arms Supermarket* (1984), along with numerous articles on arms transfers and U.S. foreign policy.

KATIE VERLIN LAATIKAINEN is coordinator of the European Union Studies Center at the City University of New York's Graduate School and University Center and a specialist on Nordic economic integration and the United Nations. Her 1995 article "Nordic EU Membership: The Swan Song of Nordic Development Assistance" appeared in *Scandinavian Review.*

TIMOTHY LUKE is professor of political science at Virginia Polytechnic Institute University, where he teaches courses in international political economy, comparative politics, and political theory. He is the author of several books, including *The Arab-African Connection* (1979, with Victor Le Vine), and of numerous journal articles in such publications as *The American Political Science Review, International Studies Quarterly,* and *The Journal of Politics.*

JOANNE O'CONNOR is a program associate at Tropical Research and Development in Gainesville, Florida, and a former research assistant at The Carter Center in Atlanta, Georgia.

ALAN RIX is professor of Japanese Studies at the University of Queensland, Brisbane, Australia. He has been involved in the study of Japanese aid since the 1970s and helped pioneer the field with his book *Japanese Economic Aid: Policymaking and Politics* (1980). His research on Japanese foreign aid, which focuses on governmental processes, most recently resulted in the publication of *Japan's Foreign Aid Challenge: Policy Reform and Aid Leadership* (1993).

PETER J. SCHRAEDER is an associate professor of political science at Loyola University of Chicago. A specialist on African politics, international relations theory, and U.S. foreign policy, he spent the 1994–1996 academic years as a Fulbright Scholar in Dakar, Senegal. He is the author of *United States Foreign Policy Toward Africa* (1994) and editor of *Intervention into the 1990s: U.S. Foreign Policy in the Third World* (1992).

DAVID I. STEINBERG is Korea representative of the Asia Foundation. A former senior foreign service officer at the U.S. State Department, he subsequently served as Distinguished Professor of Korean Studies at Georgetown University and president of the Mansfield Center for Pacific Affairs. He is the author of ten books and more than sixty articles on Asian politics and economic development.

DANIEL VOLMAN is director of the African Research Project, located in Washington, DC, and is coeditor of *International Dimensions of the Western Sahara Conflict* (1993).

JANINE R. WEDEL is an associate research professor of sociology and anthropology at the Institute of European, Russian, and Eurasian Studies at George Washington University. As a MacArthur Fellow, she traveled throughout Eastern Europe and the former Soviet Union in 1994 and 1995 conducting research on economic assistance in the region. She is the author of *The Unplanned Society: Poland During and After Communism* (1992) and other publications on the region.

ROBERT E. WOOD is an associate professor of sociology at Rutgers University. He is the author of *From Marshall Plan to Debt Crisis: Foreign Aid and Development Choices in the World Economy* (1986) and numerous articles on development policies and processes. He has recently edited, with Michel Picard, a book on tourism, ethnicity, and the state in Asian and Pacific societies, to be published by the University of Hawaii Press.

ROBERT F. ZIMMERMAN is a consultant to the U.S. Agency for International Development and several nongovernmental organizations. A former Peace Corps volunteer and USAID foreign service officer, he subsequently served as a research fellow at Georgetown University, where he authored a book entitled *Dollars, Diplomacy, and Dependency: Dilemmas of U.S. Economic Aid* (1993), underwritten by the Institute for the Study of Diplomacy at Georgetown University.

Index

About the Book

Like world politics itself, the foreign-assistance regime of the late 1990s is characterized by fundamental change and widespread uncertainty. This book confronts these changes and considers, cross-nationally, how donor and recipient states are adapting their aid relationships to the transformed geopolitical environment.

Combining the expertise of both area specialists and those focusing on general issues of political economy, the book reviews the evolving aid strategies of major donors, then considers aid issues as they affect traditional and new aid recipients. All types of aid are considered, although development assistance—the most pervasive form of foreign aid—receives greatest attention. The final chapter considers the implications of the authors' findings for global development in the twenty-first century.